Economic politics

This book raises and addresses questions about the consequences of democratic institutions for economic performance. Do institutions of accountability inside and outside government through periodic elections produce desired results? Do they lead to manipulation of the economy over an electoral cycle, or to the pursuit of partisan goals at odds with a general societal interest?

Drawing upon concrete and observable experience in the United States and occasional reference to other countries, Professor Keech suggests that there are costs of democratic procedures. But these costs are modest and bearable, and similar to the agency costs incurred whenever a principal delegates authority to an agent. Democracy does not systematically cause inferior macroeconomic policy. This inaccessible synthesis and sharp perspective on a large topical literature will be highly useful for professionals, graduate students, upper-level undergraduates, and interested citizens aiming to understand the relationship between politics and economics.

Economic politics
The costs of democracy

WILLIAM R. KEECH
University of North Carolina at Chapel Hill

CAMBRIDGE
UNIVERSITY PRESS

Published by the Press Syndicate of the University of Cambridge
The Pitt Building, Trumpington Street, Cambridge CB2 1RP
40 West 20th Street, New York, NY 10011-4211, USA
10 Stamford Road, Oakleigh, Melbourne 3166, Australia

First published 1995

Printed in the United States of America

Library of Congress Cataloging-in-Publication Data
Keech, William R.
Economic politics : the costs of democracy / William R. Keech.
p.   cm.
Includes bibliographical references and index.
ISBN 0-521-46206-1 (hbk). – ISBN 0-521-46768-3 (pbk.)
1. Democracy – Economic aspects – United States.   2. Representative
government and representation – Economic aspects – United States.
I. Title.
JK271.K318   1995
338.9 – dc20   94-11813
                                                       CIP

A catalog record for this book is available from the British Library.

ISBN 0-521-46206-1 hardback
ISBN 0-521-46768-3 paperback

To Dan and to Sarah

Contents

vii

Figures and tables

ix

Preface and acknowledgments

This book uses macroeconomic issues to address questions about how democracy works. It continues the kind of investigation I pursued in my first book, *The Impact of Negro Voting: The Role of the Vote in the Quest for Equality* (1968, 1981), which used racial issues to study the consequences of extending the franchise. It is a statement of applied democratic theory that uses economic issues to bring into focus questions about democratic institutions and practices. It brings together a body of research that has been written largely in the past fifteen years on the political dimensions of macroeconomic policy and performance. The book draws on work done by economists and by political scientists in roughly equal measure, and it is designed to present a variety of arguments fairly and neutrally.

I have taken aim at several audiences. First, the book is written to be accessible to a nontechnical audience of advanced undergraduates and thoughtful nonacademic citizens who might be interested in the relationship between politics and the macroeconomy, and in the implications for democratic theory. No special training in economics or political science is presumed. But while the book is meant to be readable by the nontechnical general public, it draws heavily on technical academic literature. As such, it makes the case that this literature is relevant to issues of broad public concern. Another audience is graduate students and faculty in political science and economics. For them, the book covers territory in the other discipline that may not be familiar, but more than this it is an argument and an interpretation of known political and economic facts and ideas. In this way, it is also designed for the colleagues who have created the literature on which I draw.

The book was drafted with the support of the University of North Carolina at Chapel Hill, which provided a research leave for the fall of 1992, and the support of Harvard University and the Massachusetts Institute of Technology, each of which provided me office space and an opportunity to extend my research leave to a full academic year by teaching a course on the topic of the book (to undergraduates at Harvard and to graduate students at MIT). An early draft was presented in May 1993 in a three-day "minicourse" sponsored by the Harvard Program in Political Economy, which is directed by James Alt and Kenneth Shepsle.

Of course the gestation period is much longer than this. My interest in economics goes back to my employment by the Brookings Institution in the early 1970s, where I learned that economists have many interesting and important ideas and theories about politics that were not part of my political science graduate training in the early sixties. My understanding of economics owes much to a Professional Development Grant from the National Science Foundation (1977-8). I am grateful to the late Jack Walker for persuading me that the University of Michigan and its Institute for Public Policy Studies was the best place to use this grant. Many people there were important to my postdoctoral education, but Paul Courant and Edward Gramlich deserve special thanks for tutoring me in economics. I have also learned a lot from the excellent macroeconomics group at UNC Chapel Hill, among whom Richard Froyen deserves special thanks.

My understanding of the topic has profited enormously from what I learned from collaboration in research projects with Henry Chappell, an economist, and Carl Simon, a mathematician and economist. I thank the National Science Foundation Division of Social, Behavioral, and Economics Research for grants through the political science and the economics programs that supported my work with Chappell and with Simon. Parts of Chapters 2, 3, 4, 6, and 8 have been worked out in papers and articles co-written with Henry Chappell, Dean Lacy, Patrick Lynch, Irwin Morris, Kyoungsan Pak, Carl Simon, and Carol Swain. Several figures were adapted from those in Richard Froyen, *Macroeconomics: Theories and Policies,* 4th ed. (Macmillan, 1993). Hyeon-Woo Lee provided invaluable research assistance. Scott Parris has continued to make me glad to be working with Cambridge University Press.

An extraordinary number of colleagues have been willing to read and evaluate the entire manuscript, providing many penetrating observations. I have responded to their suggestions as well as I could, but many of their comments made it clear how far I am from saying final words on the subject. Several others helped in many different ways. I especially thank Alberto Alesina, James Alt, Robert Bates, Nathaniel Beck, Hakan Berument, Richard Broholm, Lawrence Broz, Henry Chappell, Robert Erikson, Ita Falk, Eduardo Feldman, Bruno Frey, Richard Froyen, James Granato, Thomas Havrilesky, Sharon Keech, Margaret Levi, Peng Lian, Emily Loose, David Lowery, Patrick Lynch, Timothy McKeown, Michael Munger, Irwin Morris, Paul Peterson, George Rabinowitz, Andrew Rutten, Kenneth Shepsle, Beth Simmons, Carl Simon, Jürg Steiner, Motoshi Suzuki, John Tryneski, George Tsebelis, Peter Van Doren, Stephen Weatherford, Klaus Wellershoff, and students at Harvard, MIT, and UNC and the participants in the Harvard "minicourse." The penultimate draft was test marketed at the University of California at San Diego by Nathaniel Beck, at Harvard University by Alberto Alesina and James Alt, and at the University of Texas by Brian Roberts.

Finally, the University of North Carolina at Chapel Hill and its political science department have supported my work and intellectual growth in countless ways in the thirty years since I was first hired. Sharon Keech has done so as well. She has given this manuscript a penetrating nonacademic citizen's critique, and in many ways she has made it possible. The dedication is to our son and daughter.

PART ONE
Introduction

1 Macroeconomic politics and the costs of democracy

According to one conventional view of macroeconomic politics in contemporary democracy, governments are responsible for performance regarding inflation, unemployment, and income growth. Periodic elections give voters an opportunity to judge that performance and to approve or disapprove, choosing new leaders if performance has been unsatisfactory. From that perspective, democratic institutions provide ways to ensure both the accountability of public officials and the adequacy of government performance. A persistent or unusual problem may lead to a reform that is designed to resolve the problem, such as the creation of the quasi-independent monetary authority in 1913, or the establishment of a new set of budgetary procedures in 1974.

According to another conventional view, the democratic process is not so benign. In that view, politicians are opportunistic, and voters are naïve. Incumbents manipulate their performance to appear misleadingly good at election time, and both challengers and incumbents make unrealistic and insincere promises. Voters are myopically oriented to the present, which makes them unprepared to hold incumbents accountable for their performance over entire electoral periods, or to relate electoral choices to future well-being in a meaningful way. Economic performance deteriorates. Politicians exploiting popular discontent propose superficial reforms that fail to solve the problems, such as the Gramm-Rudman-Hollings deficit-reduction acts of 1985 and 1987.

The truth is likely to be found somewhere in between those

extreme alternatives, which I shall designate as the benign and the malignant views, and the truth is likely to vary over time and place. The purpose of this book is to address the validity of those alternative views and to map the territory in between.

THE COSTS OF DEMOCRACY

This book addresses questions about the effects of democratic institutions on economic performance, when such institutions are taken to mean generically the institutions of accountability and of government by consent of the governed through periodic elections. Do democracies produce efficient results, as Wittman (1989) contends? Or do they lead to the accumulation of special privileges and protections from market competition that reduce efficiency and growth, as Olson (1982) contends? Democratic institutions are, of course, designed to be meaningful bulwarks against tyranny and against the rulers' exploitation of the ruled. But periodic elections themselves might generate perverse incentives.

In American political institutions, the system of checks and balances and the Bill of Rights provide constraints on government and on popular majorities that may control the government. But there may be ways in which the short-term incentives inherent in a popularly based political process need further restraint. The case might be made by comparing the outcomes of a democratic process with optimal standards for those outcomes, such as a zero rate of inflation, or some target rate of unemployment. Or the case might be made by comparing the outcomes produced by democratic procedures with the outcomes produced by non-democratic systems. If the latter, what realistic alternatives are there? It is difficult to characterize authoritarian governments in a general way. I shall not make systematic comparisons between democracies, such as the United States, and known non-democratic alternatives, such as the former Soviet Union. Instead, I shall follow the suggestion of Robert Dahl's *Democracy and Its Critics* (1989) and consider "anarchy," or the absence of government, and "guardianship," or government by the wise, as abstract and generic conceptions of desirable alternative procedures. Unlike government by the wise, anarchy has some negative connotations, but Dahl is emphasizing its lineage as a leading competitor to democracy and guardianship. Here the term "anarchy" should not be taken to imply "chaos." The theory of competitive markets is a theory of how a spontaneous order, with desirable properties, emerges from the absence of government direction.[1]

For this analysis of the nature of democratic institutions and their consequences for macroeconomic policy, we shall focus largely on concrete, observable experience in the United States, with occasional attention to other countries. But though the book has this focus, it is not just a book about American economic politics. The focus on a single country has several advantages: Most of the literature in the field of political macroeconomics has been written about the United States and is therefore directly useful. Also, the focus on a single country will facilitate attention to the historical development of institutions, to the time dimension, and to the *process* of democratic politics in ways that would be less feasible if many countries were included. Both institutional choice and process will be substantively important in the analysis and conclusions.

There are also disadvantages to the focus on the United States: The United States is only a single country, and though it is an important one, it is far from typical or representative. Also, its macroeconomic experience covers only a limited range. Unlike some other democracies, it has never experienced hyperinflation.[2] It has experienced sharply rising ratios of public debt to gross domestic product, but even that experience has been tame compared with what Italy, Belgium, and Ireland have seen. Focus on a single country forgoes the advantages of systematic and explicit comparisons. Still, I hope that by the end, the reader will agree that the advantages outweigh the disadvantages.

For alternatives to democratic procedures, we shall consider incremental changes within those procedures, either toward anarchy or toward guardianship. For example, a reform in the direction of less government intervention in private markets, such as the

---

1. Of course, the desirable characteristics of competitive markets require that the government defend property rights and ensure the enforcement of contracts.
2. There was very high inflation in the colonies between 1775 and 1783, as well as in the Confederacy, caused by the printing of paper money to finance war (Sachs and Larrain, 1993, p. 728).

deregulation of the banking industry, will be considered a move in the direction of anarchy. Similarly, a reform in the direction of insulating economic policy from popular influence, such as lengthened terms for members of the Federal Reserve Board, will be considered a move in the direction of guardianship. Thus democratic institutions can include features of both anarchy and guardianship, and those institutions may perhaps be improved by trying different mixes.

Dahl's study (1989) is a normative analysis of the theoretical arguments for democracy and other candidates vying for the title of the most desirable form of government. But real-world alternatives include dictatorships, many of which are not defended (or defensible) as desirable by any viable political theory. Ronald Wintrobe (1990) distinguishes "tin-pot" and totalitarian dictatorships, on the basis of their guiding motivations. Totalitarians seek to maximize their power over the population under their control, whereas tin-pot dictators seek to minimize the costs of keeping themselves in power in order to enjoy the benefits of office. Totalitarian dictatorships include those (such as the former Soviet Union) based on Marxist ideologies that favor economic development and that pay lip service to the goal of maximizing the welfare of the people. Others (such as Nazi Germany) are based on racist or nationalistic ideologies. The tin-pot type of dictatorship, such as the Marcos regime in the Philippines, provides a more relevant comparison with democracy for the purposes of this book.

Mancur Olson (1993) provides a direct theoretical comparison between democracies and revenue-maximizing dictatorships. The latter are similar to Wintrobe's tin-pot dictators, in that both use their power to enhance their own private economic welfare. In order to make the comparison "fair," Olson assumes that the dictator wants to maximize the revenue that can be extracted from the people being ruled, whereas a democratic majority wants to maximize revenue so that it can be redistributed among that majority. Both the dictator and the democratic majority wish to enhance the society's economic productivity for selfish reasons. Both are constrained in their selfishness by the possibility that beyond a certain point, further increases in tax rates will reduce the tax base and actually *lose* revenue that could be redistributed to themselves.

Olson explains how the "encompassing interest" of a majority in increasing the income of the society at large is greater than that of a dictator, because it directly receives some of the income that is produced, as well as the redistribution that it votes for itself. So far, democracy does better by the people, even if a selfish majority wants to maximize the politically determined redistribution from the society at large to itself.

However, it does not follow that democracies will redistribute less than dictatorships, because democratic policies often are responsive to small minorities and special interests that have far less incentive than does a majority to consider "the social costs of the redistributions they obtain" (Olson, 1993, p. 571). As Olson's rich analysis makes clear, comparison of the economic performances of democracies and dictatorships is a large and complex task.[3] This book will go no further with explicit comparisons of democracies and other forms of government, but it will make use of Olson's suggestion that democratic political competition can work well or badly.

Instead of comparing democracy and other forms of government, this book will conceptualize the performance of democracy relative to "objectively desirable" policies, when such policies can be identified. Of course, there is little agreement about what policies are objectively desirable, and that fact is one of the themes of this book. However, it will be possible to characterize certain central features of democratic politics and to show how they relate to the quality of policy. When there is a systematic way in which democratic policies deviate from optimal policies, this will be considered a "cost of democracy."

The "costs of democracy" include the reasonable and unavoidable prices of things that are basically desirable. Costs are similar to prices and implicitly are to be compared to benefits. Costs are to be minimized, but some costs are likely to be the inevitable prices of things that are valuable, and they are to be understood and tolerated. Democracy is a system that operates under the logic of the relationship between a "principal" (the public) and an "agent"

---

3. An additional important feature of the comparison that is included in Olson's article is the association among individual rights (including property rights), democracy, and prosperity.

(the government). I shall argue that there are modest and bearable costs of democratic procedures, but that they are comparable to the "agency costs" that are incurred whenever a principal delegates authority to an agent. As William Bianco has said, "the problem is not representative government; rather, representative government is an example of a generic and intractable problem" (1994, p. 167).

This book will argue that democracy does not systematically lead to inferior macroeconomic policy. In some situations, however, democracy, like other systems, can produce inferior policy. Also, a democracy may face debilitating conditions that it did not create, and there are ways in which some kinds of democratic institutions may obstruct the cure or correction of such conditions. But democracy comes in many forms, and democratic performance may vary under different conditions and institutional arrangements. A common response to poor performance is to propose changes in formal institutions, such as term limits for legislators or constitutional amendments mandating a balanced budget.

I shall argue that *informal* institutional changes often are sources of performance problems and that formal changes are unlikely to be successful correctives. For example, changes in the norms and patterns of behavior were what led to our contemporary problem of federal budget deficits. Formal institutional correctives such as the Gramm-Rudman-Hollings law have not solved the problem because they have not confronted the incentives that created it. A constitutional amendment will be no more successful unless it is based on a rationale that confronts the incentives.

It is also possible that informal changes in behavior can be constructive. The most important decisions about the formal structure of the American central banking institutions were made in the Federal Reserve Act of 1913 and in revisions to that act in the 1930s. However, the institutional change that made the Federal Reserve one of the world's most independent central banks was an informal agreement called the "accord" that was implemented in 1951. The meaning of democracy in any particular context depends not only on the formal constitutional rules but also on informal institutions that define patterns of behavior.

MACROECONOMIC ISSUES PROVIDE A LENS

Macroeconomics will provide a lens through which we can focus on these questions of democratic theory. The performance issues of central concern are those regarding inflation, unemployment, and income growth. Income distribution will be peripheral, though occasionally relevant. The lens will filter out other important problems, such as the environment, racial justice, war and peace, and so on. This strategy is not meant to imply that those questions are less important than economic performance. I do mean to show that a focus on macroeconomic issues can be especially revealing about the nature of democratic processes, and not simply because they are matters of continuing concern.

Macroeconomic issues often are consensual, in that there is wide agreement on the desirability of income growth and on the undesirability of inflation and unemployment. There is plenty of disagreement as well, but compared with the bitter disagreements surrounding numerous other issues, such as abortion, for example, there is an underlying consensus on the nature of desirable standards. This fact makes it easier to draw conclusions about the performance of democratic institutions on the basis of relatively objective standards. For example, democracies (like dictatorships) may postpone hard decisions whose resolution might improve their future prospects, or they may make decisions that will provide benefits in the present at the expense of the future. Macroeconomic issues facilitate systematic attention to the time dimension of political decisionmaking in ways that help us to make inferences about costs of democracy. My concern is less how democracy performs relative to dictatorship than how democratic performance might be improved in areas in which improvement is possible.

Yet even though macroeconomic issues are relatively consensual and performance-oriented, they are, at most, a short step away from conflicts of interest. Good macroeconomic performance can make everyone better off, and poor performance can cause everyone to suffer, but the particular policy choices that are made often have distributional dimensions. And even when distributional issues do not arise, there are important differences in beliefs about the desirability and consequences of alternative policies.

There are some kinds of costs or problems of democracy that

macroeconomic issues will not highlight. These include corruption and venality, which of course are not unique to democratic systems. Macroeconomic politics is public politics; the incentives for public officials are the incentives of large-scale vote shifts and of personal and partisan reputations. The most important decisions concern large-scale movements of fiscal and monetary instruments. Any possibilities that politicians have for personal enrichment by providing narrow benefits for themselves at the expense of the public interest are not likely to loom large in the politics of inflation, unemployment, and growth. And even though this claim must be qualified by the distributive character of many tax and expenditure decisions, this is a book about very general questions regarding how well democracy works, and how reforms of democratic institutions might make it work better.

SOME ECONOMIC ISSUES

Because our focus is on economic performance, there are several issues that we must address in order to do justice to the topic:

Are there clear goals and optimal choices for policy?

There is considerable agreement about the basic goals of macroeconomic policy, but much less agreement about their relative importance and how to achieve them. Generally, inflation and unemployment are to be minimized, whereas income growth is to be maximized. Although there may be debate about the appropriate targets and the trade-offs necessary to attain such goals, there is no question that extreme values are undesirable. Hyperinflation, such as the annual inflation rates of more than 1,000% experienced in some Latin American countries, is highly undesirable. Similarly, rates of unemployment and negative income growth like those experienced during the Great Depression are also clearly undesirable. This book will argue that the relative importance of goals is defined and redefined within the democratic political process, rather than outside of it.

Does the economy regulate itself, or does it need guidance?

We must be clear about our understanding of the way the economic world works. To what extent is macroeconomic performance dependent on or subject to control or guidance by public officials? I shall try to be agnostic on this issue and to recognize reasonable alternative points of view. As we shall see, there are several viewpoints among professional economists on this issue, and there is a continuing evolution of theory. The prevailing professional position on this issue tends to change over time.

Rules versus discretion

An intuitive approach to public issues would suggest that public-spirited officeholders should make policy according to what seems appropriate at the time, that is, to use their discretion. But not all officeholders are public-spirited, and discretion may yield to opportunism and inappropriate expediency. Discretion can even be inferior when officeholders are public-spirited.

An alternative that is suggested from time to time in the literature on macroeconomic policymaking is that there should be rules to guide and restrict the behavior of public officials in order to try to eliminate opportunism or systematic biases of the democratic political process. Examples include proposals for requirements that the federal budget be balanced and that monetary authorities set money growth at a fixed rate. Such rules might be appended to the Constitution, as has been proposed for a balanced-budget amendment, or they might simply be defined by legislation.

I shall oppose a balanced-budget amendment, even though I think deficits are a serious problem, because I do not think the enforcement issues have been adequately addressed. Simply putting a goal into the Constitution does not ensure that it will be achieved or even taken seriously. The Fifteenth Amendment established the principle that the right to vote shall not be denied on grounds of race, color, or previous condition of servitude, but it took almost a century for it to be enforced. The Eighteenth Amendment, which prohibited intoxicating liquors, also failed. I am sympathetic to arguments that rules and precommitment may be superior to discretion, but I shall argue that changes in formal rules without attention to informal patterns of behavior are likely to be misguided.

Outcomes, instruments, and structure

It is important to be clear about some language and concepts. We conceive of a nation's economy as a *structure* of behavioral relationships relating the demand and supply of goods and services. Measures of the performance of this structure include *outcomes* such as inflation, unemployment, and income growth, which may be viewed as satisfactory or otherwise. Policy *instruments,* such as tax rates and money growth rates, may allow public officials some control over the outcomes, as mediated by the structure of the economy.

Different understandings of the nature of the structure and of the relationships between instruments and outcomes are at the heart of disagreements about the three issues mentioned earlier. That is, different macroeconomic theories have different answers to questions about the appropriate goals for public policy, about whether or not the economy regulates itself, and about whether or not public officials should use their discretion.

SOME POLITICAL ISSUES

There are also some political issues about which we should be explicit and clear, if only to acknowledge their importance:

What motivates public officials?

We usually do not know the answer to this question, but useful theories have been built on the basis of assuming some answer. Politicians are, from time to time, presumed to be motivated by pursuit of the public interest, or more narrowly defined policy goals, or votes, or the rewards of office, or some combination. This book will be agnostic about the motivations of politicians, but will consider seriously the alternatives. It is possible to learn the implications of different motivations by modeling politicians as benevolent dictators and as vote maximizers, for example, and then comparing the results.

The values and wisdom of the voters

Voters may be narrowly self-interested or altruistic. Voters may or may not always know what is good for them. The incentives involved in appealing to voters may or may not be constructive. Voters may or may not be able to take a long-term view of the alternatives. I shall try to be agnostic about these issues, but shall be critical of the argument that appealing for votes implies fundamentally perverse incentives on the part of political candidates. However, I do think that public preferences are at the root of some of the deficit problems that the American public deplores and that there can be a large gap between public preferences and public understanding of the consequences of those preferences.

Accountability and independence

The accountability provided by periodic elections may increase the risk that politicians will take a short-term view at the expense of long-term welfare. Alternatively, independence of the requirement that officeholders appeal to voters may facilitate a focus on the long run, but it may lead to a lack of accountability. The requirement that politicians appeal to voters may lead to a focus on simpleminded and superficial solutions to problems, to the neglect of complex and realistic solutions that more independent institutions, such as the Federal Reserve System, might offer.[4] I shall defend the independence of central banks, as well as the need for periodic elections.

The meaning of politics and the political

In ordinary usage, the term "politics" often has derogatory connotations, as if politics were inherently undesirable. Herbert Simon observed that

in our society, we have an unfortunate habit of labelling our political institutions in two different ways. On the days when we are happy with them, we

---

4. By the end of this book, I shall be emphasizing that there are two meanings of "accountable." The first is "to be subject to sanction," such as removal from office via periodic elections. The second is "to explain, report, or justify." The issue will become subtle when we consider the independence of the Federal Reserve, and whether or not it should be required to announce its targets (see Chapter 8).

call them democracy; on the days when we are unhappy with them, we call them politics. (1983, p. 99)

This book is about "politics" in macroeconomic policy, and it is intended to rise above that "unfortunate habit."

In the chapters to come, we shall be seeking out important ways in which "politics" is used to designate things that we do not like. For example, Chapter 3 describes and analyzes a theory in which incumbents are said to manipulate the economy in self-serving and opportunistic ways when elections approach, fooling the voters at the expense of the public's interests, insofar as those interests can be objectively defined. When such behavior occurs, it is certainly politics in the undesirable sense.

We shall also consider ways in which "politics" means differences of opinion and judgment among reasonable, sincere, and informed individuals, as opposed to differences in tastes and preferences. We shall find such differences in beliefs to be unavoidable at almost every stage of economic policymaking, from disagreements among voters about candidates and parties to disagreements among academic economists advising the government about fiscal or monetary policy. In this sense, politics is about the resolution of "contestable" issues. Democratic institutions provide ways in which such differences are at least provisionally resolved through rules for public discourse and policymaking that are themselves contestable and subject to change. This is one of the reasons why process is important.

IMAGES OF THE DEMOCRATIC PROCESS

We shall try to arrive at an understanding of the nature of the democratic process regarding macroeconomic issues in terms of three possibilities:

The democratic process as optimizing

We might consider that democratic processes inherently choose the best outcomes, but what would that mean? One might say that democratic processes *define* the best outcomes, but that would be begging the question. We occasionally hear it said that the cure for the ills of democracy is more democracy, implying that there are inherently desirable features in the democratic process. John Rawls's conception of "pure procedural justice" (1971) exemplifies this notion. Under pure procedural justice, the procedure is so perfect that any decision that comes out of it is rendered desirable by virtue of the fact that it emerged from the process.

An example might be May's demonstration that majority rule always makes appropriate decisions when there are two alternatives and when the preferences of all voters are equally valid (May, 1952). Majority rule is, of course, fundamental to the democratic process, and more generally a metaphor for the process. However, May's proof under these limited circumstances cannot sustain the case that the democratic process optimizes, because the conditions do not all hold.

The argument breaks down, as Arrow (1963) has shown, when there are more than two alternatives. And in economic politics, not only are there often more than two alternatives, but not all of them are neutral. For example, some scholars argue that democratic procedures systematically produce outcomes that are inferior to others. Moreover, we shall entertain the possibility that some voter preferences may be misguided.

This book will not argue that democratic processes systematically choose the best outcomes (i.e., that they optimize), for a variety of reasons: There are too many varied procedures that might be called democratic. There is too much contestability about the value of the outcomes, and we know too little about the connection between the process and the outcomes.

Arguments that democratic processes choose optimal outcomes are likely to be tautological and nearly meaningless. Still, outcomes that are produced by a fair process in democratic institutions have a provisional legitimacy that can make them acceptable until the same institutions produce different outcomes, or until the institutions are changed to some other variant of democratic procedures.

The democratic process as pathological

An opposite claim is that democratic processes may be "pathological," that is, that they lead systematically to undesirable or inferior outcomes. To make such a case, we would need to identify the standards for outcomes by which it could be made, and we would need to show the systematic connection between the procedures and the outcomes. If claims of pathological consequences are to be supportable, we shall want to know if they are true in general or true only under certain conditions, regarding, for example, voter preferences or institutional processes.

One of the tasks of this book is to identify (macroeconomically oriented) arguments that there are systematic pathologies in democratic institutions and to identify the conditions under which they are likely to occur. In fact, there are very few such arguments. This book will argue that the democratic process is not inherently pathological, though we shall identify some risks and pitfalls. If it were true that generic democratic processes systematically produced undesirable results, that would have become more obvious by now. In fact, there are undesirable *possibilities* in democratic politics, and this book is designed to identify ways to avoid them.

The liberal interpretation of voting

William Riker defended a very modest interpretation of voting in which

all elections do or have to do is to permit people to get rid of rulers. . . . The kind of democracy that thus survives is not, however, popular rule, but rather an intermittent, sometimes random, *even perverse* popular veto. (Riker, 1982, p. 244; emphasis added)

Riker criticized as incoherent and unrealistic an alternative "populist" conception of democracy wherein voting is thought to be a true and meaningful expression of popular will. For Riker, "liberal democracy is simply the veto by which it is sometimes possible to restrain official tyranny" (Riker, 1982, p. 244). Such a view occupies a broad middle ground between the views that the democratic process is either optimizing or pathological.

The reader will not be surprised to find this book taking the middle ground, for this book is designed to map the vast territory between those extremes. How much more can we say about democratic processes than that it may be possible to restrain official tyranny by rejecting incumbent public officials? Because macroeconomic topics involve performance indicators that lend themselves to comparative evaluation, we have a better chance of mapping the territory than did Riker, who considered only popular preferences, which he took to be varied without limit, and all equally valid from a democratic perspective.

One advantage of the economic issues that we shall consider is that they will allow us to relate political choices to the performance of the economy, with the possibility that the performance may be disappointing. This interpretation of democracy is compatible with maximizing long-term growth and prosperity, and also with stagnation and decline. The experiences of several Western democracies show that both things can happen in the context of periodic elections.

THE ARGUMENT OF THIS BOOK

There are costs of democracy in the sense that there are, even at best, inevitable inefficiencies to be found in any system in which agents (such as presidents) act on behalf of principals (such as voters). There may also be ways in which the incentives of the electoral process lead systematically to outcomes that are demonstrably inferior. Such pathologies are possible, but they are not inevitable features of democratic politics.

However, arguments about the costs of democracy are slippery, because there are no uncontested fundamentals against which to make evaluations. There are no Archimedean points that offer the intellectual leverage with which to judge the performance of democracies. The standards for evaluation of democratic performance are written in sand rather than set in stone. Consider these issues in terms of Charles Plott's (1991) "fundamental equation":

$$\text{preferences} \times \text{institutions} \rightarrow \text{outcomes}$$

This equation simply describes the fact that the preferences and values of voters and politicians interact in a political process taking place in electoral and policymaking institutions. This interaction produces policy outcomes.

There may also be costs of democracy in the sense that the incentives of the electoral process may prompt incumbents to seek to produce outcomes that will appear better to voters at election time than they will later from a broader and more meaningful perspective. These are costs in the sense that they are comparable to the inefficiencies associated with any principal-agent problem. These costs occasionally can be large and perhaps can be considered pathological, such as explosive growth of public debt, or hyperinflation. But obviously these outcomes are conditional rather than inevitable features of democratic politics.

The desirability of any outcome could be defined in terms of the voters as the ultimate source of authority in a democracy. Or it could be defined in terms of the institutional processes that aggregate the preferences. Or it might be defined in terms of some objective standard for that outcome. My argument will be that none of these provides an unconditional basis for evaluation. Instead, there is a logical circularity among preferences, institutions, and outcomes. That is, there is feedback from outcomes to preferences and to institutions.

Any of the three elements might be taken as a standard for evaluation purposes. Taking preferences as a fixed basis for definitive standards, we can evaluate the way institutions process these preferences into outcomes, and then compare the results to the preferences. Or taking outcomes as the basis, we can compare the outcomes produced by the political process to the "best" outcomes. Or taking the institutional procedures as definitive, we might argue that the outcomes produced by processing the preferences are legitimized or rendered desirable by the very fact of having emerged from the desirable processes, as in pure procedural justice (Rawls, 1971).

This book will argue that none of these three alternatives is satisfactory, because none of the three elements provides definitive standards that are not subject to revision in terms of the other two. Institutional processes are accepted as definitive so long as they produce outcomes that are basically satisfactory in terms of existing preferences. But when the outcomes become unsatisfactory, we may try to improve them by changing the institutions. And the preferences themselves may change when experience shows that better performance is feasible, or suggests that worse performance is inevitable.

These arguments will be developed through the remaining chapters in the following way. Chapter 2 describes what macroeconomic theories say about what is feasible and desirable for economic outcomes and for the choice of instruments. Professional macroeconomists are our main source of authoritative knowledge about how the economic world works, but here, too, there is uncertainty and disagreement, and no single set of authoritative answers. The differences in beliefs might be described as political in a perfectly respectable and non-pejorative sense, because many of their features are inherently contestable.

Chapters 3 and 4 describe the most common models of routine politics in terms of macroeconomic issues. Chapter 3, on electoral cycles, abstracts some basic features of democratic elections as institutions of accountability for incumbents, as derived from the incentive to maximize votes. This chapter describes a theory that seems to illustrate economic politics at its worst: the self-serving manipulation of the timing of economic outcomes in order to win elections.

Chapter 4, on partisan differences, abstracts some basic features of democratic elections as institutions for choosing among candidates and among alternative future policies. Partisanship models describe how differences in interests or preferences among voters or differences in partisan choices translate into differences in outcomes. Both of these standard models capture important features of reality, but they leave much unexplained about how politics influences economic outcomes. The electoral-cycle models and partisanship models also leave much unsaid about the costs of democracy.

Chapters 5 and 6 discuss sources of authority and the arguments regarding what macroeconomic policy ought to do. Chapter 5 describes and analyzes goals for economic policy outcomes as defined in public law and by economic analysis. Although it is easy to identify extreme values of, for example, inflation and unemployment that are clearly bad, I argue that the identification of specific targets as best or optimal values is inherently contestable. Provisional definitions of optimal values for growth, unemployment, and inflation rates are useful for analytical purposes, but ultimately those choices are political in a perfectly respectable and non-pejorative sense, because they are inherently contestable.

Voters constitute the ultimate source of authority in a democracy, but Chapter 6 will argue that voter preferences are seldom clearly defined. They provide only relatively loose constraints on what public officials can do, and only imprecise guidance about what public officials should do. Sometimes the electoral process seems to offer perverse incentives for politicians to follow irresponsible policies, but I shall argue that electoral incentives do not force politicians to be irresponsible in order to be successful.

Chapters 7 and 8 are about the institutions and procedures through which macroeconomic policy is made. Chapter 7 concerns fiscal institutions and policies, and Chapter 8 focuses on monetary institutions and policies. One danger of popularly based policymaking is that popular desires for public programs will not be disciplined or restrained by direct experience of the costs through taxes. Yielding to the popular temptation to evade such discipline will have both fiscal and monetary reflections.

Fiscal policy might manifest a lack of discipline by producing inappropriate deficits and excessive borrowing. Monetary policy might yield to the same temptation by printing money to cover expenditures, as an alternative to borrowing. These two chapters will analyze the ways in which such risks are handled. The formal and informal institutions have been changed and may be changed in the future in order to improve policymaking, perhaps because outcomes are deviating from the ranges of tolerable alternatives, or because a winning coalition believes that it can impose its policy preferences on the future through changes in institutions.

However, it is not clear that the people who brought about institutional changes (such as those created by the Federal Reserve Act of 1913, or by the Budget and Impoundment Control Act of 1974) always knew what they were doing. Sometimes new institutions have unanticipated consequences, and sometimes they are stopgap responses to public pressure to "do something."

Chapter 9 draws these various themes together into a conclusion that treats the interaction represented by Plott's fundamental equation as a fluid process that feeds back on itself. The interactions among these elements will involve actions and choices by human beings who express and implement preferences about which they often feel strongly. This is a kind of behavior that is best understood in the context of rational choice models, in the style of economics, and we shall make use of such models. The interactions also involve speech, persuasion, and discourse, which can take place on a high plane of ideas or at the level of demagoguery. The political process will also be considered as a setting for argument and persuasion.

Some costs of democracy are inevitable and unavoidable in the best of political systems. However, the tone of public and even academic discourse can deteriorate to a level at which arguments are not posed and answered, to a level at which arguments are replaced by utterances designed to humiliate, to divide the opposition, and to rally the troops. This might be considered pathological. Even at such a low level of discourse, the fundamental democratic institution of regular elections provides an opportunity to throw the rascals out. This is a useful and meaningful minimum provided by Riker's liberal theory of democracy. Under other circumstances, there can be discourse of much higher quality. It is likely, though not assured, that the quality of policy choices and outcomes will also be higher under such circumstances, but then again, that quality is likely to be defined and redefined in the discourse itself.

2 Macroeconomic theories and their political implications

An advantage of using the lens of macroeconomic issues through which to view democratic practice is that there is a large body of macroeconomic theory. This theory derives from the effort to understand the way the economic world works, to explain and predict, and to know what is possible and what is not. For better or worse, the unmistakable message of this chapter is that there is no single, uncontested theory of the way the macroeconomic world works. That means that political disagreement about economic issues is likely to involve differences of opinion and belief about what is realistic and feasible, as well as about what is desired.[1] This chapter shows how macroeconomic theory is, in a sense, political theory.

POLITICAL ECONOMICS AND ECONOMIC THEORY: THREE QUESTIONS

Economic theory is the source of our most authoritative understanding of the way the macroeconomic world works, and there is

1. Milton Friedman has argued that "differences about economic policy among disinterested citizens derive predominantly from different predictions about the economic consequences of taking action – differences that in principle can be eliminated by the progress of positive economics – rather than from fundamental differences in basic values, differences about which men can ultimately only fight" (1953b, p. 5). This chapter argues that there has been considerable progress in positive (as distinguished from normative) macroeconomics since Friedman wrote, but that in spite of that fact there are still major disagreements among professional scholars.

an impressive body of such theory. As such, it seeks to identify what is possible; it seeks to identify the consequences of alternative courses of action; and it "defines the norms that determine when certain conditions are to be regarded as policy problems" (Majone, 1989, pp. 23–4). But macroeconomic theory does not speak with one voice. There are competing theories, deriving from competing systems of belief about the way the world works. We shall review a sequence of these theories with an eye to their answers to the following three questions:

Does the economy regulate itself?

The answer to this question is fundamentally important, because it has obvious implications for the roles of public officials and for the issue whether government should take an active or a passive stance toward economic stabilization. The answers given to this question vary substantially across different schools of macroeconomic thought. However, the different answers usually are based on assumptions that are starting points for further analysis, rather than on conclusions derived from careful investigations.

What role does the theory imply for public officials?

Some theories suggest that public officials should follow rules, such as fixed rates for money growth. Others expect officials to exercise discretionary choice, responding to changing conditions as they emerge. Some have stressed the importance of fiscal policy, the balance of taxing and spending, and others have stressed the importance of the control of the money supply.

What are the risks of mismanagement due to political incentives?

If discretionary action is expected of public officials by a macroeconomic theory, there may be risks that such discretion will be misused, perhaps because of the incentives of the electoral process. Buchanan and Wagner (1977) have argued that that is the case with Keynesian economics. Other theories suggest that officials should follow rules for fiscal and monetary policy in order to avoid the risk of mismanagement.

In this book I shall try to be agnostic about the alternative theories and to present them fairly in their own terms. In spite of the risk of making the book sound as if it is more about macroeconomics than about politics, I present the leading alternatives early, for the following reasons. Many of the models of politics that follow assume a macroeconomic theory, and it is desirable that the reader be aware of the theoretical underpinnings of a given argument and be aware that there are alternatives. Also, many of the dynamics will be more understandable if the reader has some grasp of the theory in which given models are set.

A secondary consequence for some readers may be the impression that macroeconomics is in "crisis" or "disarray," terms that have been used by some of its own practitioners.[2] There is surely a sharp contrast between the scientific agreement that exists in the field of microeconomics (the study of individuals and firms interacting in markets) and the scientific disagreement that exists in macroeconomics (the study of the overall performance of economies). As a sympathetic outside observer, I would urge tolerance and an open mind on the part of the reader. The central point of this chapter is that regardless of how contestable they are, views of how the macroeconomy works color and influence a variety of viewpoints on politics. What follows is not meant to be a comprehensive review, but rather a sketch of the alternatives that are most consequential for understanding political models.

THE CLASSICAL SYSTEM

Macroeconomics as a subfield of economics did not exist, as we know it, before the 1930s, but at that time the prevailing view in economics regarding the issues that were to become known as macroeconomics was known as the classical system.[3] The economy was seen as a self-regulating system, even though there was, of course, a recognition that business cycles existed.[4] A key feature was that aggregate supply, or the productive capacity of the econ-

---

2. Blinder refers to "utter disarray" (1987, p. 67), and Blanchard and Fischer refer to a theoretical crisis (1989, p. 27).
3. The sketches of alternative theories in this chapter draw heavily on Froyen (1993).
4. See Keynes's ch. 2, "The Postulates of the Classical Economics" (1936).

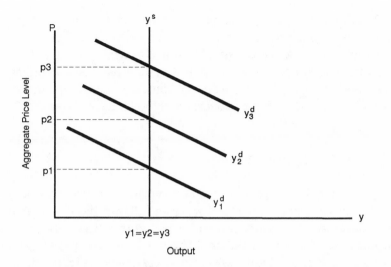

Figure 2.1. Aggregate supply and demand in the classical system.

omy, was a function of capital, labor, and technology that were fixed in the short run. The amount of output the economy would produce and the number of people employed were determined entirely by factors on the supply rather than the demand side of the economy.

The classical system explained how government manipulation of demand-side variables would *fail* to increase output. A fundamental reason was that output, or aggregate supply, was fixed in the short term. That is, the aggregate supply curve was vertical. Manipulation of aggregate demand by increasing the money supply would merely change the price level without changing output (Figure 2.1). A government budget deficit would change the balance of savings and investment in the composition of output, but not the total amount.[5]

In a world described by the classical system, there was no role for discretionary government stabilization of economic fluctuations in the form of active fiscal or monetary policy. The main role of public officials was to maintain a favorable climate for business by protecting property rights, enforcing contracts, maintaining a

5. Fiscal policy might affect output in the long run in the classical system through the effect of marginal tax rates on economic activity, or through the effect of government borrowing on real interest rates.

sound and stable currency, and balancing the government's budget. Because there was no role for a systematic, active fiscal or monetary policy, no systematic risk of mismanagement was identified. However, rigid adherence to the gold standard has been identified by some recent authors as a part of the causes of the Great Depression and as an obstruction to policies that would have ended it.[6]

EARLY KEYNESIANISM

During the Great Depression, unemployment rose to 25%, and nominal output dropped nearly 50%, from $103.9 billion in 1929 to $56.0 billion in 1932. The decrease in real output was only about 30%, because prices were falling.[7] The gross national product did not regain its 1929 level until 1939. That experience made it difficult to maintain the classical assumption that the economy regulated itself.

Keynesian economics, launched with the publication in 1936 of *The General Theory of Employment, Interest, and Money,* by John Maynard Keynes, provided an explanation for why labor markets might not clear and why massive "involuntary" unemployment could persist. Keynes contended that the

postulates of the classical theory are applicable to a special case only and not to the general case, the situation which it assumes being a limiting point of the possible positions of equilibrium. (1936, p. 3)

Keynes called his theory the "general theory" because it applied to a variety of situations, not just to that described in "the classical economics." Thus Keynesian economics *began* with the presumption that the economy does *not* regulate itself. That hardly seemed controversial in 1936.[8]

Keynesian economics explained the Depression in terms of inadequate aggregate demand for goods and services, and it proposed a way for government to use its taxing and spending powers to stimulate that demand. Although the *General Theory* said little

---

6. See Temin (1989) and Eichengreen (1992a).
7. See Froyen (1993, pp. 258–9).
8. See Keynes (1936, p. 15) on involuntary unemployment, and Hoover (1988, sec. 3.4) on the "persistence of the Keynesian problem."

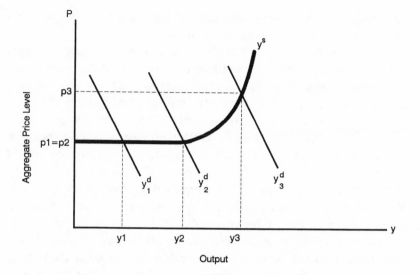

Figure 2.2. Aggregate supply and demand in the Keynesian system.

about fiscal and monetary policy, Keynes's followers developed theories by which intentional government budget deficits could stimulate aggregate demand.[9]

The political implications of Keynesian economics are several, depending on the situation. Under the conditions of inadequate aggregate demand and large amounts of unused capacity for production, an outward shift in the aggregate demand curve could be an unambiguous welfare improvement. Figure 2.2 illustrates this with an aggregate supply curve that is partially horizontal, as was implicit in early Keynesian models that assumed the price level to be fixed. If the economy is in a region where the supply curve is flat, then an outward shift in aggregate demand can increase output without increasing prices. As far as this argument goes, everybody's economic welfare is improved, while no one is hurt. Such a change is known as a "Pareto improvement."

Under those assumptions, the political problem for the Keynesians was the need to persuade policymakers of the wisdom of that course. Once recognized, the issue seemed to its proponents to be without costs and trade-offs. Politics, in that case, involved the

9. See Stein (1969, 1994). See Meltzer (1988) on Keynes's own views.

introduction of new ideas into public debate, and the argument that those ideas could help solve public problems.[10]

That was not an easy sell in the United States. President Roosevelt had met with Keynes and had not been favorably impressed. The similarity between Keynesian recommendations and the programs of the New Deal was more coincidental than intentional. Two decades later, Cary Brown summed up a careful quantitative analysis by saying that "fiscal policy, then, seems to have been an unsuccessful recovery device in the thirties – not because it did not work, but because it was not tried" (1956, pp. 863–6).

The originally proposed "full employment bill" of 1945 was of Keynesian inspiration (Bailey, 1950, ch. 2), but the process of amendment into the Employment Act of 1946 involved removal of the portions of the original proposal that had been most explicitly "Keynesian," such as using the federal budget as an instrument to achieve full employment. Congress passed the bill, but in doing so rejected Keynesian recommendations.

A weakness of Keynesian theory had been its lack of attention to the risks of inflation, which had not been a problem amidst the falling prices of the Depression. That issue was addressed in an article by A. W. Phillips (1958), who identified an inverse relationship between unemployment and wage growth across a long historical period in Britain. By extension that relationship implied a similarly inverse relationship between unemployment and inflation, which became popularly known as a "Phillips curve," such as that pictured in Figure 2.3. The trade-off between inflation and unemployment became widely understood as offering policy choices. Two leading economists cautiously described it as a "menu," and they anticipated that positions on the issue would be determined by "the tug of war of politics" (Samuelson and Solow, 1960, p. 193).

"Politics," here, implies a conflict of interests, or at least a divergence of preferences about the choices involved in the trade-offs leading to desired points on the Phillips curve. A world characterized by such an exploitable trade-off needed politics to make the choices about where to be on the curve. The economics of the Phillips curve made no judgment about what choices should be

10. See Buchanan and Wagner (1977, ch. 6).

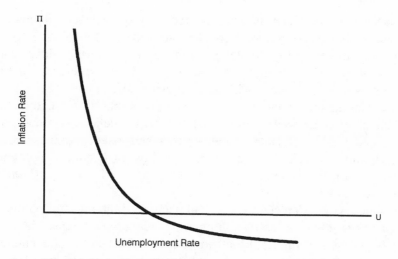

Figure 2.3. A simple Phillips curve.

made. With no "objective" economic basis for choice, *politics* became a basis for choosing among alternatives that were considered normatively neutral in economics. The political process is used to make a choice among alternatives that depend on values, preferences, and matters of taste, rather than on any authoritative or objective analysis of what is desirable. This kind of politics is benign, as opposed to malignant, in the terms identified in Chapter 1.

James Buchanan and Richard Wagner identified another, more malignant kind of politics associated with Keynesian economics. In their book *Democracy in Deficit* (1977), they did not challenge the economics of Keynes. Rather, they identified some secondary political incentives for irresponsible use of Keynesian prescriptions. They identified a kind of politics that has, in their view, adverse consequences. In the Keynesian view, the primary goal of macroeconomic stabilization policy is to stabilize output by manipulating aggregate demand, typically shifting it outward to eliminate involuntary unemployment and increase national income. Originally, that was to be done with fiscal policy, such as increasing expenditures or cutting taxes. Those actions amounted to creating *intentional* deficits in order to achieve the higher goals of stabilizing employment and output.

Once the belief in the goal of balanced budgets was relaxed, because of the identification of certain circumstances in which balance was undesirable, there were secondary political incentives to find opportunities to defend deficits. Politicians could please voters by cutting their taxes without cutting expenditures, or by increasing expenditures without increasing taxes, all in the name of stimulating the economy. Keynesian prescriptions for economic stabilization allowed a public justification for deficits that had not existed before. Buchanan and Wagner suggested that these prescriptions provided a pretext for yielding to a natural political temptation to do something that previously had been considered irresponsible.

Once Keynesian economists had persuaded the relevant political community that reductions in unemployment and increases in output were more important than adhering to the goal of annual budget balance, that goal never again had quite the same moral or political importance.[11] Furthermore, once it was acknowledged that deficits were sometimes desirable, it became much more difficult to identify circumstances in which the deficit was inappropriately large.[12]

The problem identified by Buchanan and Wagner was that in the absence of a norm of balancing the budget, the public preferred lower taxes and higher public expenditures, other things being equal. Those natural incentives to tax less or to spend more would reinforce the case for intentional deficits when they were genuinely needed to stimulate aggregate demand. However, the same incentives would create pressures to tolerate deficits for macroeconomic conditions under which deficits were not appropriate. The natural incentives to opt for low taxes and high expenditures would not change when there was *not* a macroeconomic case for intentional deficits.

Stabilization goals that would demand balancing the budget or even creating a surplus would not have the political advantage of compatible secondary incentives. Such goals would have to fight the normal incentives not to raise taxes and not to cut expenditures. Insofar as secondary incentives are operative, one would expect that budgets would be disproportionately unbalanced. That

11. The idea seems never to have lost its resilience among the public, but the attitudes of the "political community" seem to have changed. See Bratton (1994), Blinder and Holtz-Eakin (1984), Modigliani and Modigliani (1987), and Peterson (1985).
12. Chapter 5 will review some efforts to define appropriate standards.

is exactly what has happened. In the three decades since the first actively Keynesian administration was elected in 1961, there has been a surplus in just one year, fiscal 1969, which overlapped the Johnson and Nixon administrations, but was defined by President Johnson's final budget.

Even though there was no shift in the values held by the public, the informal institutions of budgeting changed when that norm for public officials was broken. After the case for intentional deficits was embraced in order to stimulate the economy in the 1960s, it became difficult to identify precisely when intentional deficits were no longer appropriate and when efforts to balance the budget might be harmful to economic performance. Judgments about when that point is reached can easily be clouded by the secondary incentives. To increase taxes or to cut expenditures when that might be appropriate for stabilization purposes runs against the secondary incentives to keep taxes low and expenditures high, and it becomes difficult to agree that such politically painful actions are necessary.

This problem of incentives identifies a potential problem for democratic politics. If deficits are harmful (and we shall see that there is disagreement among professional economists on this point), the incentives of the electoral process may not be constructive, and may even be perverse. But that is a potential rather than an inevitable malignancy in democratic institutions. If deficits were politically inevitable, we would have observed them throughout the entire democratic experience, but we have not. Budgets had been balanced as often as unbalanced over American history, until 1960. Except for wartime periods, there have not been long periods in which there have been no surpluses and in which public debt as a fraction of total output has been steadily rising, as is now the case.

Why should national budget deficits be a political problem now, when they were not a problem before? The answer, I think, does not hinge on the presence or absence of formal rules against deficits, such as those that exist in 49 of the states, or such as the balanced budget amendments that have been proposed at the national level. There was no such formal rule in the period before deficits became a problem. The answer has two components. One has to do with political norms, which were broken with the victory of Keynesian ideas in the 1960s. The other has to do with the difficulty of balancing the budget when the imbalance has grown to such a large fraction of national output. We shall return to these issues in Chapter 7 when we consider fiscal policy.[13]

The theory of economic policy

One of the achievements of Keynesian economics was "the theory of economic policy," or "traditional policy analysis."[14] That is a mathematical representation of the idea that policy instruments under the control of the government might be manipulated systematically in order to achieve given target values for outcomes such as inflation and unemployment.

The basic idea is that the complex interrelationships of a nation's economy can be represented by a structural model, that is, a system of equations that the uninitiated reader might think of as a "black box." A complete version of such a model would represent markets for labor, for goods, and for financial services and the connections among them. The relationship between a fiscal or monetary policy choice and a desired change in the economy would be defined by the equations that constituted the model of the economy. The model could be solved to identify the policy instrument choices that would achieve the outcomes that would maximize the welfare function.

This framework would seem to approach the ultimate achievement in making the public policy process scientific. Goals could be set in the political process, while the theory of economic policy would provide an objective technology to achieve them. There is no doubt that the theory of economic policy represents a very substantial intellectual achievement. However, it has been subjected to a major attack, to be described later in the section on the new classical economics.

Keynesian economics has received more attention here than do the other alternatives, the reason being that Keynesian economics is the main source of macroeconomic rationales for government

---

13. This perspective on deficits is not highly compatible with rational choice perspectives. See Alesina and Tabellini (1990) and Tabellini and Alesina (1990) for explanations that are.
14. According to Meltzer (1988), Keynes himself had little enthusiasm for this work. See Tinbergen (1952) for the landmark statement of the theory of economic policy.

intervention in the economy. Because it advocates active intervention, it is especially subject to the dynamics of political choice.

MONETARISM

Not all economists were swept away by Keynesian economics, but the objections to it were not immediately crystallized into a coherent alternative theory. Milton Friedman, the main creator of monetarism, offered a coherent alternative that for decades provided a basis for a continuing debate within economics about what could and should be done in regulating the economy. Monetarism returned to the presumption that the macroeconomy was a self-regulating system, and that presumption by itself implied that the appropriate role for government would be less than that implied by Keynesian theory. Monetarism asserted the importance of money and monetary policy, but did not advocate activist policy choices. One of its key assertions was that monetary policy could have significant effects on real economic outcomes, but that it did so with "long and variable lags" (Friedman, 1953a, p. 144). Because the lags were long and variable, one could not be sure that the stimulative effect of an increase in the money supply would be felt prior to the time the economy had already begun to recover. One could not be sure that it would not have an undesired, inflationary effect.

The general implication of such observations was that discretionary policy was as likely to destabilize the economy as to stabilize it, and should be avoided. Friedman is famous for his consistent recommendation that monetary policy be guided by rules, rather than by discretion. The rule he suggested is a rate of money growth fixed at a level designed to allow the money stock to grow at a pace that will be consistent with the overall trend for the rate of growth of the economy.

If there are political risks associated with monetarism, one such risk might be that adherence to a rule might become too rigid at a time when it was inappropriate, such as Eichengreen (1992a) and Temin (1989) have argued concerning the gold standard during the Depression. There seems to be a trade-off between the need for flexibility and the need for discipline.[15] We shall return in Chapters 7 and 8 to a discussion of rules versus discretion in fiscal and monetary policies.

Monetarism provided a basis for understanding the perverse consequences of one of the more widely discussed kinds of political manipulation. The Nordhaus (1975) model of the "political business cycle," to be described in Chapter 3, showed how the effort to create prosperity before an election might be unsustainable and might lead to lasting adverse consequences. Although Nordhaus was not known as a monetarist, the model of the economy he used was quite similar to the model articulated in 1968 in Friedman's presidential address to the American Economic Association. That address showed that the theoretical basis for the stable Phillips-curve trade-off between inflation and unemployment was weak and inadequate. Friedman introduced a distinction between short-run Phillips curves, in which there was a trade-off or inverse relationship between inflation and unemployment, and long-run Phillips curves, in which there was none.

The long-run Phillips curve is a vertical line in Phillips curve space, reflecting the combinations of inflation and unemployment that are sustainable. Because the curve is a vertical line in inflation–unemployment space, it shows that the "natural rate of unemployment" is compatible with any rate of inflation. A policy-induced increase in the money supply could lead firms to confuse a general increase in prices with a relative increase in the prices of their own products. They could respond by increasing nominal wages and hiring more workers. That would constitute a movement to the left on a short-run Phillips curve, as illustrated in Figure 2.4. As soon as workers realized that the general level of prices had risen, they would see that their real wages had declined, and employment would return to its previous level, at the natural rate of unemployment, but at the new, higher level of inflation. For Friedman, such a sequence would reinforce his earlier argument for a rule to guide a stable rate of money growth, as well as prohibition of such manipulation. His work laid the groundwork for identifying some of the risks of discretionary, politically motivated macroeco-

15. See Lohmann (1992).

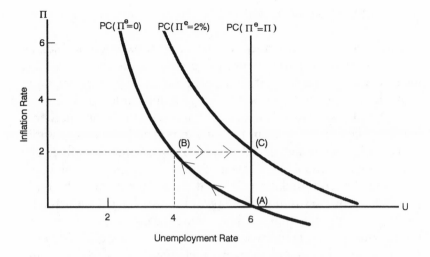

Figure 2.4. Long-run and short-run Phillips curves.

nomic stabilization policy in the form of the "political business cycle" (Nordhaus, 1975).

Keynesian and monetarist theories had divergent implications for the behavior of public officials, but neither had a theory of political motivation. Like much of economic theory, each was addressed to disinterested, public-spirited policymakers. However, the two theories led to divergent observations about the risks of political mismanagement. Keynesian theory involved some prescriptions for fiscal policy that Buchanan and Wagner (1977) argued were subject to risks of mismanagement, because the incentives of the political process might interfere with appropriate policy.

Monetarist theory involved no such prescriptions, and recommended the avoidance of discretionary policy. Monetarist theory provided a model that Nordhaus (1975) used to show the adverse consequences of political manipulation. Thus Keynesian theory proposed discretionary action that would add to the risks of politically motivated mismanagement, whereas monetarist theory recommended the avoidance of discretion and was the basis for an argument about the adverse consequences of politically motivated discretion.

NEW CLASSICAL ECONOMICS

The new classical economics, or the rational expectations school
of macroeconomics, was as emphatic as monetarism in asserting
the self-regulating character of the economy, and it was even more
emphatic in arguing that discretionary stabilization policy was fu-
tile.[16] Friedman's work had shown that attention to the microeconomic processes involved in the inflation–unemployment relationship could generate new insights and improved understanding. The
new classical school went even further than monetarism in its
search for "microfoundations," and it looked for them in the basic
premises of microeconomics. Those premises hinged on a fundamental assumption that human beings were rational, utility-
maximizing actors. New classical theory was also explicitly based
on the assumption that all markets, including labor markets, would
clear; that is, excess supply will be mopped up by reductions in
prices. For example, involuntary unemployment represents excess
supply in the labor market, which will be cleared by reductions in
wages to the "market-clearing level." In Lucas's words,

. . . there is an involuntary element in *all* unemployment, in the sense that no
one chooses bad luck over good; there is also a voluntary element in all
unemployment, in the sense that however miserable one's current work options, one can always choose to accept them. (Lucas, 1981, p. 242)

In the new classical view, there was no role for activist or discretionary stabilization policy, and the general policy recommendation
was similar to that of the monetarists: that fixed rules be followed.
In fact, new classical theory generated a rationale for a startling
claim called the "policy ineffectiveness proposition," which asserted that systematic stabilization policy was impossible. This was
an attack on the Keynesian "theory of economic policy" described
earlier.

Robert Lucas argued that the kinds of models used in that theory
"provide *no* useful information as to the actual consequences of
alternative economic policies" (1981, p. 105; emphasis in original).
The reason was that the equations in those models were not truly

16. The Great Depression poses a major problem for views that the economy regulates
    itself. See the discussions by Lucas and by Sargent in Klamer (1984, pp. 41,
    69). Conservative economists such as Robert Barro and Milton Friedman blame
    government policy.

fundamental. They did not capture invariant properties of behavior, and their parameters were likely to change in response to policy changes. For example, when a new fiscal or monetary policy is announced, economic agents may change their behavior in response to the policy, with the result that the goals of the new policy will be frustrated.

According to the new classical view, economic agents, including the public, form their expectations rationally. That is, they are forward looking and do not make repeated mistakes. From a position of economic equilibrium, businesses will respond to a monetary policy stimulus only because they confuse a general increase in prices with a relative increase in the demand for their products. Once they figure out that the stimulus came from monetary policy, rather than from a real increase in demand, they will readjust back to their previous levels of employment and output.

By extension, monetary policy can affect real behavior only by surprising people, and therefore it cannot be systematic. Policies that are not surprises will be expected by rational agents and will be neutralized. The only way for policy to be effective is for policymakers to "trick economic agents into behaving in socially preferable ways even though their behavior is not in their own interest" (R. G. Hall, quoted by Sargent and Wallace, 1976, p. 176). In effect, Lucas pointed out that macroeconomic policymaking is not decision theory in the sense of a game against inanimate nature; rather, it is a game involving other actors, who may respond strategically rather than passively to policy initiatives.

Even a public-spirited policymaker may try to create a monetary surprise that will increase output, for reasons that will be elaborated in the next section. But the people, rationally expecting it, will expect the inflation, but will not respond with the output. A credible set of rules might be designed to keep the policymakers from yielding to that temptation. We shall return to such rules in Chapters 7 and 8. Lucas did not shrink from the implication that his views imply a lesser role for economic policy advisers: "As an advice-giving profession we are in way over our heads" (1981, p. 259).

The policy recommendation of the new classicals is similar to that of the monetarists: that rules should guide policymaking. Discretionary monetary policy can only destabilize the economy by confusing people about what conditions to expect. Stable, predictable rules for monetary policy provide an environment in which markets can work more effectively than they can under the destabilizing influences of discretionary policy.

The risk of political mismanagement that is prominent in this theory is the time-consistency problem. In new classical macroeconomics, this problem offers a basis from which one can make a case for rules, but dynamic consistency is a subtle and important issue that goes beyond this variant of theory, and it deserves attention in its own right.

INTRODUCING THE TIME-CONSISTENCY PROBLEM

The time-consistency problem is an important general issue of public policy in which there is an inconsistency between the best general plan and the best thing to do at any given time. Two of the most intuitive formulations of the problem concern policy toward hostages and toward patent law. In the former case, a good general policy for all times is never to negotiate for hostages, because if that policy is believed, there will be no incentive for terrorists to take hostages. However, once hostages are taken, the incentives are strong to negotiate. Similarly, a good general policy is to encourage the development of new products by giving patents that will protect the innovators from economic competition that would drain away their incentives to create. However, once a new product exists, such as a cure for AIDS, there may be a powerful incentive to remove the patent protection and let the public enjoy the benefits of competition. In each of these cases there is an inconsistency between what is best at a particular time and what is best for all times – the difference between a best policy *ex ante* (for all conditions) and the best policy *ex post* (after conditions have been realized).

The problem is that conditions will deteriorate if it is expected that the *ex post* best policy will be followed. Even though a government announces its intention to follow the *ex ante* best policy, its determination to do so may be questioned by those who understand its incentives to deviate *ex post*. For example, a government may

announce that it will never negotiate for hostages, but if its po
is not believed, the expectation that it will negotiate will encou
the taking of hostages. Similarly, if a government policy to protect
inventions with patents is not believed, the expectation that the
government will not enforce patents will lead to fewer inventions.

The originators of this idea, Kydland and Prescott (1977), presented several examples, including one macroeconomic case, and
Barro and Gordon (1983) developed the macroeconomic implications.[17] The models assume rational behavior on the part of all
parties. The basic idea is that unemployment is too high, or national income growth is too low, even in a rational expectations
equilibrium, because of distortionary features of tax policy or of
labor markets. For example, individuals may respond to taxes by
altering their behavior from its most efficient pattern in order to
reduce their tax liability. Or collective bargaining agreements, minimum wage laws, or unemployment compensation policies may
restrict labor supply. Both patterns of behavior may reduce economic efficiency, and the policymaker may deal with that problem
by instituting a surprise burst in the money supply, designed to
reduce unemployment or increase output.

The increase in the money supply will cause an unexpected
increase in prices. Economic agents have trouble distinguishing
between a general increase in prices (i.e., inflation) and an increase
in the demand for their services or products. If they think it is the
latter, they will respond with increased economic activity, thus
fulfilling the desire of the public officials to increase output or
reduce unemployment. But if, in fact, it was a general increase in
prices, or inflation induced by the government, the effects will be
short-lived. If the tactic is tried repeatedly, over time the public
will learn to expect inflation, and will cease to respond. The result
is that there will be no change in unemployment or output, but only
increased inflation, to the detriment of everyone.

This application of the dynamic consistency problem is central
to much of the contemporary study of political macroeconomics.

---

17. One of Kydland and Prescott's examples involved government aid to people who
built on floodplains. The 1993 Mississippi Valley floods illustrated the relevance of
this example. See Albert R. Karr, "False Sense of Security and Cost Concerns
Keep Many on Flood Plains From Buying Insurance," *Wall Street Journal*, August
31, 1993.

The public and the policymakers are both considered to be "rational," in that both are assumed to seek to maximize their utility and are assumed to be capable of learning when they need to change their behavior in order to do so. In other words, both parties understand everything they need to know about their own interests and how to maximize them. But the problem still exists because the wage-setters act first, and act on their expectations of a money growth rate set by the government. The monetary authority needs to fulfill that expectation just to achieve the natural rate.

Recall that the application of this problem to macroeconomic stabilization depends on the presence of "distortions" that introduce inefficiencies into the economy. Such distortions could be caused by labor unions demanding wages above market-clearing levels, or they could be due to labor market policies, such as minimum wage laws and unemployment compensation levels, that would have similar effects of keeping unemployment too high or output too low. They could also be caused by tax policies that would interfere with economic efficiency and would have the same effect.

Because most of the models of dynamic consistency problems do not directly imply a conflict of interest between the public and the government, we might expect that the whole problem could be avoided by eliminating the distortionary taxes or labor market policies. However, Alex Cukierman has argued that "the underlying source of dynamic inconsistency can be traced in all cases to some basic conflict between policymakers and some groups within the private sector" (1992, p. 21). These could be unions that preferred wages above market-clearing levels, or groups that preferred distortionary taxes that would be borne by other groups. Although Cukierman's assertion that a conflict of interest is behind the time-consistency problem may be too strong to do justice to general examples like the hostage and patent issues, the conflict-of-interest view makes the existence of the distortions more understandable.[18]

In general, the time-consistency problem generates some insights that deserve to be introduced now, and to which we shall later return. Kydland and Prescott and Barro and Gordon have argued that the time-consistency problem can be solved by having a "rule" for the appropriate behavior, thus avoiding the "discretion" that

---

18. Another economic example involves the temptation for popularly elected governments to tax away the capital stock. See Persson and Tabellini (1990, pt. 2).

creates the problem. (Discretion in this case is the *ex post* best thing to do.) But how can rules be enforced? Would the enforcer not also be subject to the time-consistency problem? Elections might be proposed as an appropriate institution of accountability, but voters themselves might be a source of the temptation to yield. Anticipating problems like these, Barro and Gordon (1983) developed an argument suggesting that a *reputation* for following a rule may be an effective constraint on the temptation to yield to the time-consistency problem. This suggests that elections are not the only institutions of accountability for macroeconomic policy.[19]

SUPPLY SIDE ECONOMICS, REAL BUSINESS CYCLES, AND NEW KEYNESIAN ECONOMICS

There have been several notable developments in macroeconomic theory since those traced in the preceding sections. They will receive less attention here because they do not add appreciably to the articulation of alternative views on the three questions with which this chapter began, but they are considered briefly in order to suggest the flavor of theoretical developments subsequent to the theories that set out the basic political issues in macroeconomics.

Supply side economics received a great deal of attention in the 1980s, when it became known as a guide for the Reagan administration's economic policies. Some of the ideas associated with it are highly controversial, such as the idea that a reduction in taxes will lead to an increase in revenue. In terms of filling the role of a major alternative macroeconomic theory to compete with Keynesian, monetarist, and new classical theories, supply side economics is not a serious contender. However, in an important sense, supply side economics reflects a new and needed recognition that aggregate supply is an important macroeconomic issue deserving more attention than it has received for decades. In this regard, all economists are now supply-siders, in that they recognize that institutions and policies affect the incentives to produce, and thereby influence the efficiency of the economy and the amounts of goods and services supplied. The most prominent political manifestation of supply side economics is an aversion to taxes. This was reflected in

19. Note Cukierman's comparison of trigger strategy versus learning models of rule enforcement (1992, ch. 11).

the Reagan administration's Economic Recovery Tax Act of 1981 and in the continuing vigorous opposition to almost any tax increases.

Real business cycle theory developed simultaneously with the new Keynesian models. This theory is in the classical tradition in that it assumes that markets clear and that markets are efficient in achieving desirable outcomes. This theoretical view explains short-run fluctuations in the economy on the basis of changes in technology, in the cost of raw materials, and in consumer preferences. Because the fluctuations are presumed to be the desirable results of rational decisions made by individuals, there is no reason for the government to try to smooth out the fluctuations, even if it could. The role for fiscal and monetary policies in real business cycle models is not to stabilize economic fluctuations, but rather to minimize the distortionary effects of raising revenues to pay for government expenditures.

New Keynesian economics is a response to the challenge posed by new classical economics alleging that earlier versions of Keynesian economics did not have adequate "microfoundations" in theories of individual behavior. It is a theory that explains economic fluctuations and the involuntary unemployment of resources with models that are explicitly based on rational individuals who maximize their utility according to accepted postulates of microeconomics. The models emphasize the costs of adjusting prices, reasons for offering wages above the market-clearing level, and imperfect competition in markets for goods and services. New Keynesian models give modern explanations for the original Keynesian view that the economy does not automatically stabilize itself. However, new Keynesian economists do not all advocate active government stabilization policy, nor do they all agree on the relative effectiveness of monetary and fiscal policies.[20]

THE "POLITICS" OF MACROECONOMIC THEORY

This chapter has reviewed the main strands in contemporary macroeconomic theory as if they were branches of political theory.

20. See Mankiw and Romer (1991, esp. vol. 1, pp. 2–3).

That is, we have focused on the political issues in these theories: what they contend that public officials should do, and what they identify as the risks of political mismanagement. Each of the theories comprises a relatively coherent body of knowledge. Each new theory seems to have grown out of some important limitations of its predecessor, and there has been intellectual progress. Proponents of the older theories have made revisions in response to the challenges of the newer theories, and there has been an evolutionary advance of knowledge. There has also been some convergence. For example, it is possible to see Keynesian and monetarist theories as having converged in terms of structure, but disagreeing on rather narrow issues such as the sizes of various parameters in the equations on which they agree.[21]

What remains is a body of scientific thought whose diverging theories remain matters of dispute among the people who have the best professional credentials for evaluating such theories. This, I contend respectfully, is a political dispute, because it is about public issues, and because there are contending alternative viewpoints that cannot always be objectively resolved. Macroeconomic theory is contestable theory. Sometimes the interaction among these viewpoints is not conducted on a high plane. Herbert Stein observed that

although there is much talk about economic policy, there is no debate. People say what they have always believed, or what they find it convenient to say, but there is no confrontation of arguments. There is no effort to find the sources of disagreement, or to reach agreement, perhaps because the participants think that the effort to change minds and reach agreement is hopeless. Talk about economic policy has become only a way of rallying one's troops. (1994, p. 324)

As an outside observer, I think that Stein's remarks are too harsh. There has been progress in macroeconomic theory, and new developments build on the weakness of previous theory. Usually the debate takes place on a high level, and it involves a dialogue under the conventional rules of fair and objective discourse. In that regard it is often a model for what public and electoral politics should be. A distinction might be drawn between what economists study and how they study it. Economic models are models of rational choice behavior in which individual actors seek to max-

21. See Hoover (1988, ch. 1).

imize their own utility. Game-theoretic models of strategic interaction characterize how these rational economic persons may interact with each other in market and nonmarket settings. But rational actor models of strategic interaction are poor characterizations of what economists do. What they do is more like what Jürgen Habermas called communicative action, which "operates in the medium of language and is oriented toward reaching understanding" (Johnson, 1993).

Macroeconomists remain divided on the fundamental questions of whether or not the economy regulates itself and whether the proper macroeconomic role for public officials should be active or passive. However, as the theories have become more sophisticated about economic issues, they have moved steadily away from the presumption that good theory will be implemented directly without regard for the incentives of the political process. The remainder of this book addresses these incentives.

PART TWO
Models of routine politics

3 Models of accountability and opportunism: The electoral cycle

This is the first of two chapters that review the two most prominent models or theories of politics in macroeconomic policymaking: the electoral-cycle theory and the partisanship theory. These theories each capture special features of democratic politics and help us to understand democratic dynamics. In doing so, they abstract from the institutional details through which economic policy is made. Each leaves a great deal about macroeconomic politics unexamined and unexplained. The electoral-cycle model focuses on periodic elections as the democratic institution of interest, and the partisanship model focuses on dual alternatives in these elections. Both types of models connect these features of focal interest to macroeconomic outcomes: unemployment, income growth, and sometimes inflation.

In the real world, the impacts of elections and party differences are mediated through complex institutional structures of fiscal and monetary policies. For example, most of the contemporary models to be considered in these two chapters presume that governments influence macroeconomic performance through monetary policy, that is, through government control of the money supply and interest rates. Monetary policy is controlled by central banks, such as the U.S. Federal Reserve System ("the Fed"). Electoral-cycle and partisanship models often assume that the Fed obediently follows the preferences of politically motivated public officials. In fact, the Fed is considered to be one of the most politically independent of the central banks in the industrialized nations. Therefore, the idea that it is merely a transmission mechanism for politically motivated policy is problematic. Similarly, fiscal policy, that is, taxing and spending policy, has been seen as a channel for political manipulation of the economy. In the United States, these policies are the products of complex interactions among the two houses of Congress and the president. No observer of the contemporary scene would claim that there is reliable and predictable cooperation among these actors, whether or not they are controlled by the same party.

The institutions of fiscal and monetary policies are themselves (in principle) matters of choice. Their features will be the subjects of Chapters 7 and 8, respectively. Some readers may wish to look ahead to familiarize themselves with institutional details. But such details are not necessary to understand the models presented in this chapter and the next, which intentionally ignore such issues. This chapter reviews a class of models that suggest ways in which elections themselves, the main institution for ensuring accountability in a democracy, may have undesirable consequences. We begin with a simple and intuitive version.

PASSIVE VOTERS AND CASUALLY OPPORTUNISTIC POLITICIANS

Edward Tufte has offered an intuitive account of how elections may lead to cyclical policymaking. He first presents a rationale in terms of the beliefs of politicians. According to his distillation of the "politicans' theory" (Tufte, 1978, p. 9), economic movements just before an election can be decisive: Voters reward incumbents for prosperity and punish them for recession, and spurts in growth just before an election will benefit incumbents. These beliefs provide an even greater incentive to try to show better economic performance near elections than at other times, or a "motive," in Tufte's words.

Tufte provided evidence of cycles in macroeconomic outcomes. As of 1978, he found two-year cycles in disposable income, with peaks just before congressional and presidential elections, and four-year cycles in unemployment, with troughs just before presidential elections. He also found two-year cycles in transfer payments, such as veterans' benefits and Social Security. Two-year cycles were found in areas that can be relatively easily controlled by government, such as the mailing of checks and, by extension, disposable income. It is less easy for government to manipulate unemployment, which was said to follow a four-year cycle rather than a two-year cycle, rising through the first half of an administration and falling through the second half (Tufte, 1978, ch. 2).

The hypothesized motive for manipulation of such cycles is to enhance the incumbents' prospects for reelection. In fact, the incumbent party has lost six of the eleven American presidential elections since 1952; in three cases, the incumbent president himself lost. These facts suggest that there are further limits to the electoral-cycle hypothesis as a theory that integrates incumbent policymaking and electoral outcomes. If incumbents were able to manipulate economic performance in order to win elections, we might expect them to have won more often than they have. In a case like the 1980 election, incumbent defeat can be compatible with the electoral-cycle hypothesis. It has been said with tongue in cheek that in the Carter administration, the cycle was run backward (i.e., with the best economic performance at the beginning instead of at the end of the term), and President Carter's defeat could be said to confirm a theory that manipulation pays, or at least that failure to manipulate is punished.

Tufte acknowledges that the Eisenhower administrations did not manipulate the economy according to an electoral cycle, but he argues that those cases were exceptional, and he treats them as irrelevant rather than as counterexamples. In fact, Eisenhower's electoral success demonstrated that it is not necessary to manipulate the business cycle to succeed in politics. Still, the fact that the incumbent party lost six of the last eleven presidential elections does not say that incumbents do not *try* to induce electoral cycles or that they never succeed. But this record of defeat for the incumbent party clearly indicates that other things are also important.[1]

1. See Weatherford (1987) for an analysis of how a president's economic ideology and the organization of an administration's economic advising can create a variety of circumstances that can undermine the power of any single hypothesis.

   Golden and Poterba (1980) argued that the amount of stimulus that would bring meaningful political gains would be more than that observed in empirical models of the manipulation of fiscal and monetary policies.

Cyclical manipulation of the economy is not the key to understanding either election outcomes or the performance of the economy.

Regardless of the strength of the empirical evidence, Tufte provides a commentary that helps us conceptualize the "costs of democracy." He argues that the "electoral-economic cycle breeds a lurching stop-and-go economy the world over," and "a bias toward policies with immediate, highly visible benefits and deferred, hidden costs – myopic policies for myopic voters" (Tufte, 1978, p. 143). This sounds pretty bad, but the resulting instability and inefficiency are "the price we pay for having elections," according to Tufte, and should be compared with the kinds of policies that might result from having no elections at all. The implicit suggestion is that policies unconstrained by elections would be arbitrary and capricious, if not exploitative and tyrannical. But we saw in Chapter 1 that there is no single prediction of economic performance for non-democratic systems, any more than a single cyclical pattern characterizes economic performance under elections.

Tufte suggests that democratic control over economic policy is inevitably "political," but that such manipulation may be no more serious than the resulting inefficiency (Tufte, 1978, p. 149).[2] Here, then, is a preliminary statement of the costs of democracy: inefficiency that is the reasonable price for something desirable, where the undefined alternative is implied to be much worse. This view is sensible, but not completely satisfying. I shall try to define these costs more precisely and consider whether or not there are ways of minimizing them.

THE STRATEGY OF MODELING

In order to get more informative answers to such questions, we shall use simplified abstractions of important features of political processes (i.e., "models"). Models strip away inessential details that distract from our focus on the question of interest. The strategy of modeling is central to economics and is increasingly common in political science. Much of the analysis in this book draws

2. Note that Olson (1993) provides a basis for a hypothesis that some democracies may be more inefficient than some dictatorships.

on what might be called the application of the methodology of economics to political questions.

For a model of the electoral-cycle hypothesis, I shall present an initial simplification by considering the electorate as if all voters had the same preferences for economic performance, and as if economic performance was their only concern. Thus we ignore other issues and suppress possible conflicts of interest among voters. We shall consider the government as another single person, ignoring issues of collective decisions within government. We assume further that the government is motivated purely by the desire to win reelection, ignoring other reasonable possibilities. If the government fails to win reelection, it is replaced with another government that is just like it.[3] For now, we do not recognize differences among politicians, either in their policy goals or in their competence to achieve goals.

This view suggests a model in which the key interaction is across a "horizontal" divide:

government

―――――――

voters

Modeled in this way, the electoral-cycle hypothesis is a pure principal-agent problem between voters as the principal and government as their agent.[4] This interaction depends on the following factors:

1. The motivations of politicians, modeled as the single goal of winning elections or of maximizing votes. For example, George Bush once said that "I will do what I have to do to be re-elected" (interview with David Frost, January 23, 1991). Note that there may be different interpretations of this statement. Elections are the main institution through which the people express their preferences, and the statement could mean that "I will do everything I have to do in order to give the people what they want." Of course, the statement lends itself to a more cynical interpretation, such as that "I will do whatever it takes to win, regardless of principle, and regard-

---

3. For some pure theory on such an interaction, see Barro (1973) and Ferejohn (1986).
4. For an accessible introduction to agency theory in a political context, see Kiewiet and McCubbins (1991, ch. 2). See also Kreps (1990, ch. 16) for a more theoretical introduction.

less of whether or not it fulfills the wishes and needs of the voters in a broad sense." The models we shall consider will help us to sort out such interpretations.

2. The behavior of voters, modeled as voters' decisions made on the basis of past economic performance. For example, voters are often thought to ask, "What have you done for me lately?" The models we shall consider will help us assess the consequences of such a standard for voting. Later in the book we shall consider directly the evidence on how voters behave.

3. The capacity of the government to manipulate the economic outcomes to which voters respond, presumably through fiscal or monetary policy. The models to be considered will vary somewhat according to their dependence on alternatives among the macroeconomic theories reviewed in Chapter 2.

Other models with other features will be seen throughout this book. But this initial formulation of an electoral-cycle model characterizes that used by William Nordhaus in a seminal article to be described next.

PASSIVE VOTERS AND MAXIMIZING OPPORTUNISTIC POLITICIANS

William Nordhaus (1975) presents an account of how elections might lead to cyclical policymaking, an account that differs from that of Tufte. Nordhaus presents a formal mathematical model of how elections might *systematically* lead to demonstrably inferior policy outcomes. The formal model allows him to draw stronger conclusions than could Tufte, but these conclusions are contingent on the realism or verisimilitude of the model. To facilitate exposition, I shall substantially simplify what Nordhaus presents, without violating the spirit or the content of his work.

Nordhaus models goals with *objective functions,* which are mathematical equations that allow us to quantify the degree to which goals are achieved. An example of an objective function would be the well-known "misery index," which is simply the sum of the rates of inflation and unemployment. A mathematical way of stating this is to say that "misery" is an unweighted additive function of the unemployment and inflation rates: $M = U + \Pi$. For example, the misery index in the election year 1988 was 9.6, given the unemployment rate of 5.5 and the inflation rate of 4.1.[5]

Nordhaus uses two versions of the misery index as objective functions, where the only difference between the two is in the weighting of time. One, called the "vote function," is designed to show what a vote-maximizing politician will do. It is a misery index that is averaged over the period between elections, but weighted so that the part just before the election at issue counts most heavily, and the part just after the preceding election counts least. This is a way of presenting the idea that voters may forget or ignore the past and ask, mainly, "What have you done for me lately?"

The other objective function that Nordhaus uses is called a "welfare function," and it is designed to measure general social welfare, or well-being (not public assistance). This is also a misery index that is averaged over electoral periods, but it is weighted differently with respect to time. To simplify, we shall treat it as not weighted at all, that is, counting the same weight for each time period, whether early or late in the electoral period. The idea is that citizens' well-being matters at all times, not just before elections.

These two objective functions allow Nordhaus to analyze alternative kinds of behavior by the government. They will permit us to infer what a government would do if it maximized votes, and to contrast that with what it would do if it maximized social welfare. Put differently, this allows a comparison between a generic politician, who is assumed to maximize votes, and a generic benevolent dictator, or guardian, who is assumed to maximize social welfare.

For example, consider the following misery indices for the Nixon administrations:

	Unemployment	+	Inflation	=	"Misery"
1969	3.4		5.5		8.9
1970	4.8		5.7		10.5
1971	5.8		4.4		10.2
1972	*5.5*		*3.2*		*8.7*
1973	4.8		6.2		11.0
1974	5.5		11.0		16.5

The average misery index for the first administration was 9.6, but the best figure was for the election year 1972, and things got much

5. To infer misery indices for any other year from 1949 through 1992, see Table 4.3.

worse after the election. Many observers have argued that President Nixon manipulated the timing of economic events so as to maximize his chances for reelection in 1972, at the expense of well-being after the election.[6] Indeed, that experience may well have inspired the Nordhaus and Tufte scholarship, which appeared subsequently.

A politician who seeks to maximize votes might try to concentrate good times in periods just before elections. That would make sense, given that goal, if voters were thought to forget or discount what had happened early in the electoral period, and if voters were not thought to be able to relate events near the election to conditions afterward.

But what would a politician who seeks to maximize the public's welfare do? Such a politician would not concentrate the good times into periods in which the voters were paying more attention. He presumably would want to keep the misery index as low as possible all of the time, and he surely would not make things unsustainably good near elections at the expense of being worse later on.

Neither kind of public official can simply set the misery index as low as he wants, say at zero, because there are real-world limitations on what can be done. So next we need a model of the possibilities and the limitations on the achievement of either kind of goal. This is called a *constraint,* and it is a way of representing the way the economy works. The economics of the model of the constraint that Nordhaus uses are those of the natural rate of unemployment, as explained in the section on monetarism in Chapter 2. Certain features of this model are no longer widely accepted in economics, but I present it for illustrative purposes.

The essential features of the model of the economy that Nordhaus uses are that inflation and unemployment are inversely related in the short run, but not over the long run. There is a "natural rate" of unemployment, which is determined by features of the labor market and the laws regarding it. This natural rate is consistent with any rate of inflation, including zero. Efforts to drive the unemployment rate below the natural rate will create inflation; moreover, unemployment rates below the natural rate cannot be sustained without accelerating inflation.

6. See Sanford Rose, "The Agony of the Federal Reserve," *Fortune,* July 1974, p. 90.

This model is a model of intertemporal choice; it does not deal with distributional issues at all. A central feature is the way policy outcomes are dependent on what has happened before. The model explains how it might be possible for politicians to create unsustainably low combinations of inflation and unemployment before elections, at the expense of higher combinations after the elections. In other words, Nordhaus presents a theory of how politicians might appeal to voter naïveté by making things look good at election time, while at the same time their actions are such that they will cause things to be bad after the election. The way this works is illustrated in Table 3.1. Note again that this pattern hinges on a theory of the way the economy works, which may or may not be correct, as well as on other premises regarding political behavior.

Nordhaus's tightly constructed model allows him to derive powerful normative implications:

Under conditions where voting is an appropriate mechanism for social choice, democratic systems will choose a policy on the long-run trade-off that has lower unemployment and higher inflation than is optimal. (Nordhaus, 1975, p. 178)

It took radical simplification to get that answer, and the answer depends on the veracity of that simplification. Whatever its veracity, the result helps us think about the costs of democracy.

Nordhaus's model provides an explicit comparison between what happens in his stylized democracy and the "best possible policy." "Best policy" is defined by Nordhaus, and it is defined outside of the model, that is, exogenously. For Nordhaus, a superior policy is economically (technically) feasible. As he characterizes democracy, with passive voters that have no capacity to learn, superior policy is politically feasible only outside of democracy. Superior policy is feasible if a benevolent dictator, or guardian, is feasible, but we are not shown a system in which such a policymaker is a practical alternative.

This cost of democracy as conceptualized by Nordhaus seems a little more pathological than the one described by Tufte. The difference is that policy in the Nordhaus version is distinctly inferior to a feasible and clearly identifiable alternative. Also, it depends on a kind of behavior by voters that would indicate that they are not very smart, if not actually irrational. If Nordhaus were correct on all counts, we might say that the economically feasible and prefera-

Table 3.1. *Illustrating the Nordhaus model*

II is inflation, U is unemployment, M is the misery index, U^n is the natural rate
of unemployment, and Π^e, the expected inflation, is modeled as inflation in
the preceding period.

Modeling goals with "objective functions":

misery index at time $t = M_t = U_t + \Pi_t$

Modeling the way the economy works, the "constraint." What follows is a
model of an "expectations-augmented Phillips curve," with a "natural rate
of unemployment":

$$\Pi = \Pi^e - 0.5(U - U^n)$$

Assume that the natural rate of unemployment is 6% and that the policymaker
can manipulate the actual unemployment rate at will. The resulting inflation
is defined by the preceding equation.
Consider the following scenario as a possible result of an effort to maximize
votes:

	Π	Π^e	U	Misery index
Period 3	0.0	0.0	6	6.0
Period 4	0.5	0.0	5	5.5
Period 1	0.5	0.5	6	6.5
Period 2	0.0	0.5	7	7.0
Period 3	0.0	0.0	6	6.0
Period 4	0.5	0.0	5	5.5

In period 3, inflation is zero, and unemployment is at the natural rate. At 6.0,
the misery index is at its lowest sustainable rate. By reducing unemployment to 5% in the election year, the gain from lowering unemployment
outweighs the cost due to inflation, and the misery index drops to 5.5, which
is not sustainable. However, the misery index rises in the year after the
election. In order to repeat the cycle for the next election, unemployment is
raised to 7% in the second year. The average misery index is 6.25 under
such manipulation, whereas it is possible to maintain the misery index
at 6.0.

ble outcomes are not "politically feasible." But even that would be
true only so long as voters are not able to learn to avoid self-
defeating behavior. Nordhaus's voters are modeled as passive;
however, active, strategic voters might defeat the manipulative
behavior in this model.

SOPHISTICATED CITIZENS AS ECONOMIC AGENTS AND AS VOTERS

The Nordhaus model puts together three kinds of behavior: that of politicians, that of citizens as economic agents, and that of citizens as voters. Nordhaus's assumptions about politicians and his view of citizens as voters are both still widely accepted. Contemporary studies offer richer assumptions about politicians and acknowledge that they may be motivated by policy goals and by the rewards of office as well as by the desire for votes, but the vote motive is still widely acknowledged. Also, Nordhaus's assumption that voters vote in response to retrospective evaluations of recent economic performance is also widely accepted.

The weakest link in Nordhaus's model from the point of view of contemporary scholarship is that between the politician's decisions and the performance of the economy. Few informed observers believe that policymakers can manipulate the performance of unemployment or income growth with anything like the kind of precision that is assumed in the Nordhaus model of electoral cycles, if at all. The reason that politicians in his model can manipulate the unemployment and inflation rates depends on a contested, if not discredited, theory about individual-level economic behavior, specifically, an "adaptive expectations" model of the formation of inflationary expectations. Many economists think that citizens as economic agents are too "rational" to be manipulated in that way. According to "rational expectations" theory (which was originally associated with the new classical view, but is now much more widespread), citizens would see that the government was trying to expand the economy from an equilibrium, and once they realized that, they would cease to respond.

Some readers may be appropriately puzzled by the different understandings of human behavior in the disciplines of economics and political science. Patterns of behavior that most economists assume to exist and call "rational" are considerably more sophisticated than the patterns that most political scientists believe to exist. Furthermore, political scientists put far less weight on the assumption that human behavior is "rational" as a basic premise for their scholarly discipline.

For example, according to a widely accepted contemporary understanding in economics, citizens would defeat most government manipulation of the economy in their capacity as economic agents. They would be able to learn that the government was trying to stimulate the economy beyond its natural capacities, and they would defeat that effort by not responding as employers, employees, investors, and consumers. That is, according to rational expectations views of the economy, the manipulation that Nordhaus models could not even occur, because the economy would not respond, since citizens are assumed to be "rational" economic agents who could not be manipulated in that way. Later, we shall encounter more observations about voter rationality.

According to widely accepted understandings in political science, however, citizens as voters might well reward politicians for such manipulation if it were to take place, because voters are seen as responding to recent past performance. Because each discipline has its own specialized audience, inconsistencies between them are not always confronted. We shall return to this issue when we consider voting behavior, in Chapter 6. At this point, we can say that Nordhaus's model of electoral cycles in inflation and unemployment is of historical and theoretical interest. It is no longer taken very seriously in economics, though other models of electoral cycles are.

Rational expectations models of political manipulation: raising the question of competence

There have been several theoretical analyses of the interactions between the politicians who determine macroeconomic policy and citizens who are assumed to be rational in the demanding sense assumed by most economists. Such studies continue the assumption that politicians are alike in their goals and motivations. There are no divergent policy preferences, but they introduce the possibility that politicians may differ in terms of "competence."

This is an important innovation. Even in a simplified modeling world in which there are no differences in political preferences, politicians may differ in their abilities to achieve agreed upon goals. And elections are important institutions to allow voters to remove incumbents who fail to accomplish such goals. In the models that introduce competence, citizens are assumed to be rational utility maximizers and therefore to be able to interact strategically with government if necessary, rather than being passive, as they were in Tufte's and Nordhaus's studies. This by itself is an important advance. If government repeatedly manipulates the economy in order to fool voters, should we not expect that it is possible for voters to learn how to respond in their own interest?[7]

When citizens are modeled as capable of strategic behavior, the interaction between citizen and government may become a game of asymmetric information, in which the government may use superior information to achieve its goals. For example, Rogoff and Sibert (1988) and Rogoff (1990) assume that the public can monitor the government's competence perfectly after a lag. This lag introduces a temporary information asymmetry that allows the government to try to deceive the voters about its competence. Even if voters understand perfectly the motivations of politicians and the constraints under which they operate, the government still might try to signal its competence by manipulating taxes, spending levels, deficits, money growth, or the balance of government consumption and investment before elections.

It is ironic that the effort to demonstrate the appearance of competence to democratic electorates would have destabilizing consequences. Rogoff and Sibert do not draw precise conclusions about the welfare consequences of such efforts, though they do say that

elections are not necessarily a bad thing, just because they result in excessive inflation or a suboptimal distribution of tax distortions over time. By holding elections, the public gets a more competent government, on average. (1988, p. 12)

Rogoff (1990, p. 31) shows that institutional reforms may restrain manipulation, but at the expense of useful information. In these very abstract and mathematical models, incumbents are modeled as caring about both reelection and social welfare, and the relative weights of the two concerns are permitted to vary. As such, their models leave us with new insights regarding possible costs of democracy, but without clearly identified pathologies.

We might expect that sophisticated voters could in time learn to

7. See Richards (1986) and Suzuki (1991) for treatments of voters as being able to learn from the experience of manipulation.

act strategically against predictable kinds of manipulation if they understood the constraints as well as economists often assume they do. But the more enduring insight of these studies of "rational" electorates is that even at the most demanding levels of strategic interaction between voters and politicians, the government is likely to have and to exploit an informational advantage in what game theorists call an asymmetric-information game.

A very general formulation of the asymmetric-information insight is found in the work of Cukierman and Meltzer (1986). That paper is not oriented to specific policy instruments, as the Rogoff papers are, but it is grounded in the realistic presumption that the performance of the economy is not perfectly predictable, but is affected by chance. That is, it is stochastic, and its performance is affected by random shocks. Cukierman and Meltzer point out that the government will have better information than the public about the nature of such shocks and will use it in such a way as to make economic performance appear better than it actually was. They suggest that the difference between what the government does with its information advantage and what the voters would do if they shared the advantage is a "cost of democracy." This cost is not measurable or systematic. It is, in fact, characteristic of any principal–agent relationship. It is the most generic accountability problem. In their words,

our model implies that any government with private information that maximizes its probability of reelection will choose not to maximize social welfare. The public expects the government to increase its welfare before an election, at the expense of a greater loss of future welfare, and it judges the government's *competence* by its performance in advance of the election. A failure of the government to act in its own interest before the election gives an incorrect inference to the public about the government's *competence* . . . . (Cukierman and Meltzer, 1986, p. 386; emphasis added)

The cost of democracy implied is not a systematically identifiable feature, such as an inflationary bias. Rather, it is an unpredictable product determined by how random shocks affect what government can achieve. This argument offers a very general model of the costs of democracy, and it does not depend on a macroeconomic context in order to be meaningful. It does seem to presume a very finely honed and discriminating monitoring of government behavior by the public. Ironically, a less attentive public might

Table 3.2. *Average annual rates for unemployment,
growth of gross domestic product, and inflation, by year
of presidential term, 1949–92*

Year	Unemployment	GDP growth	Inflation
1	5.45	3.13	3.88
2	5.97	2.34	4.19
3	5.95	3.56	4.38
4	5.65	3.59	4.09

Source: Economic Report of the President (various years).

generate fewer "costs." We shall return to this point in later chapters, especially Chapter 6.

The systematic attention to the competence of governments is an important innovation in these studies. Competence is modeled in terms of random shocks. One would think that competence would be related somehow to the training and experience of public officials and to the similarity between their beliefs about the economy and its true structure. However, these possibilities have not yet been developed.

A BRIEF LOOK AT SOME EMPIRICAL EVIDENCE

Empirical support for the electoral-cycle idea is generally weak. Studies rejecting the idea have been appearing at least since 1978.[8] A decade ago, two leading scholars concluded that "no one could read the political business cycle literature without being struck by the lack of supporting evidence" (Alt and Chrystal, 1983, p. 125). Yet the idea remains resilient in spite of the largely negative findings.

A casual look suggests that the evidence for the electoral-cycle hypothesis is not overwhelming. Table 3.2 aggregates data on unemployment, real national income growth, and inflation, by year of the electoral cycle, for the United States in the period from 1949 through 1992, or Truman through Bush. Unemployment did rise

8. See, for example, McCallum (1978).

and fall, on average, according to the hypothesized pattern, although the lowest average rate of unemployment occurred in the first year, rather than in the presidential election year. National income growth [the annualized rate of change in the gross domestic product (GDP)] did not show the predicted two-year cyclical pattern, though it was higher in the second half than in the first half of the "average" administration. Inflation did follow a four-year cycle but seemed to peak in the third year.[9] Ironically, the lowest values for both inflation and unemployment occurred in the year most distant from the next election, rather than in the election year. The average differences are quite small for unemployment and inflation, little more than half a percentage point at the extreme. The average difference in GDP growth is larger, more than a full percentage point over the cycle. A detailed look at each administration shows considerable variation in the patterns, and the averages do not predict well for any given administration. Chapter 4 will show that partisan differences can help identify some patterns hidden within the variation.

More careful statistical studies might show evidence of electoral cycles after controlling for other complicating variables. For example, in their article "Political Models of the Business Cycle Should Be Revived," Haynes and Stone (1989) reported a sophisticated estimation of a sine-wave pattern of macroeconomic outcomes following electoral periods. Their electoral-cycle variable was significant in equations explaining income growth, unemployment, and inflation. Their results will be considered again in the next chapter, because they identified an important interaction between the electoral-cycle variable and partisanship. Without that interaction, the cycle variable predicted a difference of almost one percentage point in the growth of gross national product (GNP), almost one percentage point for unemployment, and a little over half a percentage point for inflation.[10]

Of course, it is possible that such electoral cycles exist from time to time, but that they disappear. Keech and Pak (1989) found that an apparent electoral cycle existed for U.S. veterans' benefits

---

9. In none of the cases is the difference between adjacent pairs of numbers statistically significant at the .10 level, according to a t-test for difference of means.
10. Kevin Grier (1989, 1993) has found supportive evidence in careful econometric studies. See also Williams (1990).

between 1961 and 1978, but that it subsequently disappeared. The reason for the change is easy to identify. Instead of being adjusted by Congress, benefits have been indexed to fluctuate automatically with the consumer price index since 1979. Similar results will be found for Social Security, which has also been indexed.[11]

The most extensive and authoritative empirical study (Alesina, Cohen, and Roubini, 1992a,b) analyzed the possibility of electoral cycles for economic variables in 18 Western industrial democracies in the Organization for Economic Cooperation and Development (OECD) between 1960 and 1987.[12] Those findings were largely negative, but it is instructive to report them in terms of the distinction between policy instruments and outcomes, and between real and nominal quantities. We would expect that it would be most difficult to control real outcomes, but possible to affect nominal outcomes such as inflation, and most feasible to manipulate policy instruments.

Those authors found no convincing support for electoral cycles in either unemployment or GDP, the real economic outcomes. They did find some evidence that inflation, the nominal economic outcome, followed an electoral cycle, with inflationary spurts coming after elections. There was some evidence that money growth was greater before elections in the OECD countries in general, but the supportive evidence varied by country (and was not strong for the United States). There was also evidence that budget deficits were greater before elections.

All of those findings are consistent with the idea that incumbent politicians may try, at least occasionally, to manipulate policy instruments under their control in order to enhance their prospects for reelection. The consequences for economic outcomes seem to be felt only adversely, after elections, in the form of inflation. The real outcomes (unemployment and national income growth) are not responsive to political manipulation, as would be predicted by modern rational expectations models of the macroeconomy.

Even the most positive assertion that there are cycles based on electoral periods leaves much unexplained about the behavior of economic aggregates. Moreover, there is reason to believe that

11. See Weaver (1988) for a complete discussion and analysis of the indexing of government programs.
12. See also Nordhaus (1989) and Schneider and Frey (1988).

some of the evidence for apparent electoral cycles is really a reflection of the consequence of the defeat and replacement of one party by another.[13]

IN TRANSITION

The electoral-cycle models we have discussed are models in which political manipulation regards the timing of economic events and in which the institution for accountability of the agents to the principals is the possibility of sanction through electoral defeat. The models reviewed thus far show that the very institution of control, periodic elections, may provide some perverse incentives. In each case, whether voters were modeled as passive or as sophisticated, the behavior prompted by such incentives involved an effort to make things look misleadingly good before an election, though the reality might be worse afterward.

In general, the theories of electoral cycles have generated many interesting ideas, and they have helped us to refine our thinking about the nature and risks of the electoral process. They have helped us to think clearly about the costs of democracy. As it stands, however, there is little empirical evidence that electoral cycles for economic variables are important, and there is not a well-formulated case that there are pathologies of democracy reflected in such cycles.[14] The models do help to demonstrate that the institution of public accountability in which officeholders face the possibility of removal in periodic elections may be subject to perverse incentives.

In an effort to explore the relationship between elections and macroeconomic performance in Latin American democracies, Karen Remmer found virtually no support for the hypothesis that incumbents might manipulate economic variables to make things look misleadingly good before elections. Instead, she found that competitive elections "have enhanced, not undermined, political

13. See Frey and Schneider (1978) and Haynes and Stone (1989).
14. In a mathematical argument based on the Nordhaus model, Keech and Simon (1985) found that adverse welfare consequences from political manipulation of the economy depended on the parameters of the model. Keech and Pak (1989) found no evidence that an electoral cycle in veterans' benefits contributed significantly to a growth of expenditures beyond what could be expected otherwise.

leaders' capacity to address major problems of macroeconomic management" and that they "should perhaps be seen less as threats to economic stability than as catalysts for policy reform and responsible economic management" (Remmer, 1993, pp. 393, 403).

Democratic elections are more than opportunities to evaluate the performance of incumbents. They are also vehicles for popular choice between alternatives. This is the feature that is analyzed in the models of Chapter 4.

4 Models of choice: Partisanship

Partisanship models have received considerably more attention and empirical support than electoral-cycle models. Leading scholars, such as Alberto Alesina and Douglas Hibbs, have argued that partisanship is the most fundamental basis for political influence over macroeconomic policy and outcomes. There are, indeed, systematic partisan differences, but economic movements are so fluid that party differences often are overwhelmed by larger tides of change. A limitation in most of the existing studies of macroeconomic partisanship is that they have assumed that party differences regarding goals have remained fixed or constant. That assumption has rarely been documented or demonstrated, and I shall argue that partisan goals are in fact variable. Even fixed goals may be relaxed under certain circumstances that make them unusually costly, but I contend that partisan goals are themselves variable, subject to conditions that are still only poorly understood.

Also, the institutional framework in which American parties operate is not constant. Changes in the institutions in which fiscal and monetary policies are made are likely to affect the implementation of alternative partisan goals, even if those goals were to remain constant (see Chapters 7 and 8). Most of the empirical demonstrations of partisan differences have focused on presumably fixed differences between the Democratic and Republican parties regarding control of the presidency. But a growing literature has argued that other patterns of variations in the control of office are also consequential. Most prominently, divided partisan control of the presidency and Congress can affect policy outcomes. Outside the United States, partisan competition is made more complicated in many democratic countries by the continuing presence of more than two parties. A two-party system that offers only dual alternatives is, by comparison, a radical simplification of the actual possibilities.

This chapter traces the development of models of dual partisan competition from the simple to the complex. For the most part, the later, more complex models are superior representations of the world, but all of them involve substantial simplifications that are designed to enhance understanding. The sequence of models traces two kinds of intellectual development. One is grounded in politics and involves the development of a better understanding of the nature of partisanship. The other is grounded in economics and involves a changing understanding of the nature of the choices available to policymakers. Some of the latter developments involve widely acknowledged improvements in economic understanding, whereas others involve enduring theoretical disputes in economics.

FROM ELECTORAL CYCLE TO PARTISANSHIP

Recall that the electoral-cycle models of routine politics were characterized as involving an interaction between an undifferentiated public and an undifferentiated elected official. A second set of models of routine politics deal with alternative parties competing for control of the government. Models of partisanship deemphasize or suppress any general conflict of interest or strategic interaction between politicians and voters, such as was implied by the electoral-cycle models, and instead emphasize conflicts of interests or ideology between sets of "teams" of voters and politicians. Instead of a principal–agent problem between voters and elected public officials, the partisanship model emphasizes the nature of the choices between alternatives presented in majority-rule elections. Instead of the horizontally divided interaction that defined the models in Chapter 3, the partisanship model is based on competition over a vertical divide:

team A (the Left?) | team B (the Right?)

From a normative perspective, these models speak less directly to the questions of the costs or the pathologies of democracy than did the electoral-cycle models discussed earlier. First, the basic macroeconomic differences between the parties usually are presented as normatively neutral, that is, as matters of taste. Second, there are few cases in which a dynamic process of competitive interaction between parties over macroeconomic policy is modeled so that the results are related to a general social welfare function. In fact, when partisan goals are modeled with objective functions, partisan variation is typically represented simply by different sizes of the parameters that define the relative weights that parties place on basic targets, such as unemployment or inflation. The parties are typically placed on the same normative plateau, and no superior welfare function is defined.

This is not to say that partisan competition is necessarily neutral or even constructive. Conventional wisdom suggests (as did the electoral-cycle models discussed earlier) that competitive pressures may lead incumbents to seek short-run political advantage at the expense of serious attention to long-run problems. The presence of a challenging party may add to the incentives for the incumbent to choose irresponsible policies with short-term benefits at the expense of sustainable plans.[1] The partisan models to be reviewed here are derived mostly from narrowly defined studies of routine and repetitive political patterns, and they do not, for the most part, capture this undesirable feature of partisan competition.

However, one of the issues that emerges from these models is the possibility that the options available to newly elected parties may be restricted, intentionally or otherwise, because of the actions taken by the previous incumbents. And there have been other studies showing how partisan polarization and divided partisan control of the branches of government may have adverse consequences. The reader should note that the limitation to dual alternatives considered here rules out a whole class of collective choice problems that emerge when there are more than two alternatives, as in European parliamentary systems. Those problems, which

1. See Gerber and Lupia (1993) for a general model of cases in which more electoral competition does not lead to better outcomes.

raise questions about the meaning and coherence of a popular will, as expressed in elections, will not be addressed in this book.[2]

SOURCES OF PARTISAN DIFFERENCES

Parties can differ about anything, from the relationship between church and state to foreign policy, but this book will concentrate on party differences related to macroeconomic issues such as inflation, unemployment, and income growth. In Chapter 3 we saw that some studies have recognized that governments may differ in terms of *competence* even when there are no differences in their economic goals. Conventional wisdom and popular opinion often hold that one party is better than the other at maintaining prosperity. The Democrats enjoyed that reputation for years until the 1980s, when Republicans moved ahead.

Economic issues themselves have many dimensions. Prosperity is a consensual issue, but many economic issues are divisive. The general strategy by which prosperity is to be maintained is often a basis for partisan conflict. In most countries, one party will defend the free market as the way to ensure prosperity, while another will advocate government intervention into the economy to do the same thing. Different preferences regarding the size of the public sector are related to those differing views on the free market in obvious ways. Parties with a high demand for public services usually are parties that advocate public intervention, whereas those with lower demand typically defend the free market. Basic predispositions like these are often at the heart of differences between Republicans and Democrats.

Social class differences over the distribution of income and wealth are often matters of political conflict, and are almost always potentially so. Distributional issues may underlie partisan differences in macroeconomics. In fact, that is the basis for Douglas Hibbs's explanation for why the Democrats have been more averse

2. For a compelling argument that the popular will is incoherent and undefinable, see Riker (1982). Riker also suggests that majority rule works better when the electoral alternatives are narrowed to two. See also Hirschman (1991, p. x), who argues that "curiously, the very stability and proper functioning of a well-ordered democratic society depends on its citizens arraying themselves in a few major (ideally two) clearly defined groups holding different opinions on basic policy issues." The rationale for this statement is not provided, though one can be found in Riker (1982).

to unemployment than Republicans, and vice versa for inflation. He documents the fact that lower-income, blue-collar, wage-earning workers are more vulnerable to unemployment than are higher-income, white-collar, salary-earning workers. Even after unemployment compensation, lower-income workers have the most to lose from unemployment (Hibbs, 1987, ch. 2). The distributional consequences of inflation are not as clear, but Hibbs argues that higher-income people have more to lose from inflation than do those in lower-income strata. In general, he argues that inflation is not nearly so costly as unemployment, but that insofar as it has distributional consequences, they are worse for upper-income groups (Hibbs, 1987, ch. 3).

This distributional basis for relative aversion to inflation and unemployment fits well with conventional wisdom and the reputations of the parties. Hibbs documents that the different class groupings do in fact have these "objective" interests and that the interests are related straightforwardly to their subjective preferences regarding relative aversion to inflation and unemployment (1987, ch. 4). That is, the "downscale" groups are more concerned about unemployment than inflation, and the reverse holds for "upscale groups." The downscale groups vote disproportionately for Democrats as the party with the greatest concern for and best record on unemployment, whereas the upscale groups tend to support Republicans as having comparable credentials regarding inflation.

Even though Hibbs shows that there is an objective basis for the differences between the parties concerning relative aversion to unemployment and inflation, his book also presents another theme. He argues that unemployment is a worse evil than inflation, and he suggests that a reasonable concern for the general welfare would emphasize the evils of unemployment far more than the evils of inflation. In other words, the objective basis for party differences can be questioned, and is contestable. Hibbs suggests that those who would emphasize the fight against inflation at the expense of rising unemployment may be misguided and that a stance more in keeping with the general welfare would concentrate on reducing unemployment. Whether he is right or wrong, Hibbs gives an interpretation of the general welfare, but without using something so explicit as a welfare function. As we shall see in Chapter 5, there are other reasonable interpretations of the general welfare.

Parties differ in their beliefs and ideologies about macroeconomic issues, and such beliefs may be grounded in the objective self-interests of their clienteles or may be more purely matters of judgment. As matters of judgment, they are subject to evaluation and persuasion in public discourse (Johnson, 1993). Matters of judgment may be grounded in objective circumstances and are not always purely intellectual. Both American parties are now vigorous advocates of economic growth and compete for support on that basis. They differ less in their levels of commitment to that goal than in their strategies for achieving it. Quinn and Shapiro (1991) point out that there may be important differences in the strategies that parties use to achieve such growth. They characterize Democrats as following a "consumption-led" strategy for growth, in which government policies are designed to put money in the hands of consumers. Republicans are characterized as following an "investment-led" strategy, in which policies are designed to encourage capital formation. These and other ideological differences may be rooted, in obvious ways, in the interests of the clienteles of the parties.

There is no particular reason to think that any of these bases for partisan differences in goals would be fixed. The clienteles of parties may change, and partisan issue stances may also change. A clear noneconomic example of this is seen in the changing stances of the Republican and Democratic parties with respect to equal rights for African-Americans and in the shifting partisan allegiances of American blacks. If the Democratic party was able to change from the party most identified with white supremacy to the party most identified with the aspirations of blacks over the course of a few decades, why should we not expect similar changes in economic policies and clienteles? In fact, in the nineteenth century, the Democratic party was the party of free trade and limited government, whereas the Republicans advocated trade protectionism and public spending programs. Now all of those positions have been substantially reversed. In a world as fluid as this, partisan goals with respect to inflation and unemployment are unlikely to be as enduringly invariant as is implied in some of the models to be discussed later. Changes can come about because of the addition of new clienteles, as in the case of the Democrats and blacks, or because of changes in the preferences of enduring clienteles, as in the attitudes of the business community toward public spending.

Changes in the manifestations of partisanship can occur because of conditions that change in the short term or over the long term. For example, James Alt (1985) has shown that partisan differences regarding unemployment are partly dependent on whether or not a party promised to do something about it in the preceding election campaign. Garrett and Lange (1991) have shown that increasing international interdependence has affected the strategies for intervention in the economy for governments on both the left and the right in industrial democracies, without eliminating partisan differences.

A BASIC MODEL: PARTY DIFFERENCES ON A STABLE MENU OF CHOICES

The foregoing review has recounted some things that are familiar facets of the conventional wisdom about American politics. Hibbs (1987) documented them empirically, but the most important part of his research was his systematic statistical study of the differences in unemployment and income growth rates between the parties.

The fundamental empirical results reported by Hibbs were that unemployment rates have been lower and rates of national income growth have been higher under Democrats than under Republicans. In fact, the two phenomena are widely acknowledged to be related through "Okun's law," which defines an inverse relationship between unemployment and income growth.[3] Empirically, in the period since World War II, recessions, defined as two or more consecutive quarters of negative income growth, have in fact been somewhat more likely to occur under Republicans than under Democrats, as Table 4.1 shows.

There were nine recessions in the 46 years from 1947 through 1992, or one about every 5 years. The Republicans were in office for 10 more years than the Democrats, and so were more at risk. There were two recessions in 18 Democratic years, or one every 9 years, and seven in 28 Republican years, or one every 4 years, on average. It would be quite premature to see any causality in that difference. Business cycles are not well understood, and it is clear that recessions occur irregularly. Clearly more is going on than

3. See Hibbs (1987, pp. 50–1).

Table 4.1. *Recessions in the United States since World War II, by party of presidential administration*

Period	Party
November 1948–October 1949	Democrat
June 1953–May 1954	Republican
July 1957–April 1958	Republican
April 1960–February 1961	Republican
October 1969–November 1970	Republican
December 1973–March 1975	Republican
January 1980–July 1980	Democrat
May 1981–November 1982	Republican
July 1990–March 1991	Republican

Source: National Bureau of Economic Research.

partisan change. A recession did occur at the beginning of each new Republican administration elected to replace a Democratic administration: 1953, 1969, and 1981. That could have been because of the autonomous policy choices of Republicans, if they preferred lower growth rates, or it might have been because of the circumstances under which the Republicans took over from the Democrats, perhaps after a period of high inflation, as will be explained later.

Average differences between Democratic and Republican administrations from 1949 through 1992 are negligible for inflation (4.1 vs. 4.2, respectively), moderate for unemployment (5.5 vs. 6.1), and more substantial for income growth (4.5 vs. 2.4).[4] But those averages disguise trends and the impacts of other variables besides partisanship. The main case for the argument that Republicans simply prefer lower growth rates than Democrats derives from a careful, statistically based empirical study by Hibbs (1987), in which he argued that a predictable and sustainable difference of more than 2 percentage points in unemployment rates can be expected under the Republican and Democratic parties, as well as a predictable difference of 6 percentage points in income growth rates. That is the largest difference that any scholar has found regarding unemployment. Other studies have reported smaller, but still statistically significant, differences between the parties.[5]

4. See Table 4.2 for more detail.
5. For example, see Beck (1982), the leading source for the argument that there are important differences within as well as between parties.

Yet when we consider that the rates of unemployment have fluctuated about 7 percentage points (between 3 and 11) since the end of World War II, we may conclude that the party of the presidential administration contributes only part of the variation, even if we accept the highest estimate of a sustainable 2 percentage points (Hibbs, 1987, ch. 7). The partisanship theory seems to be stronger than the electoral-cycle theory of macroeconomic politics, but it leaves much unexplained about the cyclical movements of unemployment and income growth.

The issue of compatibility with economic theory

Hibbs (1987) is not nearly so self-consciously careful as Nordhaus (1975) in presenting his assumptions about how the economy works and how that issue bears on the political model being presented. Often he seems implicitly to assume that parties are operating on a stable menu of choices represented by a naive Phillips curve. That idea represents an understanding of "the way the economic world works" that is no longer accepted by economists, though it was widely accepted by them in the 1960s.

That idea worked its way into conventional political discourse in the following manner: There was thought to be an inverse relationship between inflation and unemployment, as represented by the curve in Figure 4.1. Governments were thought to be able to choose positions on that curve and to stay in those positions. It was natural to think that a partisan government that was more inflation-averse than unemployment-averse might choose a position low on the curve, such as R, and that a party with the opposite priority might choose a position higher on the curve, such as D.

As a "menu of choices" available to a government (Samuelson and Solow, 1960; Hibbs, 1977, p. 1474), this Phillips curve is the counterpart to the "constraint" explained earlier in the Nordhaus model of electoral cycles. It defines the real-world possibilities, and the theory behind it can help explain why a goal of zero inflation and zero unemployment would not be feasible. Virtually no economists still view this static, "naive" Phillips curve as realistic, though it did seem to represent options during the 1950s and 1960s.

Note that this theory implies that when a new party takes over, the initial conditions of inflation and unemployment will be those

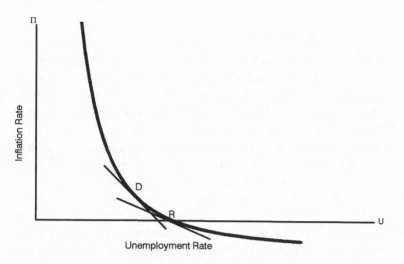

Figure 4.1. Partisan differences on a simple Phillips curve.

chosen by the outgoing party, and the new government can move directly to its own preferred point. That may take time, and one of the strengths of Hibbs's analysis is his empirical estimation of those time paths. However, there is nothing in this theory to imply that there is any restriction on the newly elected party's freedom of movement other than that the choices be on the Phillips curve and that it will take time to move to the new choice. Later we shall consider models (by Hibbs and others) that have other implications.

Hibbs's finding of steady-state differences between the unemployment rates associated with the Republican and Democratic parties is compatible with this dated theory of the economic constraint. As he acknowledged, it is less compatible with more contemporary theories (Hibbs, 1987, p. 227), none of which recognizes the possibility of governments choosing sustainably different rates of unemployment through stabilization policy. Obviously, models of the politics of economic policy will be stronger and sounder if they explicitly acknowledge and incorporate the ways in which the possibilities are limited by the structure of the economy. Later in this chapter we shall consider models that do so, but as Chapter 2 made apparent, there is no single authoritative way to do this, given the diversity of views in contemporary macroeconomic theory.

Normative issues

Most partisanship theories do not have an explicit normative model for comparing the results of politically motivated behavior with the best feasible values for social welfare functions, as Nordhaus's model of the electoral cycle does. Hibbs's theory of partisan choice is also without a similarly explicit normative model, though he does argue explicitly that unemployment is a greater evil than inflation, and implicitly that Democrats are preferable to Republicans because they produce lower rates of unemployment.

I shall lay the groundwork for a more systematic normative model by linking a welfare function to the naive Phillips curve, treating it for now as if it were a realistic representation of real-world possibilities, even though it no longer is. Consider again the misery index as a possible welfare function:

$$M = U + \Pi.$$

This welfare function can easily be turned into an "indifference curve," that is, a line that represents a set of points that are equally valued in terms of the welfare function. Such a line drawn in the Phillips curve space of Figure 4.1 would have a slope of -1, much like the line that is tangent at point D.

Because the welfare function and the derived indifference curve represent what is valued, and because the Phillips curve once represented what was thought to be possible, a point of tangency between the two would provide a solution to the problem of identifying the best possible outcome. However, the fact that the misery index is an unweighted sum of the rates of inflation and unemployment is an arbitrary simplification. Suppose someone, perhaps a Democrat, argued that a single percentage point of unemployment is twice as undesirable as a single percentage point of inflation, writing their misery index as $M_D = 2U + \Pi$. Someone else, perhaps a Republican, who argued the opposite would write their index as $M_R = U + 2\Pi$. A little calculation will show that the slope of M_D is -2, and the slope of M_R is -0.5.

This argument can be generalized by writing the misery index as

$$M = \alpha U + \Pi,$$

where α is a weighting parameter that equals 2 for M_D and 0.5 for M_R. The partisan preferences expressed by Hibbs can easily be represented by such indifference curves with different slopes. Given the stable menu of choices, parties could move from point to point on this curve, and stay at any one of them, *if* the curve represented the actual options.

In such a world, each party would have its own candidate for a social welfare function, and voters could choose between parties according to whose formulation they preferred. If there were no other issues in elections to choose between two such parties, the winning party under majority rule could be considered to have the best definition of social welfare or the public interest, according to Rawls's considerations of pure procedural justice. By this criterion, "there is no independent criterion for the right result," but given a fair procedure, such as a democratic election between two parties, the outcome or result is fair, "whatever it is, provided that the procedure has been properly followed" (Rawls, 1971, p. 86).[6]

Strategic considerations and the need for a theory of change

But where did the positions of the parties come from, and why should they be fixed and immovable? It is a strength of Hibbs's analysis that he explains the sources of partisan positions in a description of the "objective" interests of their class clienteles. But there is no recognition in Hibbs's work of the strategic considerations that will surely emerge. Suppose a party found that its most preferred positions consigned it to repeated defeats. A party that was interested in putting its positions into practice might well decide to adjust its positions in order to enhance its prospects for election. Even if a party's "true" or deep preference were fixed, it might choose its publicly stated policy position, or platform, for electoral purposes according to strategic considerations.

For example, it might choose to minimize the distance of the winning policy position from its ideal policy, by adjusting its platform just enough to maximize the probability of defeating the other party.[7] If parties were to do that and were to stick to their electoral

---

6. This view does not conceptualize any welfare costs to be entailed by parties that alternate in power. Alesina (1987, 1988a) conceptualizes such a welfare loss in terms of the goals of the parties.
7. See Alesina, Londregan, and Rosenthal (1993), Alesina and Rosenthal (1994),

platforms once in office, that behavior would imply that party differences would not be fixed. Both casual observation and systematic study (Beck, 1982) seem to support the idea that administrations will differ even if they represent a single party: Reagan was not like Eisenhower, Carter was not like Johnson, and so on. If that is the case, there will be a less solid basis for expecting that in a dual system the differences between the parties will be predictably fixed, as Hibbs (1987) and other scholars in this area have assumed.

The only theory of strategic party competition that is explicitly grounded in macroeconomic issues questions the possibility of such strategic movement on credibility grounds. Alesina (1987, 1988a) assumed that the "true" preferences of the parties were publicly known and that strategic movement toward a vote-maximizing position would be discounted as insincere. Under most circumstances the winning party would revert to its true preference after the election. Assuming that the true preferences were known, strategically defined platforms would not be credible.

In Alesina's model, moderating changes in partisan positions are possible, but they come from the interaction between the parties, rather than from an effort to adapt positions to appeal more effectively to a majority of voters. Because parties in this model are assumed to prefer to stay at a position between the two parties' ideal points, rather than alternate back and forth between those points, they may converge if their time horizon is long enough. A major disadvantage of Alesina's model is that the probabilities of the parties winning are not affected by what they do in office, but it is one of very few models of strategic competition between parties on macroeconomic issues.[8]

In the electoral-cycle model, governments were motivated solely by the desire to win elections. We saw that the empirical evidence for the idea that economic cycles follow electoral periods was not compelling, and we observed that even if it were stronger, that theory would be hard-pressed to account for the fact that incumbent parties have lost six of the last eleven elections. If the main

Chappell and Keech (1986b), and Wittman (1983) for models of electoral competition between parties with policy goals.
8. See Alesina and Cukierman (1990) for a model that shows how parties can gain mobility by a "politics of ambiguity" regarding their goals.

objective of incumbent governments is to win votes, why do they lose? Clearly something else is going on. There is a similar problem for the partisanship theory: Hibbs argues that the parties represent the interests of different clienteles, but he does not explain how they adjust or might adjust their strategies in order to win elections. Presumably parties can better please their clienteles when in office than when out, and it might pay them to adjust their policies in order to win election, but it is possible that they would not care about office so long as their goals were implemented. It would be sensible to model partisan goals as a combination of policy goals and the goal of holding office for its own sake. Such a model could take the following form:

$$\text{partisan goal} = \beta(\text{policy goal}) + (1 - \beta)(\text{officeholding goal})$$

where $0 < \beta < 1$. A goal function like this might help explain why parties lose elections as often as they do, by suggesting that they maximize their policy goals at the expense of officeholding.[9] Of course, it is possible that incumbents lose because of noneconomic issues, and it is not difficult to find noneconomic reasons that would help explain the outcomes of the six presidential elections since World War II in which the incumbent party lost. For example, the defeats of the Democrats in 1952 and 1968 were related to unpopular wars. The defeat of the Republicans in 1976 was related to the Watergate affair and defeat in war. The defeats of the Republicans in 1960 and 1992 seem to have been more purely related to economic performance.[10]

Still, most of those defeats were also associated with economic performance that reflected the risk of fulfilling the incumbent party's goals too well. They were political reflections of the following much-quoted observation:

For a generation, every major mistake in economic policy under a Democratic president has taken the form of overstimulating the economy and every major mistake under a Republican of overrestraining it. (Okun, 1973, p. 175)[11]

Party differences in unemployment and growth rates, such as those that Hibbs finds, could simply reflect shifts in targets on a stable

9. Alesina (1987) suggests that under some circumstances, parties may even prefer to lose in order to better achieve their goals.
10. See Chapter 6.
11. See also the comments by Charles Schultze reported in Nordhaus (1989).

menu of choices. If moves that go "too far" are "mistakes," this implies that there is some middle ground on the Phillips curve that will maximize votes, and a party that deviates too far from that middle ground in the direction of its supporters makes the mistakes that are characteristic of a party with its particular goals. These "characteristic mistakes" may lead to defeat that will bring the other party into office. Sharp movements in unemployment or income growth under a new party may, in part, be predictable reactions to the conditions that led to the defeat of the incumbent. Hibbs anticipated these points in the concluding observations of his chapter on electoral cycles:

Democratic administrations have been more likely than Republican administrations to get into difficulty with the electorate by pursuing overly ambitious employment goals that yield extra inflation. The Republicans, on the other hand, have more frequently suffered electoral setbacks because of their enthusiasm for disinflationary bouts of economic slack. (1987, p. 278) [12]

Specifically, the Republican wins in 1968 and 1980 followed Democratic problems with inflation after having pursued ambitious employment goals. (Of course, the 1979 oil shock was also a source of the Carter administration's problems with inflation.) The newly elected Nixon and Reagan administrations deliberately restrained the economy. Their decisions to do so might be explained by their having different targets (i.e., lower targets for growth and higher targets for unemployment). However, a decision to restrain the economy might also be explained by a goal of bringing down inflation as the most important problem. Similarly, Democratic wins in 1960, 1976, and 1992 followed Republican problems with slack in the economy. The expansions that ensued after the former two elections were consistent with the higher growth targets espoused by the Democrats and with a desire to deal with the most important problem at hand. So long as the outcomes of elections are not independent of the economic performance of incumbent administrations, efforts to explain partisan differences in economic performance without taking into account economic circumstances will not be fully satisfactory. Partisan strategies are likely to be contingent on economic conditions. [13]

12. See also Hibbs (1987, ch. 7, note 19, and pp. 277–9).
13. Subsequent work by Hibbs (1992, 1994) has developed a systematic model of this phenomenon.

The traditional naive Phillips curve defines a stable menu of choices. If that view of the options were accurate, there would be perfect mobility from point to point. If a party were defeated for going too far in one direction, its successor could simply move along the curve to another point that was more preferred. If mistakes were made, as Okun suggests, they could be easily and painlessly corrected in a world characterized by that stable trade-off. That is not necessarily true for the next models we shall consider, in which mistakes may be more costly.

PARTY DIFFERENCES IN A WORLD WITHOUT A STABLE PHILLIPS CURVE MENU

In this model, which assumes a natural rate of unemployment, mistakes are costly, though correctable. However, it is more painful to correct some mistakes than to correct others. The mistake that Okun attributed to Republicans is not difficult to correct. Overrestraint of the economy can be painlessly corrected in this model by stimulating the economy. Keynesian remedies for unemployment and poor growth are compatible with natural desires to increase spending or reduce taxes. However, the mistake one expects from Democrats is difficult to correct. Overstimulation of the economy can lead to inflation, and elimination of inflation is a costly undertaking. If the Democrats are defeated by the Republicans for making such a mistake, the Republicans may find that they must induce a painful recession. The political incentives of Keynesian stabilization policies are asymmetrical, as was suggested in Chapter 2.

As we shall see, this may help to explain a few episodes of what looks like the electoral cycle, and it provides an example of a way in which newly elected parties do not necessarily start with a clean slate. They may take office with problems left by their predecessors for them to "correct," and different parties may leave different problems.

The idea of a natural rate of unemployment

Although the idea of a stable inverse relationship between inflation and unemployment lived on in the politics of economic policy and in public discourse for some time, it came under attack a quarter of a century ago in Milton Friedman's presidential address to the American Economic Association. Friedman argued that public authorities cannot succeed in meeting specific targets for unemployment rates because of "the difference between the immediate and delayed consequences of such a policy" (1968, p. 7).

Friedman suggested that at any given time there is a single, "natural rate of unemployment," a level that is consistent with equilibrium between the supply of labor and the demand for labor. This natural rate will vary with the size and qualifications of the labor force and with public policies that affect the incentives to take jobs. For example, the natural rate might rise with an influx of untrained teenagers into the labor force, or with an increase in the legal minimum wage. It may drop with a decrease in the generosity of unemployment benefits. But it is not subject to any lasting change that could be brought about by monetary or fiscal stabilization policy. Parties that understand and accept the idea of a natural rate of unemployment might choose to lower unemployment by labor market policies, such as minimum wage laws or unemployment compensation levels, but they could not expect to achieve lasting reductions with demand management policies.[14]

Friedman argued that monetary policy might lead to a temporary reduction in the unemployment rate, by virtue of a confusion in labor markets between real and nominal wages. However, he argued that such a reduction could be sustained only by inflation, and indeed by accelerating inflation (Friedman, 1968, p. 10):

> To state this conclusion differently, there is always a temporary trade-off between inflation and unemployment; there is no permanent trade-off. The temporary trade-off comes not from inflation per se, but from unanticipated inflation, which generally means a rising rate of inflation. The widespread belief that there is a permanent trade-off is a sophisticated version of the confusion between "high" and "rising" that we all recognize in simpler forms. A rising rate of inflation may reduce unemployment, a high rate will not. (1968, p. 11)

These observations were elaborated into the idea that there is a very steep, even vertical, "long-run Phillips curve," representing

---

14. Ironically, some of the policies that economic theory says would be likely to lower "natural" unemployment rates are policies that would reduce the value of minimum wages and of unemployment compensation (Aluise, 1991).

the sustainable combinations of inflation and unemployment. This would imply that any rate of inflation, including zero, would be sustainably compatible with the natural rate of unemployment. Lower rates of unemployment could be sustained only with accelerating inflation, according to this "adaptive expectations" theory. The Nordhaus model of the electoral business cycle elaborated in Chapter 3 is a theory of cynical political manipulation based on Friedman's ideas about the difference between long-run and short-run Phillips curves. Figure 2.3 is an example.

In a world characterized by a natural rate of unemployment and a long-run Phillips curve, there is no obvious basis for party differences regarding targeted unemployment rates. Recall that with the naive, static Phillips curve, different combinations of inflation and unemployment that were on the curve were thought to be indefinitely sustainable. Under the natural rate theory, there is no sustainable unemployment rate other than the natural rate. An effort to maintain unemployment below that rate would not simply lead to a higher, but stable, rate of inflation. Such an effort would generate *steadily rising* inflation, that is, *accelerating* inflation, according to the adaptive expectations theory of inflation used in the Friedman argument described here, and used by Nordhaus in the electoral-cycle model presented in Chapter 3.

One might expect governments of either party to target the natural rate in order to preclude or minimize inflation, but as Friedman pointed out, the government "cannot know what the 'natural' rate is" (1968, p. 10). As we shall see in Chapter 8, which deals with monetary policy, that view led Friedman to advocate that government not even try to manipulate unemployment rates, but rather that it follow a rule for a fixed rate of monetary growth. (That advice has largely been ignored.)

A welfare function for a natural rate world

Recognizing that the exact location of a "natural rate of unemployment" is not known, we might still think of governments as hoping to keep unemployment at that natural rate, and to minimize inflation. Because the natural rate is thought to be compatible with zero inflation, an appropriate welfare function or misery index might look like this:

$$M = \alpha|U - U^n| + \Pi$$

where M is "misery," U is unemployment, U^n is the natural rate of unemployment, and Π is the rate of inflation. In this case, a misery index target of zero would be sustainable when unemployment was at the natural rate and inflation was zero.

A target of zero might be favored by both parties if they agreed on the nature of the limitations on the possible policies. That is, if the parties had the same understanding of the way the economic world works, they might agree on a target of zero for this modified welfare function, even if they did not agree on the weighting parameter α, which defines the relative costs of deviations of unemployment from the natural rate and inflation. As will be explained later, some of the most interesting models of policy use a natural rate, but involve target values for output growth (or unemployment) above (below) the natural rate. In this way, the time-consistency problem (see Chapter 2) is introduced into partisanship models.

Partisan differences in a natural rate world

Nevertheless, even if parties agreed on the existence of a natural rate, they might not agree on what it is. Also, they might not agree on how important it is to *reduce* inflation from an initial condition other than zero inflation. Consider the actual figures regarding unemployment and inflation in the 1980s (Table 4.2). Assume that the natural rate was about 6% in the 1980s, which approximates considerable consensus. The table shows two unweighted versions

Table 4.2. *Some misery indices for the Reagan administrations*

Year	U	$U - 6$	Π	M_n	M_o
1981	7.6	1.6	10.3	11.9	17.9
1982	9.7	3.7	6.2	9.9	15.9
1983	9.6	3.6	3.2	6.8	12.8
1984	7.5	1.5	4.3	5.8	11.8
1985	7.2	1.2	3.6	4.8	10.8
1986	7.0	1.0	1.9	2.9	8.9
1987	6.2	1.2	3.7	3.9	9.9
1988	5.5	-0.5	4.1	3.6	9.6

of the misery index, one of the form just presented, M_n, with 6% as the natural rate, and an ordinary misery index M_o, using the unemployment and inflation figures for both Reagan administrations. According to both misery indices, economic performance steadily improved throughout the Reagan years, even during the deepest recession in postwar history.

Because unemployment got worse before it got better, the change may not have been worth it to people who in 1981 had short time horizons and who cared more about unemployment than inflation. For example, if the weighting parameter α had the value of 2 for some people, say Democrats, the misery index would have gotten worse in 1982 before it got better. For some people, the human costs of unemployment and lost output are so great relative to inflation that performance such as that of the Reagan administrations is not acceptable. Hibbs, for example, argued that inflation was lowered only through "enormous costs in terms of lost output, lower incomes, and higher unemployment" (1987, p. 288). He argued that the associated gap between actual GNP and its sustainable level translated into "about 825 billion dollars' worth of 1984 goods and services, or close to $10,000 per household" (1987, pp. 289–92).[15]

Note the similarity between the experience of the first Reagan term and the pattern of a Nordhaus-type electoral cycle. Things got steadily better, so that the recession of 1981–82 was well in the past by the 1984 election. But the misery index achieved by 1984 was not unsustainable, unlike those implied in a Nordhaus-style electoral cycle, as explained in Table 3.1. In fact, it continued to drop through the next electoral period. Even though that experience may look like an electoral cycle, it can be understood as a corrective to the inflationary performance of the previous administration.

Uncertainty and "characteristic mistakes"

Of course, a partisan government may not accept the idea of a natural rate of unemployment. Even if it does, it may estimate that

---

15. The costs of disinflation can be measured with a Mundell-Sachs "sacrifice ratio," which relates the cost in unemployment or lost output to the amount of improvement in inflation. See Sachs and Larrain (1993).

the rate is lower or higher than the other party thinks. This idea can help provide an economic explanation for why incumbent parties lose. Suppose that the actual natural rate was 6%, but that Democrats, believing that unemployment is especially costly, were willing to take a risk by assuming that it was 5%. Similarly, Republicans, believing that inflation is especially costly, might choose to assume that it was 7%. These numbers, in fact, approximate Hibbs's estimates of "target" values for Democrats and Republicans. If we acknowledge the difficulty of precisely controlling the economy, the message is simply that Democrats tend to undershoot and Republicans tend to overshoot the natural rate in a world of uncertainty.

The Democratic losses of the presidency in 1968 and 1980 followed inflationary episodes that came after unemployment had been driven "too low," which might be considered a characteristic mistake of the Democrats.[16] Republican losses in 1960 and 1976 came after the opposite kind of problem: Unemployment had been allowed to drift "too high," given Republican aversion to inflation. This might be considered a characteristic mistake of the Republicans. Both parties were defeated after different kinds of poor economic performance that were characteristic of the risks inherent in their respective values and preferences.

The electoral cycle as an artifact of Republicans following Democratic "mistakes"

The best examples of the kind of electoral cycle Nordhaus identified are provided in the first terms of the Nixon and Reagan administrations. That is, each administration inherited inflation, and each induced a recession early in the term, a recession that was ending by the time of the next election. Nordhaus's nonpartisan model suggests that such a pattern is simply a result of cynical vote maximization. Another interpretation is possible, given the fact that each of those administrations began with inflationary problems

---

16. At 7.1, unemployment was not "too low" in 1980, but it had fallen from 7.1 to 5.8 in the first three years of the Carter administration. Clearly, the Carter administration's macroeconomic policies were complicated by the inflationary consequences of the 1979 oil price shock.

inherited from a defeated Democratic administration. One way to reduce inflation is to induce a recession, which reduces demand and the expectation of inflation. If that is done immediately, early in the term, the recession may well be over by the next election, at which time prosperity can be returning, with lower inflation. That may be what happened in those two cases, which have been presumed to be leading instances of the electoral cycle.[17] In other words, even the leading examples purporting to show electoral cycles may have been artifacts of another political phenomenon.

STUDIES OF PARTISANSHIP EMBEDDED IN MODELS OF THE ECONOMY

An implicit theme of this chapter has been that party differences can mean different things given different understandings of the way the economic world works, that is, of the ways in which economic reality constrains political choices. Several studies, using models built around at least three different explicit conceptions of the macroeconomy, have shown that government partisanship influences unemployment and income growth in the United States.[18] Thus far in this chapter we have considered party differences in a world with a static, naive Phillips curve, and we have considered them in a world with a natural rate of unemployment. But the natural rate theory that we have considered is not the only one. As drawn from Milton Friedman's 1968 address, as used by Nordhaus in his electoral-cycle model, and as used thus far in this chapter, this has been a natural rate model in which expectations regarding inflation are formed "adaptively," that is, as functions of past values of inflation. This view has been seriously challenged by "rational expectations." In rational expectations theory, the mistakes of overstimulation are, in principle, easier to correct than in the previ-

---

17. See Haynes and Stone (1989) and the comments by Charles Schultze reported in Nordhaus (1989, pp. 56–63).
18. Chappell and Keech (1986b) used two models of the economy, the "St. Louis" model and a rational expectations model. Alesina and Sachs (1988) and Chappell and Keech (1988a) used rational expectations models to study partisanship in income growth and unemployment, respectively. Elsewhere, Chappell and Keech (1988b) used the Fairmodel.

ous natural rate model. If expectations are rational and policymakers are credible in telling the public that they mean to eliminate inflation, a painful recession should not be necessary.

There is even less room for sustainable party differences in the rational expectations world than there is in the adaptive expectations world. As a consequence, partisan differences regarding real variables such as output and unemployment will have disappeared by the end of an administration in such a world. Under rational expectations theory, it is still believed that there are natural rates of unemployment and output. However, policymakers are seen as having even less control over unemployment, under this theory, which argues that policymakers can influence real variables such as unemployment and output only by surprising or fooling people. Because people are presumed to be too rational to be repeatedly fooled, policymakers have little control over unemployment and output, which are assumed to be normally in equilibrium at their natural rates.

Several scholars have shown that it is still possible to have party differences in the equilibrium world of rational expectations. According to one leading view of this, Democrats should produce higher income growth and lower unemployment, and Republicans should produce the reverse pattern, but such differences should be transitory, and they should come early in an administration.[19] As supportive evidence, note the following figures, from Alesina (in press); they are averages of GNP growth rates for each year of Republican and Democratic administrations from 1949 to 1992:

		Year		
	1	2	3	4
Democrat	3.3	6.2	5.0	3.3
Republican	3.0	−0.3	2.7	4.3

19. The explanation is based on the assumptions that partisan differences in monetary policy are predictable and that wage contracts overlap electoral periods. Because there is uncertainty before an election regarding which party will win, any election outcome will involve a surprise regarding the rate of money growth, and, therefore, the rate of inflation. Because labor contracts are set before the election, expectations of inflation cannot be adjusted immediately with the outcome of the election. See Alesina and Sachs (1988) and Chappell and Keech (1988b).

Consistent with rational expectations theory, the differences come early in an administration, and disappear toward the end. On the average they are small to negligible, but in the second year they are striking, though transitory.

Table 4.3 shows that unemployment figures do not follow quite the same pattern, even though in theory the two variables are inversely related through "Okun's law." The unemployment figure is actually higher in the first year of a Democratic administration. However, the difference returns to those predicted by conventional wisdom for the second, third, and fourth years, with the maximum difference coming in the third year. For unemployment, the parties are most different in the second half of the terms, whereas for income growth they are most different in the first half.

The scope for differences in unemployment and growth rates has narrowed steadily as our analysis has moved through successive developments in macroeconomic theory. The natural rate hypothesis narrowed the scope from the stable menu of choices on a static, naive Phillips curve, and the rational expectations version of the natural rate hypothesis narrowed the scope still further. Although the partisanship theory is alive and well in studies of the politics of macroeconomic policy, it does not explain much of the substantial variation in outcomes such as unemployment and growth rates.

CONDITIONAL PARTISANSHIP AND
SECONDARY PARTISANSHIP

Thus far, we have treated party differences as if they were based on fixed targets. In fact, it is likely that partisan goals are more fluid and conditional. For example, Tufte (1978, pp. 101–2) identified two rules:

1. If there is a single, highly visible economic problem that is very important to the electorate, seek re-election improvements on that problem regardless of the economic priorities of the party platform.
2. If no single economic problem is dominant, seek to improve the pre-election economy in the direction of party platform priorities.

Table 4.3. Annual rates for unemployment, GDP growth, and CPI, by party and administration, 1949–92

Party	UNEM1[a]	UNEM2	UNEM3	UNEM4	GDP1[a]	GDP2	GDP3	GDP4	CPI1[a]	CPI2	CPI3	CPI4
Total	5.45	5.97	5.95	5.65	3.13	2.34	3.56	3.59	3.88	4.19	4.38	4.09
Democrat	6.05	5.18	4.65	4.73	3.20	6.49	4.70	3.44	1.97	3.26	5.83	5.33
Republican	5.10	6.43	6.69	6.19	3.08	−0.04	2.91	3.68	4.97	4.72	3.56	3.38

Administrations	Year	UNEM1	UNEM2	UNEM3	UNEM4	GDP1	GDP2	GDP3	GDP4	CPI1	CPI2	CPI3	CPI4
Truman (D)	1949	5.90	5.30	3.30	3.00	0.06	9.98	9.56	4.53	−1.25	1.26	7.88	2.31
Kennedy/Johnson (D)	1961	6.70	5.50	5.70	5.20	2.66	5.14	4.14	5.65	1.01	1.34	0.99	1.31
Johnson (D)	1965	4.50	3.80	3.80	3.60	5.56	6.02	2.59	4.11	1.61	2.86	3.09	4.19
Carter (D)	1977	7.10	6.10	5.80	7.10	4.51	4.82	2.52	−0.54	6.50	7.59	11.35	13.50
Average		6.05	5.18	4.65	4.73	3.20	6.49	4.70	3.44	1.97	3.26	5.83	5.33
Average		5.61				4.84				2.62			
Average			5.15				4.46				4.10		
Average				4.69				4.07				5.58	
Eisenhower (R)	1953	2.90	5.50	4.40	4.10	4.73	−1.69	5.74	1.77	0.75	0.37	−0.37	1.49
Eisenhower II (R)	1957	4.30	6.80	5.50	5.50	1.51	0.35	6.30	2.38	3.68	2.48	0.69	1.72
Nixon (R)	1969	3.50	4.90	5.90	5.60	2.72	−0.05	2.90	4.99	5.46	5.72	4.38	3.21
Nixon/Ford (R)	1973	4.90	5.60	8.50	7.70	5.20	−0.63	−0.81	4.94	6.22	11.04	9.13	5.76
Reagan (R)	1981	7.60	9.70	9.60	7.50	1.77	−2.15	3.89	6.19	10.32	6.16	3.21	4.32
Reagan II (R)	1985	7.20	7.00	6.20	5.50	3.17	2.91	3.08	3.93	3.56	1.86	3.65	4.14
Bush (R)	1989	5.30	5.50	6.70	7.40	2.51	0.99	−0.74	1.52	4.82	5.40	4.21	3.01
Average		5.10	6.43	6.69	6.19	3.08	−0.04	2.91	3.68	4.97	4.72	3.56	3.38
Average		5.76				1.52				4.85			
Average			6.1				2.41				4.16		
Average				6.44				3.29				3.47	

[a] UNEM1, unemployment in first year; GDP1, gross domestic product in first year; CPI1, consumer price index in first year.
Source: *Historical Statistics of the United States.*

Hibbs also acknowledged that both parties will relax unemployment goals with rising inflation (1987, p. 253), and presumably they will also relax inflation goals with rising unemployment.[20]

One study took account of varying economic conditions using historical data. Chappell and Keech (1988b) estimated "typical" Republican and Democratic fiscal and monetary policies over the period from 1953 through 1984. Using a multiequation model of the U.S. economy, they simulated what a typical Republican and a typical Democrat would have done in each administration and compared those results with the performance of the actual incumbent. They found that the differences in outcomes caused by party differences were invariably small in size, and sometimes counterintuitive in direction.[21]

The most explicit model of contingent goal formation is that of Hibbs (1994), which builds directly on the idea that there is a sustainable rate of output growth akin to a "natural rate," and that output above that sustainable path is inflationary.[22] In this newer Hibbs theory, the difference between the parties is in the degree to which they will risk inflationary growth:

Democratic Administrations entertain higher output growth targets than Republican ones, because Democrats are more averse to needless shortfalls of output growth from potential and less averse to the risks of higher inflation that up-side mistakes might generate. (Hibbs, 1994, p. 7)

The parties are uncertain about what the sustainable path is, and they are both concerned about inflation. Hibbs argues that the parties' variable targets for nominal output "depend on fixed ('politically deep') preference parameters" and on actual and expected inflation. Thus Hibbs creates a viable theory of how immediate partisan goals vary with conditions, while at the same time main-

20. See also Frey and Schneider (1978) and Mosley (1984) for suggestions of contingent partisanship.
21. The method of inferring typical partisan policies is to estimate "reaction functions" in which choices of policy instruments are regressed on economic conditions and partisanship; see Alt and Woolley (1982) for a discussion of the assumptions and limitations of that strategy. The model of the economy was the Fairmodel. For a description, see Fair (1984).
22. This newer contribution by Hibbs quietly drops his earlier claims concerning differences between parties on the question of sustainably divergent unemployment rates. He does observe that the divergent output paths he graphs (1987, p. 228) are in levels, rather than growth rates, and thus are roughly compatible with the Alesina figures noted earlier (personal communication).

taining that these varying targets are functions of unvarying underlying preferences. This idea of fixed underlying partisan preferences is asserted without defense and can safely be viewed as simply a provisional assumption.

Such an interpretation makes much more sense for electorally motivated parties than does the idea of fixed and nonconditional goals. Any party is likely to take the stance of a general problem-solver and try to deal with the prominent problems at hand. Success or failure in doing so may have lasting influence on the identity, reputation, and even the electability of parties. The idea that the Democrats were the party of prosperity, and the Republicans the party of economic stagnation, was surely due in small part to various accidents of history from the late 1920s through the late 1960s, including who was in office when adverse shocks occurred.

Party differences as secondary consequences

The importance of partisanship in economic policy is not contingent on the size or regularity of systematic differences in outcomes such as unemployment. Parties may have more clearly defined policy differences regarding the distribution of income. Hibbs and Dennis (1988) documented the differences in income shares for the top and bottom segments of the population under Democratic and Republican administrations, showing that the distribution was more egalitarian under the Democrats. Some of those patterns may have derived from tax and transfer policies that were designed to redistribute income downward. Havrilesky (1987) argued that redistribution has disincentive effects that produce adverse electoral consequences and that governments create monetary surprises to stimulate output so as to compensate for the decline in output associated with redistribution. Through this process, some of the observed party differences in macroeconomic performance may be secondary consequences of other partisan goals. These ideas are at least superficially compatible with research based on the idea that parties have different targets for inflation and unemployment.[23]

23. See Cukierman (1992, pp. 341–3) for a commentary.

REVERSIBILITY AND LIMITING THE CHOICES
OF SUCCESSORS

Thus far in this chapter, we have considered a model in which the policy choices of defeated, outgoing governments were reversible by their successors, who could move costlessly to their goals. According to another model, it was painful and costly for the new party to correct the mistakes of its predecessor, but even in that case there was no *intentional* effort by the outgoing party to restrict the choices of its successor. However, several studies have built on the observation that incumbent governments can influence the nature of the policy that will be implemented after they are out of office, and they have presented models of how parties might do so strategically.

For example, in an article entitled "Why a Stubborn Conservative Would Run a Deficit," Persson and Svensson (1989) showed that a conservative party that expects not to win the next election can impose its preferences on its liberal successor. The key is that government consumption is negatively related to inherited debt. The losing conservatives may seek to restrict the spending proclivities of their successors by increasing indebtedness.[24]

Notable politicians (such as Senator Daniel Patrick Moynihan) and distinguished academics (such as Professor Aaron Wildavsky) have observed that that may have been a strategy of the Reagan administration. I find it doubtful that President Reagan intended to run up the deficits he produced, but a restriction on new Democratic programs may well have been seen as a welcome side effect of the huge increase in government debt in the 1980s. And clearly, that debt limits the options available to the Clinton administration.

But perverse and cynical strategies such as the one identified by Persson and Svensson are not the only ways in which politicians can assure that their preferences will live on regardless of who succeeds them in office. An early example of that was the Social Security system, set up by the Social Security Act of 1935.

Social Security was a Democratic program, opposed by Republicans, and different from the alternatives that Republicans would have preferred. It may seem ironic, but the Republicans preferred

---

24. See also Alesina and Tabellini (1990) and Tabellini and Alesina (1990).

a program that would have been targeted at the poor, that would have been funded with general tax revenues on a pay-as-you-go basis, and that would have provided immediate universal coverage for the needy. In contrast, the winning Democratic program was intended ultimately to include everybody, not just the poor; it was to be funded with earmarked taxes held in a trust fund, and it would be phased in slowly.

Why would the Republicans have wanted to target the poor, who were not part of their basic constituency? Why would the Democrats seek to incorporate the entire work force, including the upscale classes who were part of the Republican constituency? The parties appear to have reversed roles again when the Democrats preferred saving insurance "contributions" in a trust fund, whereas the Republicans favored the use of general revenues for the poor.

The answer, I think, has to do with the remarkable foresight that both parties seem to have shown concerning the long-term consequences of their preferences. Republicans seem to have anticipated that a program with annual appropriations for the poor and needy could easily be kept small, whereas a trust fund would be difficult to protect. Democrats seem to have known that if people believed that "insurance contributions" were being held in a "trust fund," they would feel entitled to those benefits and would retain higher self-esteem than if they were receiving tax revenues doled out to the needy. Obviously it would be much more difficult to limit or scale down the Democratic program in times of budgetary stringency.

Subsequent history has shown that both the Democrats and Republicans probably were correct in supporting the programs that fit with their preferences for large and small government, respectively. The Democrats, of course, won that battle. The Republicans campaigned against Social Security in 1936, but subsequently gave up direct opposition to that increasingly popular program. As Republicans predicted, the trust fund was not allowed to grow to a level at which people would be receiving benefits closely geared to their own contributions plus interest. Instead, the trust fund was tapped through a series of amendments that moved the system to a pay-as-you-go arrangement, under which most beneficiaries received back large multiples of their contributions.[25] Because of the

25. "For example, the average 65-year-old retiree in 1982 (with a nonworking spouse)

extravagant rhetoric surrounding the system, people began to feel that they had earned their benefits, quickly losing sight of the fact that they were receiving a great deal more than they had ever paid in.

For a time, the government provided increases in Social Security benefits in a pattern that suspiciously followed even-numbered years. That was one of Tufte's leading examples of an electoral cycle for an instrument under government control, until a 1972 bidding war among presidential aspirants finally exhausted the slack in the trust fund (Tufte, 1978, pp. 29–36). Since then, benefits have been indexed to go up with the consumer price index, and Social Security has become known as the "third rail" of American politics (touch it and you die). Clearly, the Democrats of the 1930s succeeded in creating a program that quickly became too big, too popular, and too entrenched to be vulnerable to future efforts to reduce or eliminate it.[26]

Social Security is a leading example of a program that limited the choices of succeeding administrations. It shows that a partisan model of political economy must take into account more than the reversible movements in inflation and unemployment, and it shows that the environment of choice that parties face changes over time, even if there are no changes in the identities and goals of the parties. I see no reason to assume that partisan stances on policy innovations will always show as much foresight as was evident in the Social Security example.

Sometimes we go down a path that reduces our alternatives in a way that is neither deliberate nor shrewd, though it may be opportunistic in the short run. In describing "how we became the choiceless society," Peter Peterson argues that the American people never made a deliberate choice for the policies that have resulted in deficits and slow growth: "The choices were never framed honestly and seriously. The American people were never provided with realistic assessments of the costs and benefits of different courses of action" (1993, ch. 2, p. 69).

recovers his lifetime contributions within nine months after retiring" (Federal Reserve Bank of New York, *Quarterly Review,* Autumn 1982, pp. 1–2).

26. The shift to automatically indexing benefits to the rate of inflation in 1974 can be seen as conservative, relative to previous practice of discretionary increases that were greater than the rate of inflation. However, it can also be seen as liberal relative to the possibility that, in some circumstances of budgetary stringency, there might have been no increases. See Weaver (1988).

DIMENSIONS OF CHOICE IN A WORLD OF ASYMMETRIC INFORMATION

The most thorough treatment of macroeconomic policymaking in a framework of asymmetric information between policymakers and the public is Cukierman's *Central Bank Strategy, Credibility, and Independence* (1992). Systematic and predictable partisan differences are discussed in only a small part of that book, but Cukierman analyzes a variety of dimensions on which policymakers may differ and over which voters may have some choice, even though their information about the nature of those choices is imperfect. Cukierman points out that policymakers differ in their relative emphasis on price stability and employment, and such preferences may change over time, even for a given policymaker. They may differ in their ability to commit to a noninflationary strategy, and they may differ in their forecasts about the state of the economy and the persistence of inflation.

All of these differences are likely to confound the clarity of otherwise predictable party differences, and these are issues on which policymakers may differ without regard to party. Therefore, this chapter on models of choice must acknowledge that partisanship is only one of the bases for choice, though it is surely the most fundamental. In Chapter 3, in discussing electoral cycles, we found that asymmetric information rendered elections imperfect institutions for accountability. In this chapter, we see that asymmetric information also renders elections imperfect institutions for choice.

COSTS OF DEMOCRACY IN PARTISAN MODELS

Partisan models have not paid much attention to the public welfare consequences of party competition and alternation. Many models use social welfare functions in which the weights on output or inflation differ by party, but there is no partisanship model that contrasts that sort of welfare function with a nonpartisan social welfare function, or with such a function for a benevolent dictatorship. The closest the literature comes to modeling the costs of bipartisan alternation in power can be seen in the work of Alesina (1987, 1988a). In his model, voters prefer a position that is between the platforms of the two parties. The parties themselves, because of risk aversion, would also prefer some averaging of their two positions, rather than the continual policy changes that result from their alternation in office. But because of credibility problems, they cannot commit to the more moderate position. As a result, they fail to converge on the position most preferred by the voters, and alternation between polarized parties continues.

This kind of oscillation, due to the parties' failure to converge to a moderate best outcome as defined by the position of the median voter, may be considered a cost of democracy. It is the cost entailed in having choices, wherein the existence of meaningful choices implies uncertainty about the outcomes. But because all of the outcomes are on a Pareto frontier,[27] the costs derive from the uncertainty, rather than from a basis for considering the outcomes inferior, from everyone's point of view, to an alternative that is feasible. There are costs entailed in having choices and having an open process of defining alternatives.[28]

A more convincing case that partisan conflict can have adverse consequences can be derived from models that go beyond the context of relatively small differences in inflation, unemployment, and growth caused by changes in partisan control of the American presidency. There are several ways in which the context of partisan conflict can vary in ways that will have welfare consequences. They include polarization of the alternatives, dispersal of power across political institutions, and the congruence of partisan alternatives with economic institutions.

Polarization

If there is a cost that derives either from uncertainty about partisan outcomes or from oscillation between alternatives, that cost will increase with increasing distance or polarization between the alternatives. However, some of the models that show adverse consequences of polarization involve a failure to agree on programs that could make everybody better off by dealing with pressing prob-

---

27. That is, there is no alternative that can make someone better off without making someone else worse off.
28. Note the Cukierman (1992) models of the welfare cost of uncertainty about outcomes.

lems, or avoiding adverse long-term consequences. These models involve situations in which different partisan actors have a veto power that can be used to prevent implementation of a painful but potentially beneficial policy change.[29]

Dispersal of power

The polarization over the distribution of the burdens of a stabilization program would not be a problem if there were no need for agreement between the actors. If winning meant that the winning party would be completely dominant, it would not matter (within the context of the model) which party won. However, in many countries there are multiple parties, and no single majority party. In those countries, coalitions are likely to be necessary to form a government and to carry out policy. When that is the case, polarization can make agreement between partisan actors more difficult and less likely. Also, the institutions that embody the separation of powers in the American sense can make partisan disagreement or polarization consequential. Roubini and Sachs argue that

> when power is dispersed, either across branches of the government (as in the U.S.), or across many political parties in a coalition government (as is typical in Italy), or across parties through the alternation of political control over time, the likelihood of intertemporally inefficient budgetary policy is heightened. (1989a, p. 905)

These themes will be picked up in Chapter 7, where budgetary policy is explicitly considered.

Congruence between partisan alternatives and economic institutions

Alvarez, Garrett, and Lange (1991) have shown that different partisan alternatives may be more effective and may lead to better performance under different patterns of organization of the domes-

---

29. See Alesina and Drazen (1991), who show that polarization of parties has consequences for the possibility of carrying out stabilization policy in the face of massive debt or hyperinflation. Their model helps us to understand political problems that are more dire than those usually faced in the United States. Unlike the equilibrium models that characterize the work of Alesina and his colleagues concerning the United States, this work acknowledges that polarization is a variable.

tic economy. Specifically, they have shown that Left governments deliver better performance in terms of growth, inflation, and unemployment in countries where there are strong and centralized unions, and Right governments perform better in those terms when there is a weak labor movement. However, in countries that do not have that "congruence" between winning parties and economic institutions, economic performance is worse. This suggests that there may be another dimension to the costs inherent in having choices. One kind of partisan alternative may be inferior and inefficient in some settings, but the determination of which one is inferior will vary across countries.

Partisan models seem to be far more robust theoretically and empirically than are the electoral-cycle models. Both are models of routine politics. As this chapter shows, there is considerable variety in the nature of partisan conflict. Partisan conflict is routine if it is repeated again and again in the same context. In fact, the context is rarely static, as succeeding chapters will show. Even partisan conflict is likely to be fluid, rather than predictable according to an equilibrium model.

PART THREE
The sources and authority of macroeconomic goals

5   The authority of
        macroeconomic goals

In Chapters 3 and 4, dealing with models of routine politics, we treated parties and voters as oriented to identifiable goals regarding inflation, unemployment, and income growth. We drew on the familiar misery index and showed how it could be modified to represent different kinds of preferences, and even to represent a conception of social welfare or the public interest. In doing these things, we accepted goals and preferences as given, as predetermined, and as clearly defined. In this chapter and the next we shall step back and ask where goals and preferences come from and how well defined and authoritative they are. In this chapter we consider official public definitions of national economic goals, as well as what economists say about various targets of macroeconomic policy.

These chapters will provide an argument that there is no basis for an unambiguous or uncontestable definition of the public interest, and there is no basis for an authoritative social welfare function.[1] This argument will undermine assertions that there are costs and pathologies of democracy. Without authoritative definitions of what public policy ought to be, there is no solid basis for comparing the outcomes of democratic politics to the best or the most appropriate outcomes. It is difficult to argue that democratic political

---

1. Note the difference between social welfare functions as used here, i.e., objective functions, and Arrow-type social welfare functions that might emerge from the aggregation of preferences. See Mueller (1989, chs. 19–20). See Asher et al. (1993) for a treatment of alternatives to the misery index.

processes lead systematically to inferior outcomes when superior outcomes resist precise and authoritative definition. In fact, the goals of public policy are defined and redefined in a continuing and fluid political process.

However, I shall suggest that even though there may not be any uncontestable targets, there are ranges of outcomes beyond which results are clearly inferior. The leading examples are hyperinflation and unsustainable increases in public indebtedness. The democratic political process might involve dynamics that take outcomes beyond the ranges of acceptability, and democratic institutions might obstruct the stabilization programs that would correct them.

OFFICIAL DEFINITIONS OF NATIONAL GOALS

Could some kind of objective definition of national economic goals, some social welfare function, be made public law? Should it? How close do the existing laws come to expressing specific goals? The U.S. Constitution expresses a basic stance on this issue. The Constitution is quite specific on the procedures through which law and policy will be made, but quite vague on goals. The closest it comes to identifying goals is in the Preamble, where "to promote the general welfare" is articulated as a goal.

The conception "general welfare" is broad and vague enough to provide no guidance at all in choosing specific goals. Implicitly, the Constitution seems to provide for continuing definition and redefinition of public purposes in a fluid political process. The Constitution is a general document with general goals, and it is difficult to imagine what might have been adopted in 1787 that would appropriately provide more specific guidance for modern economic policymaking.

The Federal Reserve Act of 1913 was much more specifically oriented to economic issues and performance than is the Constitution, but it is comparable in that it established decisionmaking bodies and procedures, but was vague on goals. That act specified that the Fed was designed "to furnish an elastic currency, to afford means of rediscounting commercial paper, to establish a more effective supervision of banking in the United States, and for other purposes." Those goals were notably imprecise.

The first law to focus specifically on macroeconomic goals was the Employment Act of 1946, whose purpose was to promote "maximum employment, production, and purchasing power." The act itself was watered down considerably from the initial bill, which was "to establish a national policy and program for assuring continuing full employment in a free competitive economy. . . ." The phrase "full employment" was dropped in the legislative process, as was the following assertion:

All Americans able to work and seeking work have the right to useful, remunerative, regular, full-time employment, and it is the policy of the United States to assure the existence at all times of sufficient employment opportunities to enable all Americans who have finished their schooling and who do not have full-time housekeeping responsibilities freely to exercise this right. (Bailey, 1950, p. 243)

In a classic, book-length case study of the legislative process, Stephen K. Bailey described and bemoaned the dilution of the original bill in the congressional process, which he described as a "kaleidoscopic and largely irresponsible interplay of ideas, interests, institutions, and individuals" (1950, p. 240). In fact, the legislative process was not always inspiring, and "there were few cases of mature economic debate between a Congressman and a witness" (p. 160). However, the process did provide an official forum for public deliberation about national goals.[2]

The Employment Act did establish the Council of Economic Advisors, to ensure that the president has ready access to professional economic advice, and provided for the annual *Economic Report of the President*. As such, it made lasting contributions in providing for systematic reporting of economic performance and providing a basis for accountability for economic performance.

A similar bill was passed in 1978 after likewise being watered down by its opponents. The Full Employment and Balanced Growth Act of 1978, also known as the Humphrey-Hawkins act, had originally proposed that government provide "last resort" jobs for the unemployed and work toward a goal of 4% unemployment by 1983. The government jobs provision was deleted in the legisla-

2. See Bailey (1950, pp. 127–8) for four interpretations of the meaning of the Senate bill, and how the subsequent House deliberations narrowed to a contest between two of them.

tive process, though the 4% goal was retained. The critics of the original bill also succeeded in adding specific inflation targets of 3% by 1983 and zero by 1988.

The real-world experience following the passage of the Humphrey-Hawkins act raised questions about the realism of those targets, and even about the wisdom of setting numerical goals for macroeconomic outcomes. In 1983, unemployment was more than double the target rate, at 9.5%, whereas inflation was close to the target for that year, at 3.9%. By 1988, inflation had dropped to 3.3% and unemployment was down to 5.4%, which might be considered tolerably within range of the targets. Such variations in performance have considerable political consequences in their own right, as Chapter 6 will elaborate. But the fact that they succeed or fail in approximating numerical targets in the Humphrey-Hawkins act is almost totally ignored in public discourse, being left for consideration in books like this.

As we saw in Chapter 2, macroeconomic theory provides no assurance that targets for outcomes such as these can be met. Without such assurance, and without better guidance on how to achieve them, the incorporation of specific numerical goals into public law renders the laws mere expressions of preferences, without regard to their realism. When we consider that the act also specified the goals of a balanced federal budget, reduced federal spending, and primary reliance on the private sector, it is obvious that the Humphrey-Hawkins act was a close approximation to the incorporation of wishful thinking into law. We have failed to achieve the targets, and many economists would tell us that they were impossible to begin with. A cynic might observe that the act was a charade that allowed members of Congress to take popular positions without following through, providing symbolic rather than concrete benefits to their constituents.

There were, however, provisions in the Full Employment and Balanced Growth Act that had lasting and probably constructive effects. Title III recognized that some of the goals and timetables might not be realistic, and it identified a series of procedures that Congress might use to deliberate over goals and the means to achieve them. They included schedules for regular reporting to Congress by the Council of Economic Advisors and by the Federal Reserve. Those reports provide the basis for semiannual public

Table 5.1. *Gramm-Rudman-Hollings deficit targets and actual deficits*

Deficit	Fiscal Years							
	1986	1987	1988	1989	1990	1991	1992	1993
GRH-I targets	172[a]	144	108	72	36	0		
GRH-II targets		144	136	100	64	28	0	
Actual deficits	221	150	155	153	221	269	290	255

[a] Billions of dollars.

hearings and debate. They are institutions for public accountability of those responsible for economic policy.[3]

The most recent examples of the effort to identify specific, official macroeconomic goals in legislation are the Balanced Budget and Emergency Deficit Control Acts of 1985 and 1987, known after their sponsors as the Gramm-Rudman-Hollings acts (GRH). The numerical targets in these laws are for the federal budget deficit. (The original act of 1985 was declared unconstitutional on a technicality, and a new version was passed in 1987.) Because the federal budget is much more directly controllable by the government than are unemployment and inflation rates, the GRH law is, in a sense, more realistic than the Humphrey-Hawkins act, at least from the point of view of economic theory.

That is, no one seriously claims that outcomes like inflation and unemployment rates are under direct government control. At best they can be influenced by fiscal policy or monetary policy instruments, which are under direct control. Federal budget deficits are, in contrast, much more nearly under direct government control, through taxing and spending laws. Even though federal tax receipts and expenditures are themselves products of the interaction of laws that are under government control and economic fluctuations that are not, budget deficits are far more directly subject to government control than are inflation and unemployment rates.

However, the effort to enforce a balanced budget has been even less successful than the Humphrey-Hawkins effort to achieve 4% unemployment. Table 5.1 identifies the deficit targets in the two

3. See *Congressional Quarterly Almanac*, vol. 34 (1978), pp. 272–9.

versions of the GRH law, and compares them with actual experience. The gaps between the targets and the actual deficits have become larger and larger, in spite of the fact that the laws had specific enforcement mechanisms designed to carry out *automatic* cuts if the government did not achieve the targets through its discretionary decisions. Although those targets may have been economically realistic, they apparently were not politically realistic.

The GRH law demonstrates that numerical targets with enforcement mechanisms provide no assurance of success even when the targets are, within certain limits, under the control of public officials. The problem with achieving the unemployment targets of the Humphrey-Hawkins act was that they probably were not economically realistic; that is, they were not feasible under the constraints of economic reality. The problem with the budget targets of the GRH law was one of political rather than economic feasibility. That is, Congress and the president were not able to agree on a program of expenditure cuts and/or tax increases that would reduce the deficit by degrees that would approximate the targets. These authorities seem to have been operating under powerful political constraints that limited their capacity to achieve the targets. Such constraints involved failure to reach agreements across parties and across branches of the government that would reduce expenditures or increase taxes, and they involved the fear that proposals to cut specific expenditures or to raise taxes not only would not achieve agreement and cooperation but also would be exploited by partisan opponents in the next election. Specific actions to reduce the deficit often appear to be politically suicidal.

Under recent circumstances, then, voluntary agreement on taxing and spending decisions that would reduce deficits seems not to have been politically feasible. But the fact that continuing large deficits are not always features of democratic politics suggests that the conditions of political feasibility may vary. We shall return to an analysis of the political incentives surrounding deficit creation and reduction in Chapter 7.

The GRH declining deficit targets were quietly abandoned in the Budget Enforcement Act of 1990. In signing that agreement into law, President Bush undermined his credibility by violating his famous pledge: "Read my lips: no new taxes." The law was actually a substantive victory for the president in several respects (Collender, 1992, ch. 2), but the fact that it was accompanied by a tax increase made it seem a major political and symbolic defeat, given his campaign pledge. Although the 1990 act does not state visible and inflexible targets for anything, it may be more realistic in terms of achieving certain goals, such as a limitation on the growth of federal spending.

Our record of experience with laws that identified specific numerical goals for unemployment and budget deficits should, at the very least, give pause to anyone who would advocate a constitutional amendment that would require a balanced federal budget. Regardless of the worthiness of the goal, experience has made it clear that identification of goals in public laws provides no assurance of their achievement. Those who would propose such laws should consider carefully whether or not it is within the power of the government to meet those goals, whether or not they can design a credible enforcement mechanism, and whether or not the identification of one official goal will entail costs by detracting from other goals.

There is a deeper problem with legislated goals for public policy that is captured in the title of a recent article: "Congress Is a 'They,' not an 'It': Legislative Intent as Oxymoron" (Shepsle, 1992). Drawing on social choice theory, Shepsle points out that any given majority is likely to be one of many possible majorities based on the same preferences. As Jerry Mashaw has put it,

statutes are . . . the vector sum of political forces expressed through some institutional matrix which has had profound, but probably unpredictable and untraceable, effects on the policies actually expressed. There is no reason to believe that these expressions represent either rational, instrumental choices or broadly acceptable value judgments. (Mashaw, 1989, p. 134)

Legislated goals for public policy *could* reflect a broad, well-informed, and stable consensus on values, but there is no assurance that they will. They may reflect an arbitrary stopping point in the legislative process that could be bettered by some other proposal if the process were allowed to continue, or they may reflect superficial agreement on goals that would appear questionable if the full costs and implications of their achievement were seriously considered. The American experience in placing specific macroeconomic goals into law has reflected little well-informed, stable consensus, but many arbitrary stopping points and superficial agreements.

GOALS AS UNDERSTOOD IN ECONOMIC ANALYSIS: OUTCOMES

In this section we shall review a series of macroeconomic goals in their own right, as well as some of the considerations that a genuine national deliberation on goals should address. The main, standard goals for macroeconomic outcomes are maximization of growth in income, output, and consumption, and minimization of unemployment and inflation.

Income, output, and consumption growth

Probably the most comprehensive and consensual contemporary measure of economic performance is growth, specifically growth in national income, total output, or consumption, all of which are empirically related. In contemporary economics, growth is largely an uncontested goal, but it was not always so in the past, and may not always be so in the future. In *The Rise and Fall of Economic Growth,* H. W. Arndt (1978) found an interest in growth and material progress among classical economists from Adam Smith to John Stuart Mill, but that "hardly a line is to be found in the writings of any professional economists between 1870 and 1940 in support of economic growth as a policy objective." In that intervening period, most attention went to problems such as "the theory of value and distribution, welfare economics, monetary and trade cycle theory, all these treated almost entirely on static assumptions" (1978, p. 13).

"Economic growth" returned as a major objective of public policy, and as a preoccupation of economists, after World War II, reaching its high point in the 1960s. During that period, the literature acknowledged that growth involved some issues of preference for the present, to the neglect of the future, and that growth might well impose costs in terms of inflation, the international balance of payments, and inequality, as well as noneconomic goals. But even at that peak of interest, according to Arndt, "no economist was

foolish enough to think of economic growth as an 'end in itself' "
(1978, pp. 80–1).

Arndt characterized the arguments of those with major reserva-
tions about the goal of economic growth (the critics, the revolution-
aries, and the prophets), concluding that

> what the debate over economic growth has achieved is wider recognition that
> the trade-offs between the objective of a high rate of economic growth and
> some other objectives need to be reconsidered. (1978, p. 153)

In my reading of the contemporary scene, this recognition has been
lost both from public political discourse and from most professional
economic analysis. Growth issues now dominate both the partisan
debate and macroeconomic analysis. Perhaps growth as a goal is
questioned most sharply when growth performance is strongest, as
in the 1960s. Since the early 1970s, growth in American national
income has stagnated, and as growth performance has deteriorated,
it seems to have risen as a topic of economic analysis and of
political debate. Growth of national income is now a central concern of economists, politicians, and the public, but historical perspective makes it clear that growth comes and goes as a goal. As
Tibor Scitovsky has said, "the national income is at best an index
of economic welfare, and economic welfare is a very small part and
often a very poor indicator of human welfare" (1992, p. 145).

Growth is a central issue today because it has risen to the top of
the agenda in a fluid political process, not because anyone has
made an authoritative case that maximizing growth should be a
central goal of public policy without regard to trade-offs with other
concerns. What those concerns are and how their trade-offs are
defined are questions to which there are no single, lasting, authoritative answers. In a democratic system, these are questions that
are answered in different ways at different times, depending on
what the most significant problems of the day seem to be. If the
rates of national income growth were higher, I expect that the
prominence of the goal would fade, to be replaced by issues of
equity or the environment or other alternatives, in ways that are
not easy to predict.[4]

Amartya Sen (1993) has pointed out that some very basic indica-

---

4. For an analysis of the fluidity of national political agendas, see Kingdon (1984).

tors of well-being, such as infant mortality, life expectancy, and famine, are only loosely related to national income. His argument makes it clear that maximization of income growth at the expense of distributional considerations can be a limited and perhaps limiting goal, rather than an appropriate index of all good things.

Unemployment

Minimizing unemployment is another leading goal of economic policy. Unemployment is well known to be inversely related to income growth, and policies designed to reduce unemployment often are the same as those designed to increase growth. The rate of unemployment is the fraction of the labor force out of work and looking for jobs. Note that this rate is relative to the size of a base that is not fixed. The labor force as a fraction of the total U.S. population has risen substantially since World War II (from 59.7% in 1950 to 66% in 1991) because of the increased participation of women and teenagers. Thus the unemployment rate is imperfect as a constant measure of the economy's capacity to provide jobs.

The unemployment rate is also imperfect as a constant measure of human suffering. At any given time, some of the unemployed will have been out of work for extended periods of time, whereas others will have only recently joined the ranks. Also, people enter and leave the labor force for a variety of reasons, and the search for a job may reflect different degrees of need. In addition, the pain of unemployment may be cushioned to various degrees by unemployment compensation or public assistance.

Still, unemployment is a more direct indicator of human suffering than is a low rate of income growth. Even though minimizing unemployment seems desirable, other things being equal, zero unemployment is not a reasonable target. One way to understand this is to recognize that much unemployment is *frictional unemployment,* wherein people sometimes are voluntarily unemployed while looking for better jobs. For such people, unemployment might not seem as bad as working at a job that did not suit their talents or interests. In a free society there will always be some unemployment of this type, and this fact alone justifies not having a goal of zero unemployment.

Structural unemployment is defined on the basis of a mismatch between the skills and training of available workers and the demands of available jobs. An example is the unemployment that has resulted from the declining number of manufacturing jobs in the contemporary economy, leaving large pockets of unskilled labor in former manufacturing regions. This is a serious economic problem, but it is not highly amenable to solution by the fiscal and monetary stabilization policies that are the concern of this book.

Cyclical unemployment, a third type, is the kind of unemployment that comes with recessions and disappears with expansions of the business cycle. It is the kind that has been thought to be responsive to fiscal and monetary stabilization policies. As shown by the review of macroeconomic theories in Chapter 2, there has been a great deal of controversy in economics over just what, if anything, can be done to correct cyclical unemployment.

There is no doubt that unemployment has serious costs. These costs can be measured in terms of lost output for the economy as a whole. They can be measured in terms of lost income for the individuals and families directly affected. These costs have been borne disproportionately by those in the lower economic strata. Finally, the costs can be measured in terms of indicators of psychological consequences, as measured by various indicators of mental health.[5]

Even though there is little good and much bad to be said about unemployment, there are no clear, objective answers about how low unemployment ought to be, and what public officials should do about it. There is little dispute that there is a "natural" or equilibrium rate of unemployment at any given time, but there is considerable dispute about where it is, what causes it, and what should be done about it.[6] Ironically, Democratic programs designed to benefit the working class are likely to raise the natural rate. Minimum wage laws raise the price of labor and are likely to reduce the demand for it. Generous unemployment compensation reduces the incentive for the unemployed to accept jobs they do not like. Both policies place upward pressure on the natural rate of unemployment. There are deep and legitimate disagreements among economists about what can and should be done through economic stabili-

5. See Schlozman and Verba (1979) for a book-length treatment of the political consequences of unemployment. See also Summers (1990).
6. See Summers (1990, chs. 8 and 9).

zation policy to reduce unemployment. These disagreements are largely scholarly and intellectual, but in an important sense they are political as well, because they involve differences in values and judgments that often cannot be resolved outside of a political process.

Inflation and price stability

Minimizing inflation is the last of the three leading public goals for macroeconomic performance. The fact that it is the last to be considered does not necessarily imply that it is last in priority. Inflation is a general increase in the money prices of goods and services and a decline in the purchasing power of the currency. As such, it has to do with numerical values for prices and wages, with no necessary connection with "real" variables such as unemployment or income growth.

The most common indicator of inflation is the rate of change in the consumer price index (CPI), a number that represents the dollar price of a standard bundle of goods and services that are thought to represent typical tastes and needs. This index is normalized to 100 for a base year, and inflation is calculated as the annual rate of change in this index. The CPI currently used by the U.S. government is based on 100 for the period 1982–84, and had risen to 146 by the end of 1993. During that period, annual inflation rates were as low as 1.9% in 1986 and as high as 5.4% in 1990 (*Economic Report of the President,* 1994).

Annual rates of inflation in the United States rose to double digits just after World War II and in 1979, 1980, and 1981. Rates can be negative, indicating deflation, or a general decrease in prices and an increase in the purchasing power of money. This is rare in the contemporary era, having happened last in the mid-1950s. In some countries, inflation can rise to four digits or more, indicating hyperinflation. For example, inflation in Argentina in 1989 was nearly 5,000%.

Inflation is not the same thing as the cost of living, but rather is an indicator of *change* in that cost. If inflation is truly general, there will be the same percentage increase in the price of everything, including wages and salaries earned and goods and services purchased. If this is so, high rates of inflation can be compatible with a constant capacity to purchase and a constant standard of living, so long as incomes keep pace with prices. To see this, think of the value of the dollar being arbitrarily doubled or halved, or being multiplied or divided by 10. There would be no "real" difference in the purchasing power of the dollar. The change would be "nominal," rather than real.

What are the costs of inflation? What difference does it make if these arbitrary numbers are changing? There are several ways to answer these questions, and most of them imply that inflation has "real" costs even though it fundamentally involves only numerical values. Douglas Hibbs (1987, ch. 3) reported a massive data analysis in which he empirically estimated the consequences of inflation for real income growth, for the distribution of income, for corporate profits, and for savings. For the most part, he found that the consequences and costs of inflation were minimal.

For example, his findings for the postwar American experience showed that inflation had negligible consequences for growth in real disposable income. He showed that inflation was moderately advantageous for the income shares of lower-income strata relative to higher-income strata and that it adversely affected corporate profits only after taxes. Hibbs used those findings to make an interesting and subtle argument about the "true costs" of inflation. He argued that

it is unlikely that the measureable consequences of inflation . . . explain satisfactorily the common belief that rising prices pose a serious problem. . . . less tangible and partly psychological factors are probably more significant in accounting for concern about inflation than are easily identifiable objective costs. (1987, p. 118)

Hibbs was suggesting that inflation not only measures nominal rather than real changes but also has "psychological" rather than real consequences. Note the difference between this use of the term "psychological" and the earlier use regarding unemployment. Here, "psychological" implies that the costs of inflation are imagined, rather than real or objective. In the previous usage, the psychological costs of unemployment in terms of family stress, admissions to hospitals, and even suicides were very real. I shall argue later that the costs of inflation can be real, though not easily measured.

Hibbs made an interesting, almost tongue-in-cheek argument about the costs of inflation:

> The biggest costs are *indirect* costs, flowing from the consequences of monetary and fiscal policy reactions to inflation, rather than the direct effects of rising prices *per se*. (1987, p. 123)

That is, he argued that inflation entails large costs because of the fact that policymakers induce recessions to get rid of inflation. The costs come from the recessions (through unnecessary unemployment and lost income) rather than from the inflation itself. Hibbs suggested that society would be better off if the public and public officials would ignore inflation and not incur the costs of reducing it by inducing recessions.

There is a well-documented public aversion to inflation, and I contend that it reflects real rather than imaginary consequences. It is true that the costs of inflation are difficult to measure precisely, but this does not mean that they do not exist. Inflation interferes with the efficiency of prices as indicators of relative value and as signals for what people should do to use their resources efficiently.[7]

Think of prices as carrying information about the relative values of things that are bought and sold in the market. When the demand for or supply of these things shifts, their prices will change in ways that will reflect an increase or decrease in value relative to other things that have prices. These kinds of changes are continually taking place because of changes in tastes and in the availability of the factors of production.

When inflation occurs, the general increase in prices can easily be confused with the relative changes in prices that are continually taking place. This confusion leads to inefficiencies in the economy that are difficult to measure, but are nevertheless likely to be real and consequential. Because they are so difficult to measure, their evaluation becomes a matter of judgment, and quite likely a subjective and contestable judgment. As such, this judgment can be called *political,* for two reasons: because it is likely to be associated with a person's values and interests, and because there is no authoritative source for a public, objective evaluation.

7. See Fischer (1986) for analysis and assessments.

Considered without regard to other goals, a zero target for infla-tion makes sense in a way that a zero target for unemployment does not.[8] Other things being equal, lower inflation is generally better than higher inflation. But the effort to reduce inflation, or to achieve a target of zero, is not likely to be unambiguously desir-able, because other things are not equal. Reductions in inflation are likely to come at the expense of (temporary) costs in real variables such as unemployment, as was illustrated in the figures presented in Chapter 3 regarding the misery index in the 1980s. Chapter 2 showed that there are several ways in which these trade-offs can be defined.

Hyperinflation

There is no precise definition of where hyperinflation begins and inflation that is merely high ends, but there is no doubt that hyper-inflation represents a pathological condition (Cagan, 1987). When prices increase at rates of thousands of percent per year, the utility of money as a means of exchange breaks down, and an economy retreats into a barter system. Hyperinflation was experienced in several European countries after World War I and in Latin America and Israel in recent years. The elimination of hyperinflation makes virtually everybody better off. But is hyperinflation as a pathologi-cal condition equivalent to being a pathology of democracy? It would be if democratic institutions and processes had an inflation-ary bias that led to hyperinflation. There may well be an inflation-ary bias to democratic institutions under some (but obviously not all) circumstances. However, so far as I know, the case has not yet been made that democratic institutions have had a causal influence in the creation of the hyperinflations that have existed. There is reason to believe that democratic institutions may obstruct the implementation of painful stabilization programs that are designed to eliminate hyperinflations (Alesina and Drazen, 1991).

Growth, unemployment, and inflation are all legitimate and ap-propriate areas for macroeconomic policymaking. There are good

8. There are sophisticated arguments that optimal rates of inflation should be above zero, for example, as a nondistorting tax (Barro, 1979), or as a way to change relative wages without reductions in nominal income.

reasons for the public and for politicians to want to increase growth and reduce unemployment and inflation. However, even if there were no trade-offs between these and other goals, there are no obvious, authoritative numerical targets that public policy ought to aim for, with the possible exception of inflation. But the fact is that these three goals may conflict with one another, as well as with other goals not discussed here.

With no external authority for individual goals, or for objective functions that could define optimal combinations among goals, we must consider that public goals are to be formulated and reformulated in a public political process. Each formulation is likely to be subject to subsequent reformulation. This fluid dynamic is likely to be an inevitable feature of macroeconomic policymaking in a democracy.[9]

GOALS AS UNDERSTOOD IN ECONOMIC ANALYSIS: INTERMEDIATE TARGETS

Growth, unemployment, and inflation will continue to be the outcomes of interest in this book, because they are the ultimate indicators of macroeconomic performance. However, economists and the public often recognize other variables as indicators of the health of an economy. Among these are the balance of the government's budget, interest rates, the balance of trade, and the exchange rate. These are sometimes thought of as intermediate targets, because they are more subject to government control than are the ultimate goals regarding growth, unemployment, and inflation, and also because they are of less intrinsic interest and value.

The balance of the federal budget is the intermediate target that receives by far the most attention in the United States. Almost everyone has an opinion about it. There is a very large gap between the opinions of the public and those of economists on the issue whether or not the budget should be balanced. For the public, the goal of a balanced budget has been strongly supported as long as opinion surveys have been taken. Furthermore, the public also

9. This argument is similar to an argument in favor of discretion as opposed to rules. I do not mean to exclude the possibility that policymaking might be improved by precommitments that may be similar to rules. See Shepsle (1991).

consistently favors an amendment to the Constitution to require a balanced budget.[10]

Although the balance of a government's budget is a common goal in conventional wisdom, it is less important in economic analysis. Macroeconomists are in fact quite divided over the desirability of balanced budgets and the consequences of deficits. These differences follow the different schools of macroeconomic theory. The classical school favored balanced budgets, whereas the Keynesians saw intentionally created deficits as appropriate means to stimulate the economy out of a depression or recession. Monetarists disagreed; they favored a balanced budget as one of the rules that should guide government policy. At least some new classicals think that deficits do not really matter, because rational agents will simply save to cover the future tax liabilities implied by deficits.

Those views all were expressed before the explosive growth in deficits that began in the early 1980s. Even though the national debt as a fraction of GNP had been higher than 100% after World War II, that number steadily declined, reaching 33.5% in fiscal 1981. Since then, it has risen, reaching 68% in 1992 (where it was in Eisenhower's first term). The unadjusted size of the national debt has quadrupled since 1980 (from less than $1 trillion to more than $4 trillion). That growth has led many economists who previously had been casual about deficits to view them with alarm. Charles Schultze has characterized three contemporary professional views on the basis of wolves (the deficit is like the wolf at the door), termites (the deficit is slowly doing major damage to our future prospects), and pussycats (the deficit is no problem at all). From among the advocates of those views it is possible to identify a diverse group of economists who think that goals for the deficit should not be allowed to distract us from our concern with the issues of growth, unemployment, and inflation. Still another diverse group thinks that the deficit is a very important problem, but probably very few economists would say that it is important for the budget to be balanced every year.[11]

The nominal surplus or deficit is based on the relative sizes of

10. See Bratton (1994), Blinder and Holtz-Eakin (1984), and Modigliani and Modigliani (1987).
11. See Rock (1991) for a compendium of views.

Table 5.2. Selected data on U.S. federal deficit and debt, fiscal years 1946–93

Year	Surplus (+) or Deficit (−)[a]	Surplus or Deficit as % of GDP	Interest[a]	Interest as % of expenditure	Interest as % of GDP	Interest as % of deficit	Total debt[a, b]	Total debt as % of GDP[b]
1946	−15,936	−7.5	4,111	7.4	1.9	−25.8	270,991	127.5
1947	4,018	1.8	4,204	12.2	1.9	104.6	257,149	115.4
1948	11,796	4.8	4,341	14.6	1.8	36.8	252,031	102.2
1949	580	0.2	4,523	11.6	1.7	779.8	252,610	96.2
1950	−3,119	−1.2	4,812	11.3	1.8	−154.3	256,853	96.6
1951	6,102	1.9	4,665	10.2	1.5	76.5	255,288	81.4
1952	−1,519	−0.4	4,701	6.9	1.4	−309.5	259,097	76.1
1953	−6,493	−1.8	5,156	6.8	1.4	−79.4	265,963	73.1
1954	−1,154	−0.3	4,811	6.8	1.3	−416.9	270,812	73.6
1955	−2,993	−0.8	4,850	7.1	1.3	−162.0	274,366	71.3
1956	3,947	0.9	5,079	7.2	1.2	128.7	27,693	65.5
1957	3,412	0.8	5,354	7	1.2	156.9	272,252	62.1
1958	−2,769	−0.6	5,604	6.8	1.3	−202.4	279,666	62.4
1959	−12,849	−2.7	5,762	6.3	1.2	−44.8	287,465	59.9
1960	301	0.1	6,947	7.5	1.4	2308.0	290,252	57.6
1961	−3,335	−0.6	6,716	6.9	1.3	−201.4	292,648	56.6
1962	−7,146	−1.3	6,889	6.4	1.2	−96.4	302,928	54.6
1963	−4,756	−0.8	7,740	7	1.3	−162.73	10,324	53.1
1964	−5,915	−0.9	8,199	6.9	1.3	−138.6	316,059	50.5
1965	−1,411	−0.2	8,591	7.3	1.3	−608.9	322,318	48
1966	−3,698	−0.5	9,386	7	1.3	−253.8	328,498	44.7
1967	−8,643	−1.1	10,268	6.5	1.3	−118.8	340,445	42.9
1968	−25,161	−3	11,090	6.2	1.3	−44.1	368,685	43.5
1969	3,242	0.4	12,699	6.9	1.4	391.7	365,769	39.5

Year								
1970	−2,842	−0.3	14,380	7.4	1.5	−506.0	380,921	38.7
1971	−23,033	−2.2	14,841	7.1	1.4	−64.4	408,176	38.8
1972	−23,373	−2	15,478	6.7	1.3	−66.2	435,936	38
1973	−14,908	−1.2	17,349	7.1	1.4	−116.4	466,291	36.6
1974	−6,135	−0.4	21,449	8	1.5	−349.6	483,893	34.5
1975	−53,242	−3.5	23,244	7	1.5	−43.7	541,925	35.9
1976	−73,732	−4.4	26,727	7.2	1.6	−36.2	628,970	37.3
TQ	−14,744	−3.3	6,949	7.2	1.6	−47.1	643,561	36.2
1977	−53,659	−2.8	29,901	7.3	1.6	−55.7	706,398	36.8
1978	−59,186	−2.7	35,458	7.7	1.6	−59.9	776,602	36
1979	−40,183	−1.7	42,636	8.5	1.8	−106.1	828,923	34.1
1980	−73,835	−2.8	52,538	8.9	2	−71.2	908,503	34.4
1981	−78,976	−2.7	68,774	10.1	2.3	−87.1	994,298	33.5
1982	−127,982	−4.1	85,044	11.4	2.7	−66.4	1,136,798	36.4
1983	−207,818	−6.3	89,828	11.1	2.7	−43.2	1,371,164	41.3
1984	−185,388	−5	111,123	13	3	−59.9	1,564,110	42.3
1985	−212,334	−5.4	129,504	13.7	3.3	−61.0	1,816,974	45.8
1986	−221,245	−5.2	136,047	13.7	3.2	−61.5	2,120,082	50.3
1987	−149,769	−3.4	138,652	13.8	3.1	−92.6	2,345,578	52.7
1988	−155,187	−3.2	151,838	14.3	3.2	−97.8	2,600,760	54.1
1989	−152,481	−2.9	169,266	14.8	3.3	−111.0	2,867,537	55.4
1990	−221,384	−4	184,221	14.7	3.4	−83.2	3,206,347	58.6
1991	−269,521	−4.8	194,541	14.7	3.5	−72.2	3,598,993	63.9
1992	−290,398.	−4.9	199,421	14.4	3.4	−68.7	4,002,669	68.2
1993	−254,670	−4	198,811	14.1	3.2	−78.1	4,351,223	69.1

^a Millions of dollars.
^b End of year.

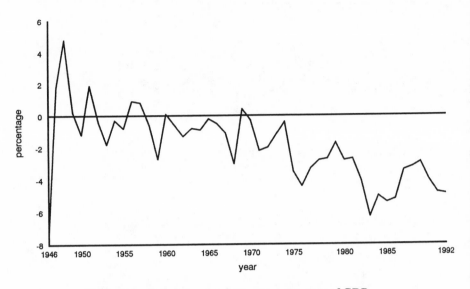

Figure 5.1. U.S. federal deficit as a percentage of GDP.

revenues and expenditures. Even if public policy is designed to produce a balance between the two, business cycles and exogenous shocks can throw them out of balance. For example, an economic downturn automatically leads to increases in expenditures for unemployment compensation and decreases in revenues, because of lost income among the newly unemployed. These "automatic stabilizers" operate in a countercyclical fashion to cushion the impact of a recession, whereas balancing the budget every year would have an opposite, procyclical effect.

Liberal and Keynesian economists have always seen these automatic stabilizers as desirable, but even leading conservative economists have come to accept them, including their implications of occasional deficits. For example, Milton Friedman's famous article "A Monetary and Fiscal Framework for Economic Stability" (1953a) advocated automatic stabilizers based on transfer payments and a progressive income tax. Robert Barro (1979) defended occasional deficits on grounds of the revenue smoothing hypothesis, which states that governments can and should plan equal marginal tax rates over time, to minimize distortionary effects on people's incentives to work and consume. Such rates will be set to cover the expected stream of expenditures, which will be exogenously

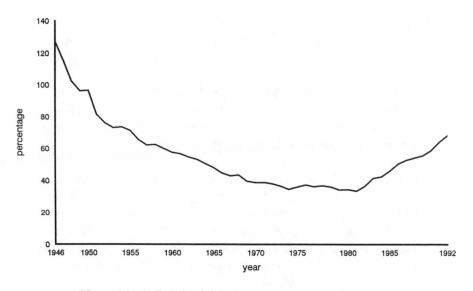

Figure 5.2. U.S. federal debt as a percentage of GDP.

determined, presumably in a political process. Because unanticipated shocks like wars and recessions will affect the path of expenditures, deficits will be allowed to fluctuate in a way that will
meet government budget constraints over time, without demanding
distortionary adjustments in taxes.

A nominal balance of the government's revenues and expenditures is a thoroughly arbitrary target, although it is very appealing
politically because it is simpler than any other target and thus is
more widely understood among voters.[12] A cash flow deficit of zero
is a focal point for agreement in a way that no other goal is likely
to be.

Only a few of the arguments in favor of a balanced budget
present this goal as an end in itself. Such arguments are likely
to be based on aphorisms, such as Adam Smith's analogy with
households: "What is prudence in the conduct of every private
family, can scarce be folly in that of a great kingdom." The most
convincing arguments that deficits are harmful hinge on the consequences of deficits, rather than on deficits as a goal in their own

12. Economists on the left, such as Robert Eisner, and on the right, such as Robert
    Barro, agree on certain accounting issues that imply that zero is a meaningless and
    arbitrary target. See Eisner (1986).

right. Deficits are said to cause inflation and rising interest rates in the short run, and reductions in growth in the long run: They may cause inflation, because increases in aggregate demand relative to a supply that is fixed in the short run are likely to increase prices. They may cause interest rates to rise, because increases in deficits increase the demand for lendable funds, the price of which is an interest rate. These arguments have lost force because the enormous increases in deficits in the Reagan-Bush years have been associated with decreases in both inflation and interest rates.

Deficits and the associated indebtedness are said to be at the expense of long-run growth and capacity to produce, because savings that might be invested in productive capital are diverted to government borrowing. Although that belief is very widespread among economists, there is considerable disagreement about what level of deficits will seriously threaten the other, more important economic goals (Rock, 1991).

The idea that a budget should be balanced for every period, such as every year, is based on conventional wisdom, such as that quoted earlier from Adam Smith. It has no sounder basis than its inherent appeal, and than its analogy with households. But that analogy is misleading, because of the differences between governments and households. It is also misleading because even conservative and prudent households have always gone into debt for certain purposes, such as the purchase of housing.

Budget balance over the business cycle was a more relaxed standard that received attention in the years after the Keynesians began advocating intentional deficits. Thus, a deficit in a recession would be inevitable, because of the automatic stabilizers and the desirability of a countercyclical policy. A prominent suggestion in the postwar era was that such deficits be balanced with surpluses in good times. Budget balance at full employment was a still more relaxed standard. It recognized that deficits were desirable in recessions, but avoided the issue of "paying off the debt." That standard made the definition of "full employment" implicitly important, but failure to agree on a definition made the standard ineffective as a guide.[13]

13. See Stein (1969, 1994).

Rising debt-to-GDP ratios

Most targets for deficits are contestable by reasonable and informed people. However, a compelling "minimum standard for deficit reduction is that federal deficits should be low enough that an unchanging fiscal policy should *not* result in steadily rising debt and interest burdens" (Gramlich, 1991, p. 184). Such a condition would be a good candidate for a pathology. A steadily rising ratio cannot be sustained without adverse consequences. In spite of some models that illustrate how the normal political process may have a bias in favor of deficits, there is too much history of budget balance to think that such is an inevitable feature of democratic government. In parallel with the arguments regarding hyperinflation, mentioned earlier, the case has not been convincingly made that democratic institutions cause rising debt/GNP ratios. We have enough experience with such institutions to be confident that any such connection is not simple and deterministic. Exogenous shocks have had much to do with rising debt/GDP ratios in the OECD nations since 1970 (Roubini and Sachs, 1989a,b). However, there is reason to believe that certain features of democratic institutions systematically obstruct stabilization programs that are designed to resolve such situations. Specifically, divided government and fractionalized party systems are associated with failure to resolve such problems.[14]

THE NATURE OF GOALS IN A SYSTEM OF DEMOCRATIC ACCOUNTABILITY

This chapter has shown that there is no obvious source in law or in economics for definitions of public economic goals that are fundamentally authoritative. We have found no source of authority for single goals nor for objective functions such that we can use them as benchmarks for evaluating the performance of the political process. There are no authoritative social welfare functions.

Ironically, the closest we might come to a consensual goal is balance in the federal budget, because that has been an official goal

---

14. See Roubini and Sachs (1989a,b), Grilli, Masciandaro, and Tabellini (1991), and Poterba (in press).

in legislation (e.g., Gramm-Rudman-Hollings) and is widely and consistently supported by the public. However, a little analysis and reflection will seriously undermine the validity of budget balance as an indicator of economic health. In fact, deficits persist in the face of declarations in law, dire predictions by public officials, and soundings of public opinion. This persistence may indicate that the political process is reflecting some real and meaningful preferences that are not being articulated in the public rhetoric.

Public purposes are defined within the political process, not outside of it. To paraphrase Arthur Okun, a nation's constitution (and perhaps even its laws) should not try to settle forever the precise weighting on economic goals. The constitutional arrangement "should rely on the democratic political process it establishes to select reasonable weights on specific issues as they arise" (Okun, 1975, pp. 93–4). This stance presumes that the political process operates in a reasonable and healthy fashion. In the preceding two chapters, models of electoral cycles and partisanship did not provide compelling arguments or evidence that the political process is unreasonable or pathological. The next three chapters will consider the political process in regard to voting and the making of fiscal and monetary policies.

6   Voters, elections, accountability, and choice

Voters are the ultimate authority in a democracy. Their preferences and behaviors are the fundamental sources of legitimacy for policymakers, who get their power through elections. Their preferences and behaviors also place constraints on what elected politicians can do. The electorate is the source for the authority of constitutional rules of procedure and for the authority of official statements of public goals. When there is ambiguity about what goals are appropriate for public policy, voter choices can resolve them at least provisionally. When there is ambiguity about which potential officeholders have correct or appropriate beliefs about the way the economic world works, voter choices can determine which ones will get to test their views against experience.

All this would be true in a world of ideal democratic citizens, but it is true in the real world as well. Yet the effort to maximize one's share of the votes of even ideal citizens can lead to opportunism, according to some of the models of political economy we have reviewed. And whereas ideal citizens may be public-spirited and fully informed, real-world voters may not have either of those qualities. This chapter will assess what we know about how voting behavior is affected by macroeconomic issues, as well as the implications for policymaking.

Most real-world voters are not well informed about political issues; they sometimes are characterized as being vulnerable to cynical manipulation by opportunistic politicians. However, I shall suggest that politicians do not need to be opportunistic in order to succeed: Voters will tolerate a wide variety of policies and out-comes, and politicians have considerable latitude for alternative choices, many of which are consistent with successful electoral careers. Pandering to voters' worst instincts is a realistic possibil-ity, and it may even be rewarded. But such pandering is not a necessity for political survival. It is, of course, easy to conceive that responsible policymaking will be punished at the polls, but that is not necessarily so. Voters do not usually *demand* irresponsible policymaking, and they do not necessarily do so.

THE HEAVY BURDEN OF THE SIMPLE ACT OF VOTING

An individual's vote must settle on a single choice following the consideration of many different kinds of preferences and judgments that may be in tension or even incompatible. Thus a vote may be only a crude reflection of a great deal of information. Because they allow voters to "throw the rascals out," elections enable voters to hold incumbent elected officials accountable for the past per-formance of the government. (This is what was going on in the electoral-cycle models in Chapter 3.) At the same time, the election is the institution through which voters choose among alternative future governments. (This is what was going on in the partisan choice models in Chapter 4.)

Consider the information that might be communicated in a single vote in a presidential election between two candidates, an incum-bent and a challenger. If the voter approves of the past economic performance of the incumbent, and also prefers the choices offered by the incumbent to those offered by the challenger, the choice is clear. The same is true if the voter disapproves of the past perfor-mance and prefers the challenger. In both these cases, the meaning of the vote is unambiguous, even though the vote is carrying two kinds of information.

However, suppose the voter disapproves of the incumbent's per-formance, but does not prefer the options presented by the chal-lenger. A vote for either candidate garbles this message, and such a vote is indistinguishable from the votes in the simpler unambiguous cases.[1] If we knew that voters always voted retrospectively, essentially by evaluating the performance of incumbents, we could interpret the meaning of elections accordingly. Or if we knew that voters always voted prospectively, by choosing among the expectations for future policy and performance, that would also simplify the interpretation of elections. But there is evidence for both patterns, and there is no reason to assume that all voters use the same decision rule, nor even that any one voter uses the same rule all of the time.[2] Not voting might be a way of expressing both disapproval of the incumbent and dislike of the challenger, but nonvoting because of distaste for both alternatives is not, on its face, distinguishable from nonvoting that derives from the indifference of those who would be satisfied with either alternative.

The addition of new alternatives does not necessarily help, because this may simply divide a majority that disapproves of the incumbent, so that he may win anyway. If the simple act of voting is overburdened in an artificially simple case like this, imagine how many more complex opinions must be distilled in an ordinary election in which considerations of partisan loyalty, candidate appeal, and other policy issues are also relevant. All these considerations may combine in ways that vary from voter to voter. When we consider the rich set of institutional alternatives regarding parliamentary and presidential systems, two-party and multiparty systems, the possibilities for ambiguity become still greater.

No wonder it is difficult to infer mandates from elections. In fact, I contend that in a narrow sense, mandates almost never exist. The narrow sense of "mandate" is "an authoritative command or instruction," presumably regarding a policy choice (*American Heritage Dictionary*, 1992). Referenda give such commands by virtue of clear popular majorities, choosing between the binary alternatives of a proposal and a status quo. For an election of persons to

1. A less likely possibility is that the voter prefers the policy preferences of the incumbent, but believes that the challenger will be more competent to guide the economy. A single vote cannot carry this message clearly either. One reason I expect that this possibility is less likely is that judgments of competence and judgments of the appropriate policy preferences are likely to be closely intertwined in macroeconomics.
2. See Sniderman, Brody, and Tetlock (1991, ch. 9) for a report of research that shows that different groups use different decision rules. See also Rivers (1988).

give such a command, a clear majority would have to express itself clearly about the policy choice through its choice among persons. The majority would have to choose the person because of a policy position with which he or she was identified. I know of no concrete case of such a mandate.

The term "mandate" will not go out of use because of this argument, however. A weaker definition is also meaningful: an "authorization given by a political electorate to its representative" (*American Heritage Dictionary,* 1992). Public officials who win elections have mandates, in this sense, to do what they see fit, subject to the authority of the office. This means that even if some of the support received by winning candidates came *in spite of* their stands on certain issues, they still are "authorized" to carry out their goals. Otherwise, public officials would be virtually paralyzed in the absence of mandates in the narrow sense. "The voice of the people can be about as readily ascertained as the voice of God" (Huntington, 1968, p. 106).[3]

RETROSPECTIVE AND PROSPECTIVE VOTING

In spite of all of this complexity, I shall argue in this book that the most consequential feature of elections can be understood in a very simple way. Seen in this way, elections are meaningful exercises in accountability even when they are not inspiring exercises of public discourse. It is now conventional wisdom to understand presidential elections as being influenced by retrospective evaluation of the economic performance of the incumbent administration. Many studies have reported "unmistakable" evidence that voting in presidential elections responds to economic performance, and one study has reported that economic performance is an even better predictor of the outcome than is a measure of the relative personal appeal of the presidential candidates (Erikson, 1989).

Some scholars go so far as to claim that information about economic performance allows them to predict the outcomes of presidential elections better than can public opinion polls intended to directly measure voters' intentions (Fair, 1988). There is something

3. See Kelley (1983, ch. 7) for a useful discussion of mandates.

to this, though there is also reason for humility among forecasters.[4] But even when different defensible models provide different predictions, as is sometimes the case, almost no careful student of the issue would deny that past economic performance is an important determinant of election outcomes. There is, however, a considerable range of interpretations of the meaning of this fact.

Two leading alternative interpretations are those of V. O. Key, Jr. (1966), and Anthony Downs (1957). The Key view has been designated the traditional reward–punishment theory by the leading student of retrospective voting (Fiorina, 1981). This view imposes little burden on the electorate:

The patterns of flow of the major streams of shifting voters graphically reflect the electorate in its great, and perhaps principal, role as an appraiser of past events, past performance, and past actions. It judges retrospectively; it commands prospectively only insofar as it expresses either approval or disapproval of that which has happened before. (Key, 1966, p. 61)

Key recognizes that voters have policy preferences, but he discounts the importance of policy choice in elections. He does address the contrast between the experience of the past and promises for the future:

Voters may reject what they have known; or they may approve what they have known. They are not likely to be attracted in great numbers by promises of the novel or unknown. Once innovation has occurred, they may embrace it, even though they would have, earlier, hesitated to venture forth to welcome it. (Key, 1966, p. 61)

Thus, Key recognizes that voters may take a leap in the dark when they reject incumbent parties. His interpretation was presented as a realistic description of American voters, but it was not meant to denigrate. In fact, the title of Key's book makes that doubly clear: *The Responsible Electorate: Rationality in Presidential Voting, 1936–1960*. The charitable quality of his view was further clarified by his statement that the "perverse and unorthodox argument of this little book is that voters are not fools" (1966, p. 7).

In contrast to Key's use of empirical data for inferences about how voters actually decide, Anthony Downs articulates a theoretically grounded argument about "The Basic Logic of Voting" (1957, ch. 4). In his theory, the vote is a future-oriented comparison of

4. See Greene (1993).

the streams of utility income to be expected from government activity under alternative parties. Downs is explicit about the future orientation of his theory. To "ignore the future when deciding how to vote . . . would obviously be irrational, since the purpose of voting is to select a future government" (1957, p. 40).

However, the most solid basis for an assessment of future utility under the incumbent party is its performance in the current period, "assuming that its policies have some continuity" (1957, p. 39).

As a result, the most important part of a voter's decision is the size of his *current party differential,* i.e., the difference between the utility income he actually received in period t and the one he would have received if the opposition had been in power. (1957, p. 40)

Downs's theory of the logic of voting is emphatically future-oriented. But note that both elements of the information that Downs's voter would use are based on the past: the utility "received" in the past and the utility the voter "would have received" in the past.

Downs implicitly assumes that the future will be a projection of the past, whether the projection is based on a continuation of the incumbents' policies and performance or a continuation of the counterfactual conditions that would have prevailed if the opposition had been in power. For Downs, the past is important because he sees it as the most useful available guide to the future. The relationship between past and future is seen as simple extrapolation or projection. Downs shows no awareness of the possibility that opportunistic incumbents might manipulate conditions before elections in ways that would mislead voters about the conditions that would obtain after the election. That is, a Downsian voter could be quite vulnerable to a Nordhaus-type electoral cycle. Of course, there is no reason to be sure that voters as characterized by Key would not also be vulnerable to such manipulation, though Key's vagueness about standards leaves the question more open.[5]

It would be a mistake to exaggerate the differences between the views of Downs and Key. Downs (1957) cites Key's earlier work three times, though Key (1966) does not mention Downs and does

5. The idea that incumbents would manipulate the economy in this way was not common among political scientists or economists when Downs and Key wrote. The idea, probably inspired by the 1972 election, became widespread only after the publications of Nordhaus (1975) and Tufte (1978).

not seem to be aware of his relevance. Each scholar acknowledges, at least implicitly, the central theme of the other: Downs discounts the value of platforms and promises relative to actual performance, and Key implicitly acknowledges that some voters might respond to promises. But still, as Fiorina asserts, the difference is important:

> . . . under the Downsian view elections have policy implications. . . . Downsian retrospective voting is a means to prospective voting. . . . But under the traditional theory, elections have no policy implications other than a generalized acceptance or rejection of the status quo. (1981, p. 13)

In fact, as a general rule, most judgments about the future are related somehow to the past, and most judgments about the past are not totally divorced from implications for the future. We should not expect to find that voting is purely retrospective or purely prospective. Most votes will involve some mixture of the two elements, and the mixture is likely to vary among voters. The next sections will present an overview of the evidence regarding the importance of the past and the future in voting as it relates to the economy. Even though there is ample evidence that voters are at least somewhat future-oriented when they vote, I shall argue that some important features of elections are better understood from Key's perspective. This is partly because, as Downs readily acknowledges, information about the past is much more solid than information about the future. But there is another reason: Sometimes elections produce innovations that are quite surprising by almost any standard.

EVIDENCE OF RETROSPECTIVE JUDGMENTS

There is plenty of evidence that past economic performance affects the vote share or the popularity of incumbent presidents. This is, at least superficially, evidence in support of Key's view that voters are retrospectively oriented. But there is also reason to believe that information about the past is used as a guide to the future, which implicitly supports a Downsian view. The most basic evidence of the importance of past performance is that a measure of recent real national income growth is a very powerful predictor of the vote

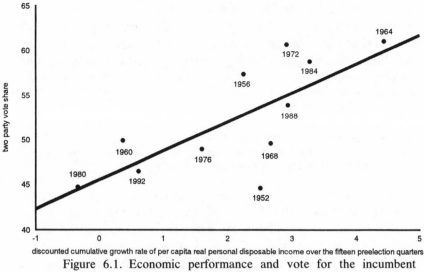

Figure 6.1. Economic performance and vote for the incumbent party's presidential candidate.

share of the incumbent party's presidential candidate. For example, Erikson argues that

> one can better predict the presidential vote division from income change during the previous administration than from the voters' relative liking for the two candidates! . . . Evaluations of candidate personal characteristics aside, the vote is determined almost entirely by the amount of prosperity that the incumbent party delivers. (1989, p. 568)

The economic performance variable that Erikson uses is a quarterly measure of per capita growth in disposable income, discounted over the presidential term so that recent performance counts most heavily. Erikson's model does include a measure of candidate appeal, which is also significantly related to vote share, but not more strongly than the economic performance. Figure 6.1 shows the results of a bivariate regression of the two-party vote share on the same measure of income growth used by Erikson, and originally used by Hibbs (1987, ch. 6). Incumbents lost each of the four elections in which the cumulative and discounted growth was below 2%. As the elections that are away from the line show, economic performance is not a perfect predictor. The incumbent party lost in 1952 and 1968 in spite of economic growth that normally would have made for a solid reelection.

A more complicated model of presidential voting (Fair, 1978,

1988, 1990) includes inflation, the party of the incumbent, and whether or not the incumbent is running, as well as income growth. This model accurately "predicted" the winner of sixteen of the nineteen elections from 1916 through 1988. The only ones it missed were the very close elections of 1960, 1968, and 1976, and in each case the error was less than 2%. However, the model predicted a solid victory by President Bush in 1992.

Even though the predictive value of these studies is contestable, there is little doubt that economic performance affects presidential election outcomes. Prosperity is always good for incumbents, and recession and stagnation are always bad. However, other factors can overwhelm economic performance. Incumbents or their heirs can be rejected even under conditions of prosperity, as in 1952 and 1968, and they can be reelected even under conditions of indifferent economic performance, as in 1956 in the United States and 1992 in Britain. The economy is only one of many causal influences on election outcomes.

Economic conditions like those just discussed seem not to have the same impact on congressional elections that they have at the presidential level. The seminal study of the effect of economic performance on voting (Kramer, 1971) was a study of congressional elections. In a memorable exchange, George Stigler (1973) challenged Kramer's findings on both theoretical and empirical grounds.[6] Subsequent research leaves little doubt that voting for president is influenced by economic performance, but controversy continues regarding the impact of the economy on congressional elections. Erikson argues that "with proper specification, per capita income growth is not significantly related to the congressional vote" (1990, p. 373), but Jacobson (1990) contests that finding. At best, evidence of the impact of the economy on congressional elections is sensitive to specification decisions in a way that its impact on presidential voting is not.

Most quantitative studies of the impact of economic performance on American elections have focused on the twentieth century.

6. Stigler (1973) argued that economic performance should not be a basis for voters' decisions, but if it were, it should be based on the entire electoral period, rather than on just one year. He showed that Kramer's findings evaporated when economic performance was measured over the two-year electoral period, and he used that fact as evidence in support of his assertion that economic performance should not be a basis for political competition, because prosperity is not a partisan issue. He contended that distributional issues should be a basis for partisan competition.

However, there is reason to believe that incumbents have been punished for poor economic performance well before anyone would think that they could have had any influence over it. For example, incumbent presidents or their parties' nominees were defeated after several of the major economic downturns of the nineteenth century, in the elections of 1840, 1860, 1884, and 1896.[7]

More refined inferences of voter preferences

Elections are the authoritative expressions of voters' wishes, but there is a limit to the information that can be squeezed out of them, because American national elections are held at two-year intervals. Presidential approval has been measured in a series of public opinion polls that began in 1935. Since 1953, the question "Do you approve of the way [president's name] has been handling his job as president?" has been asked at a rate that averages over once a month (Edwards, 1990). These polls yield a data series that provides a much richer source of inference about the connections between different economic conditions and political responses than can be inferred from elections.

For example, Douglas Hibbs has used these studies to infer the relative aversion of the public to inflation and unemployment, among other things. Consider an equation that relates presidential popularity to unemployment and inflation rates:

$$\text{approval} = a + b(\text{inflation}) + c(\text{unemployment})$$

The coefficients b and c, which we expect to be negative, show how popularity varies with inflation and unemployment, respectively. If the coefficients were the same, that would imply that the public was equally averse to inflation and to unemployment. That would imply a slope of -1 in the Phillips curve space described in Figure 4.1. If b were twice the size of c, that would imply that voters found a point of inflation to be twice as distasteful as a point of unemployment. That would imply a slope of -2. We can call the lines defined by these ratios indifference curves; they reflect the relative aversion to inflation and unemployment.

7. See Keech and Lynch (1992). See Miller and Wattenberg (1985) for survey-based measurements of the balance of retrospective and prospective judgments in elections from 1952 to 1980.

Hibbs found that the slopes of such "marginal rates of substitution" differed among partisans. He found that for Democrats, the slope was -1.1, and for Republicans the slope was -0.65 (Hibbs, 1987, p. 177). If possible combinations of unemployment and inflation were characterized by a static Phillips curve trade-off, that would imply that Democrats would choose a point such as *D,* and Republicans a point such as *R,* in Figure 4.1.

Inferring incentives for manipulation by vote-motivated politicians

Just as the approval polls permit a more refined assessment of voters' tastes regarding inflation and unemployment, they provide a more refined measure of the time horizon over which citizens evaluate past performance. Some of the controversies over the impact of economic conditions have been confused by this issue. For example, Kramer (1971) had originally assessed the impact of the most recent year's economic performance on congressional votes, whereas Stigler (1973) had assessed the impact of performance over the entire two-year term. Stigler thought that his unweighted two-year measure was an obviously superior measure of performance, but he did not consider the possibility that voters might discount the past in the spirit of the ancient question, "What have you done for me lately?"

Hibbs and other scholars have used the presidential approval series to infer the relative weights that citizens place on conditions that vary in their distance from the present. The standard that has become widely accepted is a weight that declines quarterly from a full weight for conditions in the quarter before an assessment to approximately 0.8 for the quarter before that. The weighting formula is a geometric lag, where the parameter $0 < g < 1$, which is 0.8 in this case, is multiplied by itself one additional time for each additional quarter back into the past. Because the parameter can vary between zero and one, a value of 0.8 might seem relatively high. However, when multiplied by itself several times, it rapidly approaches zero. The weight for the first quarter of the year before the election year would be g to the sixth power, or 0.26. The weight for the first quarter of a presidential term would be close to zero.

If that is the rate at which voters discount the past, even Downsian future-oriented voters might seem very much like those characterized in Nordhaus's model of vote-maximizing politicians manipulating naive voters. The crucial features are that they evaluate incumbents in terms of past economic performance, with the greatest emphasis on the recent past, and then project forward. The temptation Nordhaus identified for a vote-maximizing politician was to exploit a presumed possibility of making things look misleadingly good just before the election, at the expense of being worse after the election. For example, a misery index would be lower before the election than after, and a Downsian projection of past performance to the future would be misleading. Voters who heavily discounted the early part of the term would be vulnerable to such manipulation.

The reason that the past might be a misleading indicator of the future is the complicated and time-dependent trade-off between unemployment or income growth on the one hand and inflation on the other. In the natural rate world that Nordhaus modeled, unemployment below its natural rate or income growth above its natural rate will have delayed inflationary consequences. The main reason that voters were seen as vulnerable to manipulation was that the models used to estimate their preferences assumed that voters would reward reductions in unemployment and increases in income growth without regard to their natural rates, and without regard to their inflationary consequences. That feature was not an explicit assumption in the scholarship, but it was simply the simplest and most direct way to model voter responses to economic conditions.

The implication that voters are naively retrospective and vulnerable to manipulation was tested against an alternative hypothesis by Chappell and Keech (1985a), who conceptualized a model of voters who would reward reductions in unemployment or increases in income growth only to their natural rates. In that model, voters would not reward unemployment reduction or income growth that had inflationary consequences, and they would even tolerate economic slack that brought about reductions in inflation. For such voters, vote-maximizing policy is not irresponsible and does not generate inferior outcomes. Chappell and Keech tested and compared their model of sophisticated voters against the standard model that implicitly assumes vulnerability to manipulation. In those tests, the model that presumed voters to be sophisticated performed at least as well as, and sometimes better than, the alternative. Those findings cannot be interpreted as robust support for the hypothesis that voters are sophisticated and invulnerable to manipulation, but they do strongly suggest that *responsible policymaking will not necessarily be punished by voters.*

As a theory of voting behavior, the strength of the sophisticated voter model left a puzzle. The performance of the sophisticated voter model was only marginally better than that of the naive voter model. Direct evidence about voter information and understanding of the relevant trade-offs is not very supportive of the sophisticated voter hypothesis.[8] These facts suggest that the sophisticated voter hypothesis is most compelling when considered as a suggestion that voters behave "as if" they were sophisticated. But this leaves open the question of why voters are able to act in a sophisticated way without sophisticated cognitive processes.

Motoshi Suzuki has illuminated this puzzle by suggesting that under certain conditions, the two models are observationally equivalent. The responsiveness of output growth to unanticipated demand shocks or inflationary surprises may vary across countries and across time within a country. In settings (or "regimes") in which unexpected policy shifts have large impacts on output, vote-motivated politicians might have an incentive to manipulate the economy. In those settings, the difference between naive and sophisticated voters will be consequential. However, in settings in which government policy has little impact on real growth, voter sophistication does not matter very much.

Suzuki (1991) distinguished two such settings or regimes in the United States. The period from 1961.I through 1974.II was characterized as a stable period in which the two models of voting behavior could not be distinguished, whereas the period from 1974.III to 1985.IV was characterized as an unstable period in which they could. In empirical tests, Suzuki found that the two models performed comparably well and were indeed indistinguishable in the first period. However, he found that the sophisticated model was outperformed by the naive or adaptive model in the second period. Directly, these results imply support for "nonrationalist" perspec-

8. See Gramlich (1983).

tives on voting behavior. However, Suzuki suggested that voters may learn only what they need to learn in order to hold incumbents accountable for economic performance. Because the economic regime has returned since 1985 to the stability that characterized the earlier period, voters may not have been rewarded for the effort to learn new decision rules that would make them less vulnerable to manipulation (Suzuki, 1991). In a study of Japanese voting, Suzuki suggested that voters were able to learn strategic behavior in response to the emergence of manipulative behavior by politicians.[9]

Suzuki's important work suggests that an observed pattern of economic voting behavior is likely to be conditional. If the economy does not respond to policy manipulation, or if politicians do not try to manipulate it, naive and sophisticated voting will be difficult to distinguish. And even if economic and political conditions make sophisticated voting appropriate, it may take time for voters to learn. We are far from having conclusive observations on voter vulnerability to cynical manipulation of economic performance.

Both the model of naive performance evaluation and that of sophisticated performance evaluation are based on past performance, and are in that sense retrospective, and in keeping with Key's views. But the model of sophisticated performance evaluation is implicitly future-oriented, in that it is consistent with behavior that would avoid adverse future consequences. This feature makes it consistent with a reformulated Downsian view in which information about the past is used as a guide to the future.

The impact of voters on economic policymaking should be viewed less in terms of what voters demand than in terms of what they will tolerate and reward. Voters are not the initiators of public policy; they are more like an audience whose approval is necessary for a show to continue. The question is not what kind of show they demand, but whether or not the shows that are produced will receive good reviews and continued support.

There is no compelling evidence that voters characteristically punish responsible policymaking that is not opportunistic. We have seen that there is no single best economic policy that is uncontested among fair-minded and informed people. There are many policies

9. Suzuki (in press). See also Richards (1986).

that may be legitimately defensible and that may receive voter support. Only some of these should be considered irresponsible, and the case is yet to be made that there is strong voter demand for inferior policy.

PROSPECTIVE VOTING

Several studies have found evidence that voters are forward-looking as well as retrospective. For example, in his study *Economics and Elections,* based largely on western European voters (i.e., Britain, France, Germany, Italy, and Spain), Michael Lewis-Beck found that "future expectations about what economic performance a government will deliver emerge as a decisive individual vote determinant" and that "prospective economic policy evaluations have at least as strong an immediate effect on individual vote choice as retrospective economic evaluations do" (Lewis-Beck, 1990, pp. 82–3, 122, 133). The evidence for that inference came from sample surveys in which voters were asked for their evaluations of past economic performance and their expectations about future economic conditions. Lewis-Beck presented regression analyses in which he compared future-oriented and past-oriented judgments in terms of their capacity to predict vote choice.[10]

If prospective judgments are important determinants of voter choice, where do they come from? How valid are they? How do voters know what to expect about the future performance of government? There are several possible grounds for judgment about the future consequences of alternative choices. One is that future expectations are based on some kind of extrapolation from past performance, as Downs suggested. Another is that they are based on a more sophisticated way of forecasting the future. (A third possibility, that future expectations are based on campaign promises, will be considered in a later section of this chapter.)

If judgments are based on a simple extrapolation from the past, a clear distinction between retrospective and prospective voting cannot be made. Models based on such inferences are quite respectable. For example, when Kramer (1971) formulated the semi-

10. For related evidence on the United States, see Kuklinski and West (1981) and Lewis-Beck (1988).

nal study of the relationship between economic performance and voting behavior, he did so in an explicitly Downsian, future-oriented framework. The measure of future economic performance to be expected from reelection of the incumbent party was a measure of actual recent past performance (in the election year), which was considered to be the best available indicator. Because the inference was made from aggregate economic data (and did not involve surveys), we do not have direct evidence of how voters were using that information, nor is there evidence whether or not past performance was consciously used as a basis for judgments about the future. The more sophisticated and strategic standard of voting modeled by Chappell and Keech (1985a) is implicitly future-oriented, in that such voters do not reward policy that seems desirable at the time but implies undesirable consequences in the future.

MacKuen, Erikson, and Stimson (1992) have presented an argument that voters are future-oriented in a very sophisticated way. They assert that "economic conditions affect presidential popularity only to the extent that economic conditions alter expectations of the economic future" (1992, p. 603). They show that expectations of the future are not simple extrapolations of past performance, however. They argue that there is independent informational content in these expectations, which comes from the leading economic indicators, as filtered through news media. This remarkable finding makes a case that the orientation of voters toward the future depends on the economic news, which in turn depends on the index of leading indicators of economic performance.

Party identity and policy voting

All of the models in the foregoing accounts of voting have treated incumbents as if they had no identity that was independent of their performance, but we know that that is an oversimplification. Parties have reputations as being best able to deal with particular problems. There is a theory of "policy" voting that is to be distinguished from retrospective voting. In that theory, voters react to conditions by choosing the party that has the best record of concern and performance regarding the most salient problems. For example, voters might support Republicans in conditions of high inflation, because that party is known for being effective in dealing with that problem. Or voters might support Democrats in conditions of high unemployment, for a similar reason.[11]

RETROSPECTIVE VOTING AND INNOVATION IN ECONOMIC POLICY

American presidential elections are simultaneously contests between challengers and incumbents (or their heirs) and contests between candidates from parties with identities and histories. But these identities can change substantially. The identity of the Democrats changed dramatically in 1896, when the gold standard advocate Grover Cleveland was replaced by the free silver advocate William Jennings Bryan as the party's candidate for president. The most dramatic lasting change in the identity of the Democratic party came with the election of Franklin D. Roosevelt in 1932. President Roosevelt presided over a revolution in American government and policymaking that was so fundamental that one leading scholar has designated the period since then as the Second Republic.[12]

The identity of the Republican party may never have changed so dramatically as had that of the Democrats in those two episodes, but there is little doubt that the Reagan presidency marked a significant departure from previous Republican administrations. In some respects, Reagan's election represented victory for a conservative wing that had been losing all the postwar nominating contests except that of 1964, when the conservative Barry Goldwater was soundly defeated in the general election. But there was more innovation in Reagan's program than simply the proposals and policies of the party's Taft-Goldwater wing. "Supply side economics" and the predominance of the goal of reducing taxes over the goals of reducing expenditures and balancing the budget were new features of Republican economic policy.

The policy innovations of Roosevelt's New Deal and of Reagan's

11. See Kiewiet (1981, 1983).
12. See Lowi (1979).

supply side revolution were dramatic departures from their previous partisan identities, as well as from the policies of the party that each replaced. Still, I contend that those innovations are best understood in terms of Key's point that voters

are not likely to be attracted in great numbers by promises of the novel or unknown. Once innovation has occurred, they may embrace it, even though they would have, earlier, hesitated to venture forth to welcome it. (1966, p. 61)

That observation is least controversial with respect to the 1932 election, but I shall argue that it is also true for 1980.

In 1932, Roosevelt ran a remarkably conventional campaign. He promised to balance the budget, which Herbert Hoover had failed to do, but in general he gave no indication of the flood of innovations that were to come. The 1932 election is easily interpreted as a negative retrospective judgment of the Hoover administration. In 1936, after four years of new policies that radically changed the nature of American government and policy, voters again had a chance to approve or disapprove, and Roosevelt was reelected in a landslide. Voters approved in retrospect what they had not actively chosen four years before.

One need not argue that voters did not think about or care about what kind of president Franklin Roosevelt would be. Choosing him involved taking a substantial risk, perhaps even a "leap in the dark." Knowing what we know now, we could even argue that the 1932 campaign was misleading in suggesting that Roosevelt was not a radical innovator. In retrospect, the "risk" of major innovation was greater than it seemed at the time.

The first Reagan administration was more predictably innovative than the first Franklin Roosevelt administration. Governor Reagan was outspoken in advocating change, promising major cuts in taxes and domestic expenditures, and increases in defense spending, along with a balanced budget. But it would be too facile to conclude that the American public actively chose those changes, even though they seemed to endorse them in the landslide election of 1984. Just as Roosevelt's victory in 1932 can best be understood as a rejection of Hoover, so Reagan's victory in 1980 can best be understood as a rejection of Carter.[13]

13. See Hibbs (1982).

Both of those elections involved retrospective voting against incumbents whose performance was seen as inadequate, and they both involved some risk in the choice of the alternative. Quattrone and Tversky (1988) have provided some insight into the reasons why voters might take such risks without clear knowledge of what to expect. They argue that risk aversion is common for people who expect positive outcomes. For example, during a period of prosperity, voters will be less inclined to take a risk and vote for a challenger whose policies and skills are not well known.

However, as negative outcomes become more likely, risk aversion gives way to risk acceptance. In political terms, as incumbents become associated with economic downturns, voters may be more likely to seek risks in the form of the unknown economic leadership of the challenger. Quattrone and Tversky observe that

incumbents are usually regarded by voters as less risky than the challengers, who are often unknowns and whose policies could drastically alter the current trends, for better or for worse . . . the less risky incumbent should fare better when conditions are good . . . in contrast the election of the challenger offers a *political gamble that is worth taking when "four more years" of the incumbent is viewed as an unsatisfactory state.* (1988, p. 724)

When conditions are satisfactory, a challenger may seem like too much of a risk, but as conditions deteriorate, the risk involved in rejecting an incumbent for an unknown challenger may seem more and more palatable.

If these interpretations are correct, major changes in policy are likely to be somewhat like mutations in evolution. From the point of view of the electorate as a whole, such changes are not actively chosen from a clearly defined set of alternative future programs. Instead, they "happen" as a result of the rejection of incumbents. They happen at the initiative of those who take over, and only sometimes can their direction be foreseen by even careful study of what challengers say they will do.

CAMPAIGNS, INCENTIVES, AND ACCOUNTABILITY

The foregoing observations do not lead to a claim that electoral campaigns are meaningless exercises. There have been systematic studies showing a connection between platforms and promises on the one hand and policy innovation on the other.[14] In spite of this, there are several reasons to discount the predictive value of campaign promises.

1. They typically are so vague as to predict very little. For example, candidate John F. Kennedy proposed "let's get this country moving again." Candidate Richard Nixon proclaimed that "I have a plan to end the war." Candidate Bill Clinton promised "change."
2. They often are not credible. President Franklin Roosevelt assured the public in 1940 that "your boys will not be sent into any foreign war." Both Jimmy Carter in 1976 and Ronald Reagan in 1980 promised to balance the federal budget in the next four years. Candidate George Bush reached a new height in explicitness: "Read my lips: no new taxes."
3. Some of the most dramatic policy innovations come from people who might be most expected to oppose them. In a sense, Richard Nixon built his career on cultivating hostility toward Communist China; yet he was the president who took the initiative to lay the groundwork for opening diplomatic relations and bringing the People's Republic into the community of nations. Cooperation with China would once have been a politically risky move that would have made the initiator vulnerable to charges of being "soft on communism." Because Nixon had impeccable credentials as an anti-Communist, he was in a safer position to take that initiative than someone who did not have such strong credentials. There were similar ironies in Nixon's establishment of price and wage controls in 1971.

A complete and reasonable view of elections should at least provide room for potential influence from each of the elements we have been discussing. There should be a place for retrospective evaluations, for consideration of promises, and for independent sources of information about the future. There is no reason to believe that any of these elements should always have the same impact regardless of circumstances. In fact, it is quite likely that the relative balance of retrospective and prospective judgments will be affected by conditions. Very bad conditions are likely to

14. See Budge and Hofferbert (1990).

prompt negative retrospective voting regarding incumbents. Very good conditions are likely to prompt positive retrospective voting. In between the very bad and very good, there may be more careful attention to comparisons between the record and promises of the incumbent and the promises of the challenger.[15]

Consider the implications of my interpretation of the electoral process. This view implies that the accountability aspect of elections is more meaningful than the choice aspect, partly by default. Voters can know well what they are accepting or rejecting when they vote on an incumbent. But forward-looking choices often are not clear, and often they are even misleading, for the reasons stated. Elections, at best, offer only a blunt instrument of popular control.

But this interpretation is far from implying that elections are meaningless just because they do not always offer clear choices, or because their outcomes do not always allow unambiguous interpretation of meaning. The anticipation of possible rejection at the polls is a powerful motivator for politicians. It is often, if not always, a constructive incentive. Recall from Chapter 1 the "liberal interpretation of democracy" presented by William Riker. In his interpretation,

all elections do or have to do is to permit people to get rid of rulers. . . . The kind of democracy that thus survives is not, however, popular rule, but rather an intermittent, sometimes random, even perverse popular veto. (1982, p. 244)

According to Riker, even democracy that is no more inspiring than that is the most desirable *realistic* form of government. This book's interpretation of American democracy in practice is compatible with Riker's view, but in mapping performance regarding economic issues, I am developing a picture that is less negative.

Retrospective voting is compatible with innovation in politics in two ways. The backward-looking rejections of incumbents can enhance the prospect for innovations that might not be chosen by an otherwise risk averse electorate. I contend that retrospective voting makes possible more innovation than would more purely prospective voting. The fact that the innovations themselves will be subject to retrospective evaluation makes the process of innovation

15. I am grateful to Peng Lian for a number of these suggestions about the conditional nature of retrospective and prospective voting.

accountable. The anticipation of possible rejection at the polls is a powerful mechanism of accountability.

This book began with an analysis of a model that showed how this anticipation might lend itself to opportunistic behavior that would reduce public welfare through the creation of an electoral business cycle. That hypothesis was based on the possibility that vote-maximizing incumbents would exploit naive retrospective evaluations by voters with short memories. The evidence in favor of that model is not strong, to say the least. Some of the reasons for the weak evidence have to do with the fact that the economy is not so easy to manipulate. Very few analysts still believe that public officials have the capacity to manipulate the economy with the precision needed to create an electoral cycle.

Other reasons have to do with the motivations of politicians. They may not in fact all be vote maximizers, and even among those who are, not all may think that the way to do it is through manipulating the economy. We saw in Chapter 3 that partisan politicians may have policy goals that they try to implement in office, and they may appeal for votes to the extent that it helps them win office and implement other policy goals.

But the strong evidence that voters respond to recent economic performance does not necessarily make a strong case that voters are manipulable, or that politicians could get away with opportunistic electoral cycles if they could actually create them. There is reason to doubt that voters provide a strong incentive for politicians to attempt manipulation, and even if they did, there is reason to believe that voters could learn what was happening and would change their behavior. The simplest reading of the bulk of studies of retrospective voting suggests that voters respond most strongly to income growth and that they pay attention to recent experience at the expense of the more distant past. This is exactly the kind of voter whose support Nordhaus's opportunistic politician would maximize. But the studies of economic voting by Chappell and Keech and by Suzuki also raise questions about voter vulnerability to repeated manipulation over the electoral cycle.

Still, there are occasional examples of cynical manipulation that can be seen as a response to electoral incentives. When this does happen and leads to inferior outcomes, what comes first, voter demand or politicians pandering? Do voters really demand irre-

sponsible behavior? Nothing in my reading of the extensive literature on voting on economic performance provides a strong case
that voters will not reward performance that involves a sustainable,
noninflationary path of economic growth. I contend that irresponsible behavior by politicians is conditional, rather than an inevitable
response to voter incentives.

Voters do respond to superficial appeals, and they do heavily
discount the past. This could make them vulnerable to manipulation from time to time. But whereas voters may reward irresponsible behavior, they do not generally demand it. In fact, there is no
reason to believe that any single level of economic performance is
demanded for political success. Voters learn to want what they
know that they can get. Voting behavior is consistent with both
rising and falling expectations (Alt, 1979). Voters and the electoral
process may contribute to or support national conditions for
growth and development, or those for stagnation and decline.

In one respect, retrospective voting with short memories allows
politicians to do constructive things that can improve outcomes.
Recall the path of the misery index through the first Reagan administration described in Chapter 4. The recession early in the Reagan
administration permitted inflation to fall in a way that made for a
much lower misery index by election time. If voters had weighted
all periods equally, they might not have tolerated that. Similarly,
painful austerity programs designed to eliminate deficits or inflation
may be feasible only with long electoral periods, in which the pain
can be forgotten by election time. Key's view of retrospective
voting suggests that voters may well accept sacrifices they would
not choose. Would voters have prospectively chosen the 1980s
recession to reduce inflation if that had been promised in the 1980
campaign? Krugman (1992, ch. 5) says no, and I agree. But would
they retrospectively approve of the choice? Clearly they did. Slack
between principal and agent can be used constructively as well
as perversely.

PART FOUR
Institutions and processes

7 Discretion and accountability in the fiscal policy process

Fiscal policy consists of public decisions about government expenditures and revenues. Spending policy and taxation policy have always been of interest in their own right, but at least since the 1930s, spending and taxing and the balance between them have been seen by at least some economists as having controllable consequences for the performance of the macroeconomy. For example, Keynesians have advocated active discretionary manipulation of the size of the budget deficit (or surplus) to stabilize the economy, to reduce unemployment, and to shift the path of economic growth. The Kennedy-Johnson tax cut of 1964 is seen by Keynesians as a successful example of how fiscal policy can increase prosperity by increasing aggregate demand. Supply side economists have acknowledged the success of that tax cut, but explain its success in terms of increasing aggregate supply, rather than demand. They would defend the Economic Recovery Tax Act of 1981 on the same, supply oriented grounds.[1]

Causality goes in the other direction as well. That is, the performance of the economy has an effect on the size of the government's deficit (or surplus). Specifically, when the economy expands, revenues may rise faster than expenditures, thus reducing a deficit. And when the economy goes into a recession, expenditures may rise

---

1. A leading alternative hypothesis about fiscal policy is that the government plans for equal marginal tax rates over time in order to minimize the distortionary effects of taxation on private decisions to work, invest, and consume. In this view, deficits are, and should be, passive adjustments to economic shocks (Barro, 1979, 1986).

(e.g., because of increased unemployment compensation claims) while revenues fall, because of declining incomes and reduced economic activity. Both these effects are countercyclical, which means that a system of expenditure and taxation programs can automatically stabilize economic fluctuations. This would not always have been the case, but with a sizable public sector based in part on a system of transfer payments and progressive income taxation, it has been so for some 50 years.[2]

DISCRETION, AUTOMATIC POLICY, AND RULES IN THE POLICY PROCESS

The distinction between *discretionary fiscal policy* and automatic fiscal policy introduces an issue that will occupy us in this chapter and the next (which is on monetary policy). "Discretion" involves the capacity to act on one's own, using one's own judgment. At best, this implies the judgment of the benevolent dictator, or guardian, who by definition knows the best thing to do. At worst, it implies the judgment of the opportunistic public official who makes improperly expedient decisions. In terms of the time-consistency problem, discretion means doing the best thing at the time, rather than following an optimal plan.

Discretionary decisions could be improper by a variety of standards, such as favoring narrow interests at the expense of broad interests, or inappropriately favoring the present at the expense of the future, not to speak of being venal or corrupt. Democratic institutions are designed to ensure that there will be accountability for officials who are empowered to exercise discretion, but as we have seen in the analysis of electoral cycles, the very institutions of accountability may have perverse incentives if policymakers try to exploit the inattention of the voters or the asymmetries of information between themselves and the electorate.

There are two alternatives to discretionary policymaking. One is *automatic policy,* such as the automatic stabilizers described earlier. Here, the institutions of progressive taxation and of entitlement-based transfer payments ensure that there will be a

---

2. See Stein (1969).

countercyclical response to economic fluctuations, even without discretionary intervention. Automatic policies do not deny the possibility of discretionary decisions to supplement or even to counteract them. They simply assure that certain actions will be taken without any conscious decision to take new action. Automatic policies are not necessarily desirable.

The second alternative to discretion is *rule-based policy*. Like automatic policy, rules do not involve discretion, but unlike automatic policy, they are meant to exclude discretion in favor of a presumably superior standard that decisionmakers will follow. The most commonly advocated rule for fiscal policy is a constitutional amendment prohibiting deficit spending under most circumstances. Another rule, known as "tax smoothing," is less a prohibition than a guideline for policy. It implies that taxes be fixed at a level designed to cover expected government expenditures over the long term and that deficits be allowed to fluctuate secondarily (and automatically) in response to unplanned events such as wars and economic shocks. In monetary policy, a rule for a fixed rate of money growth is a standard proposal.

Various rationales have been provided to support different rules, and rules in general. One is that the limitations of knowledge and information are likely to make discretionary policy worse than policy that follows a simple rule, even without raising questions about the motives of public officials. This is the basis for Milton Friedman's case for a fixed rate of money growth (1960). A second rationale is that the discretionary behavior of politicians in an electoral process is not to be trusted, and the institutions of electoral accountability do not adequately restrain irresponsible and shortsighted policymaking. This is the basis for most arguments in favor of a constitutional amendment to require a balanced budget.[3] A third rationale that is common in contemporary economics concerns the time-consistency problem, wherein the best policy for all times, *ex ante,* may not be the best policy for a given time, *ex post.* This, too, has been a basis for proposals for a fixed rate of money growth.[4]

Regardless of the rationale, rules may be contingent or noncon-

3. See Buchanan and Wagner (1977) for an example.
4. See Kydland and Prescott (1977) and Barro and Gordon (1983). See Keech (1992) for a review of several arguments for rules in macroeconomic policy.

tingent. A noncontingent rule is one that would prescribe policy regardless of conditions, and without feedback from performance. For example, a fixed rate of money growth is generally prescribed as a noncontingent rule. An example of a contingent rule is provided by the proposals for a balanced budget amendment that specify that the rule can be relaxed in wartime, or by a two-thirds vote of Congress.

The more a rule is contingent on conditions, the more similar it becomes to discretion. In the extreme, a state-contingent rule could aspire to specify exactly what a benevolent dictator or guardian would do under whatever circumstances might arise. There are two problems with this. First, as we have seen, it is not easy to define objectively what a benevolent dictator should do. Almost all decisions about macroeconomic policy inevitably involve choices that are inherently contestable, and hence political. Second, the more contingencies a rule has, the more difficult it is to know whether or not it has been followed. This is because it becomes more complicated and difficult to see whether or not the decisions appropriately matched the contingencies specified in the rule. Problems of accountability and enforcement become both more important and less clear if rules are contingent. The information asymmetries between the public and the policymaker become more and more significant, and they imply larger costs of democracy due to principal-agent issues.

Procedural "justice" and legitimization by process

In American national politics, there are few noncontingent rules specifying the desired outcomes of the policymaking process, though there are numerous ways in which laws make fiscal outcomes automatic. Not all of these are desirable. In general terms, authoritative decisions about fiscal goals and policies are made through a political *process*. Even if the goals and policies cannot be defined as authoritative in their own right, they gain authority and legitimacy through a political process grounded in constitutionally defined public institutions. Elected governments make authoritative policy that may work well or not so well. They are accountable for their performance at the next election. This process is continuing and iterative, so that most choices are subject to revision in the light of experience. New elections can select new public officials to set new directions.[5]

This description of the political process echoes John Rawls's conception of pure procedural justice, wherein a perfect process transmits desirability and moral force to an outcome (1971, pp. 83–90). But the institutions through which the political process takes place are themselves not perfect. They are subject to criticism and revision. Institutions and procedures are themselves matters of political choice. Procedural institutions can be revised when they are seen as needing improvement, from a variety of perspectives, which might range from changing the standards of political legitimacy to specifically macroeconomic issues. Given an existing set of institutions, we may think of the political process as one of procedural legitimization rather than procedural justice.

Can the means justify the ends?

The institutions through which American fiscal policy is made include the most fundamental in the polity, namely Articles I and II of the Constitution, which define the roles of Congress and the president in taxing and spending policy. Fiscal institutions also include legislated procedures, such as those prescribed in the Budget and Impoundment Control Act of 1974. These procedural institutions are not perfect in any noncontestable sense, but because they are official, they transmit legitimacy and authority to the policy choices that are made through them. They are the "means" that at least provisionally justify the policy choices, or the "ends" that emerge.

The rules of sport provide an analogy. A game, such as a basketball game, is a procedure designed to determine a winner between two teams, each of which has its own supporters. A game can be seen as a procedure designed to determine which is the better team. No one doubts that inferior teams occasionally upset superior teams. Otherwise there would be much less interest in sport. However, regardless of other considerations, a victory is an authoritative determination of superiority in that game, and an opera-

---

5. This conception of the political process echoes Simon (1978) on procedural as opposed to substantive rationality.

tional definition of which was the better team at the time of play. The official procedure defines and legitimizes the result.

Similarly, constitutional and legislative institutions are authoritative ways of determining which policy should prevail among alternatives, each of which has its own supporters. The alternative that prevails is not necessarily superior in a normative sense, but it is official and legitimate if it emerges from the mutually agreed procedure. Just as different teams may win on different days, different policies may emerge under different circumstances, even though the rules do not change.

But the rules may change. For example, in both professional and college basketball, originally all field goals were worth two points, regardless of the length of the shot. Countless games were won and lost under that rule. Some time ago that rule was changed in order to add interest to the game. Now field goals shot from behind a designated semicircular line count three points, and all others count two, as before. Not everyone favored the new rule, but once it was adopted, it was accepted as an authoritative way of scoring goals and determining the winner of the game. Many outcomes would be the same under both the old and new rules, but others would surely be different. The new rule would affect the outcomes of some games if they were played in exactly the same way. But of course the new rule affects the strategy and the play of the game, so differences in outcomes are likely to be fewer than they would be without adjustments in strategy. The point for our purposes is that the outcomes are authoritative and legitimate, given the rules in place at the time of play, and regardless of the fact that the rules are not necessarily the "best possible rules." And the best possible rules in a democracy are undefinable.

Public institutions and public policy are, of course, far more consequential than sport. Moreover, there has been meaningful, serious analysis of the relative merits of alternative institutions and policies. But such analysis is usually contestable, and the resolution takes place within the existing procedural institutions, which can themselves be changed. These institutions are changed from time to time, usually with the expectation that the change will improve outcomes either for the public as a whole or for the winning coalition. The point of my analogy is that there is a reciprocal and provisional quality to the interaction between procedures and policy. *Neither* provides normative bedrock, an Archimedean point from which all else can be evaluated.

This chapter will analyze the institutions in which fiscal policy is made. The next two sections deal with formal institutions: the relevant parts of the Constitution and the relevant legislated institutions. But institutions are not necessarily legislated or formal; they can be informal patterns of behavior, or norms, and these will be analyzed as well. For each, we shall consider whether or not the institution is neutral with regard to fiscal policy issues and how decisionmakers are accountable under it.

CONSTITUTIONAL INSTITUTIONS OF FISCAL POLICY

The fundamental constitutional institutions of fiscal policy are the basic institutions of American national government, the separated powers and checks and balances between the legislative and executive branches, as defined in the Constitution. Congress has constitutionally defined "power to lay and collect taxes" and "to borrow money on the credit of the United States," as well as to spend money for various purposes (Article I, section 8), subject to presidential veto and congressional override of such vetoes.

The separation of powers and countercyclical fiscal programs

The institutions of separated powers apparently were neutral regarding taxing and spending in the pre-Keynesian era, before intentional deficits were considered (by some) to be appropriate, because there was nothing in the separation of powers that inherently obstructed achievement of balanced budgets under most circumstances. Between 1787 and 1929, the government budget was in surplus about two-thirds of the time, with most exceptions arising from wars or recessions.[6] From 1930 through 1946 there was only one surplus (1930), but from 1947 through 1960 there were seven surpluses and seven deficits. Since 1961, fiscal 1969 has been the only year of surplus.

6. See Stein (1978).

This experience suggests that there may be different behavioral "regimes" for dealing with deficits within constant constitutional institutions. However, Barro (1986) has demonstrated that in the period from 1916 through 1982, which includes each of the periods mentioned earlier, a single model derived from the tax-smoothing hypothesis can explain the entire range of deficits in terms of temporary bursts in public expenditures, such as those associated with wars. Nonetheless, I shall argue later that different patterns of fiscal policymaking exist in different periods.

In a Keynesian world where activist fiscal stabilization policy is appropriate, the separation of powers may become a problem. This separation reduces the speed with which the government can respond to economic conditions, because agreement must be reached between the two houses of Congress and (short of veto-proof majorities) between the president and Congress. This feature distributes blocking and delaying powers, and it stands in the way of immediate action.

At a minimum, the separation of powers adds to the length of the "long and variable lags" that Milton Friedman has identified in stabilization policy (1953a, pp. 144–8). These lags are divided into the "inside lag," between recognition of a problem and policy action, and the "outside lag," between action and result. The structure of American government lengthens the inside lag of fiscal policy. This fact derives from the rationales for the separation of powers. James Madison observed in *The Federalist* 62 and 63 that if bodies chosen in dissimilar ways can agree at all, they are more likely to agree on something good. Alexander Hamilton had a more negative way of putting a similar point, observing in *The Federalist* 73 that the advantage of defeating a bad law is worth the risk of defeating a few good ones.

In the eighteenth-century environment in which Madison and Hamilton wrote, inside and outside lags were far from anyone's imagination. We can assess the contemporary fiscal consequences of these institutions of separated powers for Keynesian stabilization policy by reviewing the history of fiscal action in the postwar era. In general, all such actions were taken after recovery had begun. Bruce Bartlett has identified the dates of passage for all of the postwar countercyclical fiscal programs. None of them was finally enacted before the date the preceding recession ended, according to subsequent "official" dating by the National Bureau of Economic Research (NBER). Specifically, for the recession beginning in November 1948 and ending in October 1949, President Truman proposed an eleven-point program on July 11, 1949. Only one of the points was enacted, an Advance Planning for Public Works Act, signed in October, the month the recession ended. No fiscal action was taken to stem the recession of July 1953 to May 1954.

Congressional Democrats passed three countercyclical bills to deal with the 1957–58 recession, and President Eisenhower signed them. A highway bill was signed in April, the month the recession ended, and unemployment compensation and rivers-and-harbors bills were passed later that summer. The brief recession of April 1960 to February 1961 spanned two administrations. President Kennedy proposed several measures in February 1961, and an unemployment compensation bill was enacted in March. The Area Redevelopment Act was passed in May, and a Social Security bill was passed in June.

The recession of December 1969 to November 1970 led to one major legislative act, the Public Works Impact Program, enacted in August 1971, almost a year after the recession had ended. The recession of November 1973 to March 1975 prompted several pieces of legislation, the first of which was passed the month the recession ended. That law included tax rebates and extended unemployment benefits, along with some tax changes.

No action was taken regarding the January–July 1980 recession other than to remove credit controls. However, the Reagan administration did adopt two countercyclically oriented programs for its recession. The Surface Transportation Assistance Act was enacted in January 1983, and the Emergency Jobs Appropriations Act was also passed in the year after the recession had ended.[7] The recession of 1990–91 prompted a Democratic proposal, which President Bush vetoed. President Clinton's stimulus program, which was submitted after the recession was officially over, was defeated in Congress.

This history is a powerful demonstration of the inside lag in

7. This material is drawn from "If It Ain't Broke, Don't Fix It," a *Wall Street Journal* op-ed article by Bruce Bartlett, December 2, 1992, and from a memorandum he prepared in the Treasury Department, dated December 7, 1991.

stabilization policy following the occurrence of a downturn and preceding the recognition of the problem and countercyclical fiscal action. There is no example of a program that was passed before the final month of the recession it was designed to correct. Although the fact that the government was divided between the parties was relevant in most of the recessions, it is not clear that unified partisan government helped a great deal in speeding a response (as in 1948–49, 1953–54, and 1980). Although it is not clear that parliamentary governments would act faster, the need to secure agreement among the two houses of Congress and the president surely adds to the inside lag.

For supporters of timely, discretionary fiscal stimulus to deal with recessions, this experience is surely discouraging. However, those advocates might defend such programs as enhancing the nascent recovery. Advocates of rules might argue that this experience reinforces their claim that discretionary policy is likely to destabilize, rather than stabilize, the economy, though their claim was not demonstrated by the experience described earlier. For those, such as monetarists and new classicals, who would argue that the countercyclical programs are misguided, a blocking capacity is likely to seem desirable, echoing the rationale of Alexander Hamilton about the desirability of defeating bad laws. However, if those were bad laws, they were not all defeated. Several were merely delayed, and that may have made them even less desirable.

For a time, when economists had more confidence in the power of fiscal policy, there were suggestions for institutional changes designed to reduce the inside lag without changing the basic structure of American government.[8] Some of those proposals would have given the president the power to make small proportional changes in tax rates at his discretion, and subject to congressional veto. But as two leading economists observed two decades ago, "no such proposal has ever seemed close to enactment" (Blinder and Solow, 1974, p. 45). At present, it is difficult to imagine such a thing even being proposed. There is considerable distrust between the two branches in this era that has seen more government that is divided than unified by party. Also, there is a lack of interest and

8. See Portney (1976) for an example.

confidence in fiscal policy, because of the sizes of the deficits and the public debt, and because of developments in macroeconomic theory.

In spite of all of these cautions, there seems to be powerful public pressure during a recession to "do something," if only to show evidence of government concern for the suffering associated with economic downturns. Stimulus programs, such as those of presidents Kennedy and Clinton, are sometimes proposed after a recovery has begun, with the goal of speeding or improving the recovery. A recession may provide a convenient pretext to do something a government wishes to do anyway. In any case, the separation of powers seems to slow the timing. For those who argue that fiscal stimuli are misguided, too little too late may ironically be better than speedy and decisive action.

Divided government and deficits

The period since 1952 has seen more divided partisan control of the national government than any previous period of comparable length in American history (Fiorina, 1992, pp. 6–10). It has also seen the largest sustained peacetime deficits of any previous period. Mathew McCubbins (1991) has developed a theoretical model to show that divided government causes deficits. The basic idea is that the two parties have sharply different spending priorities, with the Democrats favoring domestic programs, and the Republicans favoring defense. According to McCubbins, each party is able to block increases in the other party's favored programs, but each party would prefer to let both parties' programs grow over having both restricted to current levels. With Republicans able to block tax increases, the default was growth in both defense and nondefense spending, without accompanying tax increases.

McCubbins (1991) provided evidence to support his interpretation,[9] but Alt and Stewart (1990) applied that hypothesis to the entire history of American government and found that it fit poorly with previous experiences of divided government, such as those in the nineteenth century. It seems, provisionally, that divided

9. Barro provides a sardonic critique as a commentary, included in McCubbins (1991).

government may be causally associated with deficits, but the association is at best conditional rather than inevitable.[10]

The constitutional status of the income tax

Article I says that representatives and direct taxes shall be apportioned according to population, which would seem to rule out income taxes. Such taxes were used to fight the Civil War, but the Supreme Court subsequently declared them unconstitutional in *Pollock v. Farmers Loan* (1895). Therefore, it took the Sixteenth Amendment to the Constitution to begin modern government's heavy reliance on income taxes. Because the income tax is a visible tax, this may have something to do with the increasing percentage of deficit years in the twentieth century. In the nineteenth century, the tariff, an invisible tax, was the main source of government revenue, and raising revenue through tariffs was not nearly so risky politically as raising taxes through an income tax.

Discretion, rules, and accountability

Countercyclical stimulus programs such as those reviewed earlier are classic examples of discretionary policy. Their desirability is highly contestable. For those who like them, the blocking and delaying that American constitutional institutions facilitate are impediments. For those who oppose them, these institutions are useful. When overall performance is deemed unsatisfactory, however, these institutions do not facilitate accountability. None of the responsible agents was pleased with the deficits that began to emerge in the 1980s, but none was effectively held accountable. Republicans and Democrats blamed each other, and the president and Congress blamed each other. But it would be difficult to argue that any of the responsible officials were punished for the deficits.[11] The American system of separated powers obstructs electoral accountability. This fact has been recognized since Woodrow Wilson's

10. See Roubini and Sachs (1989a) and Grilli et al. (1991) for a cross-national perspective. See Alt and Lowry (in press) and Poterba (in press) for analyses regarding the American states.
11. Bratton (1994) has shown that deficits undermined support for President Reagan, but that Democrats were not expected to do better.

time and has prompted many proposals for general constitutional reform.

The United States has had little direct experience with rules as alternatives to discretion. However, the original constitutional requirement about direct taxes could be considered a rule against income taxes. This rule was effectively followed for most of the period before the Sixteenth Amendment was ratified in 1913, but it was ignored during the Civil War and after. The institution that enforced the rule was the Supreme Court, in the *Pollock* case, though it had looked the other way during wartime. That experience may be relevant to the prospects of enforcing a balanced budget requirement as a constitutional amendment.

LEGISLATED INSTITUTIONS OF FISCAL POLICY

Legislated institutions of fiscal policy define the procedures by which fiscal policy is made in greater detail than Articles I and II specify. These procedures often are defended as neutral or as designed to achieve general public purposes. Sometimes they reflect the efforts of winning coalitions to extend the reach of their legislative victories beyond their time in office, either by "stacking the deck" in some way or by making certain desired outcomes automatic.[12]

Institutions of centralization and coordination

Although the separation of powers may have consequences for fiscal policy, it was chosen for far broader purposes than fiscal policy as we know it. Ancillary institutions may be created or amended through legislation in response to the problems of the day. From time to time, "reform" movements have gained strength and prompted major innovations in the procedures by which fiscal policy is made. Such movements achieved success in 1921 and 1974. The basic issue was the coordination between spending and revenues. For most of American history before 1921, spending and taxing decisions were quite independent, at least formally. The

12. See Stewart (1989) for such an argument.

substantive committees and the appropriations committees in Congress made the spending decisions. The revenue committees made the taxing decisions, usually by setting tariffs. Other than what took place in the minds of the members and on the floor of Congress, there often was no institutional coordination of those decisions.[13]

The Budget and Accounting Act of 1921 changed that situation. That act was the culmination of a desire by reformers to impose a more centralized and hierarchical process on federal taxing and spending. The act was a reflection of dissatisfaction with the results of the more decentralized process that had characterized budget policy before that time. It reflected a concern with deficits that had begun to mount even before World War I and that had become far larger as a result of the war. It reflected an intellectual climate associated with the Progressive movement, which preferred government structures that were "centralized, rational, and streamlined" (Stewart, 1989, p. 215). The act created an executive agency, the Bureau of the Budget, which would assemble government agencies' requests for appropriations and adjust and coordinate them with each other and with projected revenues before sending the entire package to Congress as the president's budget. Congress would then act on that proposed budget, which theoretically had been derived from a synoptic approach designed to take into account all relevant considerations and package them in a coherent manner.

That act sounds like a neutral, public interest, good-government-oriented innovation, and it was presented that way. However, Stewart (1989) has seen it (along with other innovations that preceded it in the nineteenth century) as a procedural device by which a contemporary majority tries to impose its wishes on its successors. In this case, the majority was interested in restricting government spending, and the institutional device was one that assured that a complete set of programs would be considered together as a package. Stewart has presented a compelling defense of his hypothesis, though it remains possible that some of the support for the Budget and Accounting Act was in fact genuinely based on more neutral, good-government rationales.

13. But see Fisher (1975, ch. 1) and Stewart (1989, pp. 16, 32).

Regardless of the interpretation of the motives of those who passed the Budget and Accounting Act of 1921, Stewart raises a general question about the nature of institutional choice, to which there is likely to be no single answer. Surely it is sometimes true that changes in institutions are, as he suggests, efforts of contemporary majorities to impose their views on those who will come after. But surely it is also sometimes true that institutions are efforts to achieve more generally beneficial solutions to problems of collective action. Stewart's view is one that gives considerable credit to the winning majorities for an understanding of the consequences of their design of institutions. Still another possibility is that the consequences of institutional change cannot always be readily anticipated. Surely some reformers have been surprised and disappointed at the unanticipated consequences of their activity.[14]

The Budget and Impoundment Control Act of 1974 was a similar innovation. That act reflected dissatisfaction with the way the procedures set up by the Budget and Accounting Act of 1921 were working, as well as the fact that deficits seemed to be out of control. Most importantly, it was a reflection of divided control of the government and of the conflict between the Democratic Congress and the Republican president, Richard Nixon. Nixon had been using the executive power to override spending decisions made by Congress, by impounding, or refusing to spend, some of the money that Congress had appropriated. The president had also publicly criticized Congress for lacking fiscal discipline.

The 1974 act responded to that situation by placing restrictions on the authority of the president to impound funds appropriated by Congress. More to our point, the act created a legislative counterpart to the Office of Management and Budget, into which the Bureau of the Budget had evolved. That new Congressional Budget Office was designed to make Congress less dependent on the executive branch for information about fiscal policy. It also set up a new budget calendar, new committees, and a new set of procedures that were designed to facilitate congressional control over taxing and spending.

Some of the purposes of the 1974 act had been to ensure that

14. For example, it is unlikely that those who passed the Campaign Finance Reform Act of 1974 anticipated the ways in which it would lead to proliferation of political action committees.

Congress could take an overall, "top-down" perspective on taxing and spending and to reduce federal deficits, which had become a topic of increasing concern. As Gilmour put it,

the budget reforms adopted since 1974 have increased the power of congressional majorities: helping overcome a lack of coordination in budgeting that weakened Congress vis-à-vis the executive; providing Congress with procedures that permit adopting a far more coherent budget policy than previously possible; and enabling Congress to exercise more deliberate control over the budget and deficit. Now what majorities want to accomplish with the deficit, they can. (Gilmour, 1990, p. 224)

Yet almost nobody professes to be satisfied with the results of the budget process. "Judged by nearly any conceivable output criteria, the budget process has not solved the budget problem" (Gilmour, 1990, p. 225).

The key to understanding this puzzle is in the relationship between the preferences reflected in the desire to "solve the budget problem," known as a "top-down" perspective, and those that are reflected in specific spending and taxing decisions, known as a "bottom-up" perspective. A member of Congress (or a citizen, for that matter) may wish to spend more on needed programs, but at the same time wish to have the overall level of spending curtailed. The Congress may well have a majority of such individuals. A majority that wishes to curtail spending may well be an ambivalent majority when it faces the consequences of overall cuts for specific programs. Both as individual members and as an institution, Congress reflects an ambivalence about the incompatibility of preferences regarding taxes, spending, and deficits.

Since the 1974 Budget and Impoundment Control Act, presidents have continued to present unbalanced budgets to the Congress, even as some of them have advocated balanced budget amendments to the Constitution. And Congress has continued to pass unbalanced budgets, even given the presence of the institutions that force top-down consideration of the overall consequences of the sum of spending and taxing decisions. A likely explanation for this is that these decisionmakers prefer the budgets they pass to budgets that would reduce expenditures or increase taxes.

The implication for the choice of procedural institutions is as follows: Forcing the decisionmakers to confront the long-term or overall consequences of the sum of their specific decisions does not ensure that the general considerations will prevail over the specific considerations. David Stockman has argued that Congress and the people are getting what they really want when they pass the expenditure programs (and deficits) that have been emerging from the congressional process (Stockman, 1986, pp. 376–94). In effect, the use of discretion in the procedures set up by the Constitution and the acts of 1921 and 1974 may not lead to outcomes that are satisfactory by some standard, including perhaps even some of the standards used by the decisionmakers in question.

The problem may be due to a conflict between individual or district preferences and the public good, as in a prisoner's dilemma. Several theoretical models have developed rationales for why the public sector might be "too large." Most of them emphasize distributive politics. In these models, committees composed of members who have high demand for public projects control the legislative agenda, producing concentrated benefits for their constituents, but distributing the costs over the whole population. Because majority rule permits those who enjoy the benefits of public programs to share the burden with those who do not, there are possibilities that the political process will choose inefficient programs whose benefits are less than their costs.[15] Because most of these models implicitly or explicitly assume that taxes cover the benefits, they do not directly address the incentives for budget deficits.[16]

In any case, there is an apparent disjuncture between the individual taxing and spending decisions that members of Congress make and their satisfaction with the aggregated results of those decisions. The dissatisfaction with such results is not effectively redressed by periodic elections as a system to hold accountable the public officials who make fiscal policy. These processes may not be effective for ensuring that policy is congruent with reasonable overall or long-term views of what is appropriate and desirable. This dissatisfaction has led to proposals for rules that would limit discretion and ensure achievement of a desired goal. We shall consider these

15. See, for example, Shepsle and Weingast (1981, 1984), Weingast and Marshall (1988), and Baron (1991).
16. For rational choice models of deficits, see Alesina and Tabellini (1990) and Tabellini and Alesina (1990).

later in the section on precommitment institutions. But before doing that, we shall consider another set of legislated institutions.

Entitlements and indexation

Traditionally, government expenditures have had to go through two processes: authorization and appropriation. A subject-matter committee, such as a public works committee, might recommend authorization for a project that would cost money (e.g., authorizing a flood control project), whereupon it could be passed by Congress and become law. But the passage of that law would not bring action until another process appropriated funds to pay for it. The appropriations committees traditionally did that according to "roles," by which the House Appropriations Committee served as a tightfisted "guardian" of the public purse, and the Senate Appropriations Committee was an "appeals court" for those who felt unjustly denied in the other committee.[17]

Such decisions are discretionary rather than automatic. They may be operative for one year or several years, but they are not permanent. The advocates for certain programs who wanted to impose a more lasting quality on the programs they legislated developed a practice called "entitlements." This is legislation that authorizes expenditures to eligible recipients "permanently," or at least until the law is changed. The unemployment benefits described earlier as part of the system of automatic stabilizers provide an example.

The Social Security Act of 1935 authorized a program of unemployment compensation and provided that persons whom the law defined as eligible could automatically receive benefits for a specified period. The terms of eligibility have changed from time to time, and the levels of benefits have changed, but the basic structure of the law has remained. The amount of expenditure in any given year is not defined in Congress through the appropriations process but is determined by the number of individuals who are eligible and report to the government to demand their benefits. Social Security retirement benefits, veterans' benefits, and Medicare and Medicaid benefits are structured as entitlements.

---

17. See Fenno (1966) and Wildavsky (1964) for the classic descriptions of this system.

Entitlements provide a way for the winning majorities who establish such programs to ensure that the programs will outlive the (possibly) temporary tenure of those majorities. They ensure that money will be expended without regard to the availability of revenue. They put a heavy burden of initiative on those who would change the existing programs. Entitlements are pro-expenditure institutions, as compared with arrangements in which either the authorization or the appropriation is structured to expire after a given period.

Inflation may erode the real value of the legislated entitlement amounts, in which case the real worth of such a program can decline. One way for a legislature to deal with eroding real values in a program is to have regular increases in the nominal value. Some of the most dramatic early evidence of an electoral cycle was seen in the increases in Social Security and veterans' benefits in election years (Tufte, 1978, ch. 2). Members of Congress were able to take credit for maintaining or even increasing the real value of the benefits.

Indexation is an alternative mechanism to deal with the same problem. If benefits are indexed to inflation, their real value will automatically stay constant, also without regard to the availability of funds (Weaver, 1988). As such, indexation is neutral, given the existence of a program. Relative to regular increases in the real value of benefits (as seemed to be the congressional practice in the 1960s and 1970s), indexation is conservative and is a limitation on the growth of expenditures. But relative to the erosion of real value due to inflation, indexation is a pro-expenditure institution.

Entitlements, indexed and otherwise, are automatic devices to keep certain expenditures from decreasing. There had been, until recently, a counterpart on the revenue side. Tax laws are almost always "permanent" in the same way as entitlements. They usually are structured to last until they are changed. The default is their continuation. The income tax passed in 1916 was "progressive" in that it provided for increasing rates of taxation for higher levels of income. Progressive income taxes without indexation will produce automatic increases in revenue under conditions of inflation. When the nominal value of income rises with inflation without increasing its real value, the recipient may rise into a higher tax bracket and therefore pay a higher rate of tax on effectively the same income.

With inflation and without indexation, a progressive income tax provides for automatic revenue increases.

The anti-tax Reagan administration, of course, realized that and successfully proposed the indexation of tax brackets in the 1986 Tax Reform Act. On the revenue side, indexation has an effect that is opposite to its effect on the expenditure side. Indexation of tax brackets keeps tax rates down by keeping them from automatically rising with inflation, whereas indexation of benefit programs keeps benefits up by preventing their value from eroding with inflation. Without indexation, inflation increases the value of revenue from progressive taxes, while eroding the value of expenditures.

Institutions of precommitment

When the processes of fiscal policy are seen as producing an undesirable pattern of outcomes, we may hear suggestions for rules that will predetermine the outcomes of the process. The leading example of such a rule is the proposal for an amendment to the Constitution to require a balanced federal budget. Other examples are the Gramm-Rudman-Hollings (GRH) law and the Budget Enforcement Act of 1990.

We may view a member of the public or of Congress as having multiple, incompatible preferences. The preference for a small public sector and a balanced budget may be incompatible with preferences for expenditures on a variety of programs. The history of passing budgets that emerge from piecemeal decisions about individual programs seems to reveal a collective congressional preference for these programs, even if the institutions force a confrontation of preferences that are incompatible.

Those who wish to go further in the direction of imposing top-down perspectives on the budget process have supported rules for outcomes that may be seen as institutions of precommitment, such as the GRH law and the Budget Enforcement Act of 1990. The GRH law defined specific deficit targets that would decline to zero, and it identified specific automatic procedures to ensure spending cuts in case Congress lacked the will. Those procedures were full of loopholes, and GRH has not come close to achieving its goals.

Yet Robert Reischauer, the director of the Congressional Budget Office, doubts that other processes could have done as well:

GRH may not have brought the deficit cows back into the barn, but it has kept them from stampeding over the cliff. It may have encouraged budget makers to resort to optimistic economic assumptions and other sleight of hand, but it has also focused public attention on their expediencies and made them somewhat uncomfortable.

The lesson of the last five years is that process reform, by itself, cannot guarantee that significant deficit reduction takes place. *No budget process can force those engaged in it to commit what they regard to be political suicide.* The nation, therefore, will probably have larger than desired deficits until the political costs of continued large deficits are perceived to exceed those of spending cuts and tax increases. (Reischauer, 1990, p. 232; emphasis added)

The problem was that those provisions were not "incentive-compatible." They were at odds with the day-to-day political incentives of the policymakers, especially those in Congress. Moreover, they were not readily enforceable. The deficit targets were targets in the projections for planned spending, not for final, actual expenditures. That made the law vulnerable to overly optimistic projections.

The Budget Enforcement Act of 1990 (BEA) is also not admired, but there is more reason to believe that it has limited spending. The BEA set up pay-as-you-go procedures for increases in domestic expenditures (favored by many Democrats) and for military increases (favored by many Republicans). By blocking the switching of funds across that divide, the BEA imposes fiscal discipline on the congressional advocates of both domestic and military expenditures. The BEA has worked to prevent the savings in the military budget from being shifted to domestic programs, and Congress has defeated proposals to break the agreement and shift those expenditures. Still, the BEA has not succeeded in reducing deficits. In fact, they have increased since its passage, largely because of the automatic stabilizers and a weak economy. Without the BEA, it is likely that the deficits would have increased even more.

The experience with these institutions of precommitment illustrates that there are problems of accountability with them as well as without them. There is no evidence that anyone has been punished for failure to comply with the GRH targets, but conventional wisdom suggests that there could be plenty of punishment for raising taxes or cutting entitlements. The closest approximation to an electoral punishment regarding contemporary fiscal policy was the defeat of President Bush. Chapter 6 showed that the cumulative real income growth under the Bush administration was below the figures for all administrations since 1948 except those of Carter and Eisenhower (II), and no administration has been reelected with such performance. However, the breaking of his pledge ("Read my lips: no new taxes") doubtless worked against him as well, but it would be too simple to argue that he was punished simply because he went along with increased taxes.

In my judgment, the fact that he went along with a budget deal that included some tax increases was less significant than the fact that doing so was at odds with what was probably the most visible and unambiguous promise a winning presidential candidate has made in recent memory. President Bush allowed his behavior to undermine his credibility. If the budget agreement is considered to have been a reasonable way to limit spending, the mistake was in making the pledge in the first place. He may have felt that he had to make that pledge to be elected, in view of the fact that he has acknowledged publicly that he would "do what he had to do" to be elected.

The experience with GRH makes it clear that changing the formal institutions of fiscal policymaking by passing a rule cannot prohibit public officials from following the incentives of electoral politics when such incentives are at odds with the general goals of reducing annual deficits and slowing the growth of the national debt. The problem was not that GRH was not in the Constitution; the problem was that it was not enforceable. In Reischauer's words, these formal institutions cannot force politicians to commit political suicide. But the definition of political suicide depends on the expectations and preferences of voters, which will vary over time, as the next section will suggest.

INFORMAL INSTITUTIONS: PATTERNS OF DISCRETIONARY FISCAL POLICYMAKING

Normally, the level and composition of public expenditures will be determined in a political process that will reflect popular preferences for the size and composition of government programs. A government has three possible ways to pay for these expenditures: taxation, borrowing, and printing money. The "government budget constraint" defines this relationship:

$$G \equiv T + dB + S$$

where G is government spending, T is taxes, dB is borrowing (wherein d refers to change, and B refers to bonds), and S refers to seignorage, the possibility of generating revenue by expanding the money supply (e.g., paying the government's bills with money the government simply prints).

Note that each of these four variables is subject to government control, but they vary in their political salience and visibility, and they vary in their logical and causal primacy. The expenditures are the benefit, and presumably are of primary political importance. Friedman, for example, proposed that the volume of government expenditures be determined "entirely on the basis of the community's desire, need, and willingness to pay for public services" (1953a, p. 136). As previous parts of this book have suggested, it is not a simple and unambiguous task to identify the proper volume of spending. There seems to be a gap between the political community's desire and need for public goods and services and its willingness to pay for them. Barro (1986) suggested that government expenditures are exogenous and therefore are causally prior to items on the right-hand side of the foregoing identity, but later we shall consider the possibility that spending is affected by the availability of the resource variables on the right-hand side.

Among those variables, taxes are likely to be visible and politically painful. Borrowing may be a way of covering expenditures that is less painful in the short run. However, it is still visible and easy to measure in nominal terms. Seignorage is even less visible, and not at all easy to measure.[18]

Expenditures and revenues are determined by popularly elected legislatures in representative democracies. With qualifications for the automatic character of some spending and revenue policies mentioned earlier, they are more or less *actively* chosen. Debt and seignorage, in contrast, may be relatively *passive* responses to the failure of governments to cover expenditures with taxes.[19] If there is a shortfall of revenues, the government may be able to borrow the difference by selling bonds. Alternatively, a compliant central bank can expand the money supply to cover a revenue shortfall.

---

18. See Klein and Neumann (1990).
19. See Andrabi (1993) for an elaboration of the distinction between active and passive.

The distinction between active and passive is a matter of degree, not a simple binary choice. The question is the difficulty the government has with each source of revenue. Elected officials may be reluctant providers of revenue because of the political costs to them of raising taxes. So long as investors are willing to lend money to the government, borrowing may be a relatively passive option. For the U.S. government it is surely easier to borrow money than to raise it in taxes, hence a more passive choice. Whereas a compliant central bank may readily issue credits to a government, an independent central bank may resist such demands. In the United States, with a relatively independent central bank, borrowing is a more passive option than is seignorage. Insofar as it is easier to raise money through debt and seignorage than with taxes, these alternatives are likely to be passive responses to the failure of governments to match expenditures with taxes. However, as we saw in Chapter 4, debt might also be actively chosen as a strategic variable to limit the spending choices of the next government.

If the desired level of expenditures is taken as given, the government may choose how to allocate the cost among taxes, borrowing, and seignorage. However, there are other alternatives. The government may consider revenues as given and adjust spending to the available revenues. And, of course, revenues and expenditures may be jointly determined. If there is a balanced budget constraint and no seignorage revenue, we might expect expenditures and tax revenues to be jointly determined. There is reason to expect that these phenomena do not always follow a single pattern.

Historically defined regimes

There have been several different patterns of fiscal policymaking in American history, but one overall phenomenon explains a great deal. Up until the current era, the main reason for public borrowing by the federal government had been military. The United States incurred large debts in fighting each of our wars. After each war, the debt/GNP ratio declined steadily. That pattern is predicted by the tax-smoothing hypothesis presented by Barro (1986).

However, there is some variation that is not predicted by the tax-smoothing hypothesis. According to Cary Brown, up until World War II, the avowed policy was to repay or liquidate public debt, which he calls a creditor-dominated policy. Since that war, inflation and economic growth, rather than debt retirement, have brought the debt/GNP ratio down, which he calls a debtor-dominated policy (Brown, 1990, p. 229).

Moreover, there were other patterns within the period before World War II. For much of American history, government revenues were not defined by the need to cover expenditures. They were determined by a protectionist trade policy, which produced large revenues from the tariffs imposed on imported goods. In the early years of the nation, before the Civil War, the dominant Democratic party opposed public expenditures at the federal level; tariff revenues were used to pay down war debts, and sometimes large amounts were turned over to the states (Brown, 1990, pp. 230–3).

For most of the period between the Civil War and the Great Depression, the Republicans dominated national politics and pursued a program of public expenditures for internal improvements. Even so, revenues often outpaced expenditures, leaving large surpluses in many years. Those revenues, which were secondary consequences of protectionist policy, created political "problems" for the mostly Republican administrations. Nineteenth-century Republicans did not have the aversion to public spending by the federal government that had characterized the Democrats in the early part of that century, and revenues were used for internal improvements and veterans' pensions, as well as for paying down the Civil War debt. According to one nineteenth-century observer, Henry C. Adams,

the Arrearage Pension Acts, by which the treasury was relieved of its plethora of funds, find their true explanation in the desire of Congress to maintain inviolate the system of protective duties. This could not be done in the face of an ever increasing surplus, and protectionist politicians did not dare to advocate the abolition of the whiskey tax; it only remained for them to spend the money. (Brown, 1990, p. 236)

This case shows that it is at least possible for revenues to be causally prior to expenditures, and in certain circumstances spending can rise to match the available revenues.

After the passage of the income tax amendment in 1913, revenue raising became more visible (though less regressive), and there was no longer a "problem" of revenues outpacing expenditures. Most obviously in the case of the two world wars, expenditure needs drove, or causally influenced, increases in both taxes and deficits.

Characterizing fiscal policy since the New Deal

Nominally, the United States has almost always followed a publicly avowed policy of balancing the federal budget. That was the policy of Franklin Roosevelt, in spite of the fact that there was not one balanced federal budget during his presidency. [Cary Brown has observed that Keynesian deficit spending did not fail during the prewar portion of the New Deal; "it was not tried" (1956).] That was the policy of the Truman and Eisenhower administrations, during each of which the deficit years were roughly balanced by surplus years. Although President Kennedy paid lip service to the concept of balanced budgets, his was the first administration to run up an intentional deficit in peacetime for the avowedly Keynesian goal of stimulating economic growth.

Economists had long struggled with standards for budget balance that would recognize the importance of automatic stabilizers and of intentional deficits when the economy was below "full employment." Instead of annual balance, they proposed balance over the business cycle, and balance at full employment. But none of those standards had the clarity and simplicity of balance between nominal revenues and expenditures. Even though the public rhetoric regarding deficits did not change much, there seems to have been a shift after 1960. James Buchanan and Richard Wagner (1977) identified the Kennedy administration as the turning point after which Keynesian economics was self-consciously applied, and after which the balanced budget norm was effectively broken. Once politicians accepted the idea that deficits were occasionally to be desired, that gave them an opportunity to justify politically popular endeavors that would earlier have been considered too expensive. Keynesian economics held that sometimes it was economically wise to cut taxes or to increase expenditures even though there was no surplus (see Chapter 2).

In the absence of a clear-cut standard for when the economy was sufficiently healthy that intentional deficits were not needed, zero deficit as a simple standard for self-discipline was lost. Not only did Keynesian theory provide a justification for intentional deficits; it also provided a warning that increases in taxes or reductions in expenditures could pose significant risks for economic performance. Accordingly, there has been only one year of surplus in the more than 30 years since the end of the Eisenhower administration. For the period between 1961 and 1981, that pattern probably reflected the asymmetric incentives of Keynesian economic policy as identified by Buchanan and Wagner.

In the Reagan-Bush years, there was a substantial change in fiscal policy.[20] In the Reagan administration, deficits grew dramatically in nominal size, and somewhat less dramatically as a fraction of Gross Domestic Product (GDP). Total federal debt as a fraction of GDP, however, doubled from 33.5% in 1981 to 68.2% in 1992, after a more or less steady decline subsequent to World War II. That resulted from large tax cuts during the Reagan administration, repeated "automatic" increases in entitlement spending, and a shift in the stance of the Republican party regarding taxes, the new stance being that the commitment to low taxes could override the party's commitment to balanced budgets.

Part of that change in Republican fiscal ideology seems to reflect a belief that taxes cause spending, that increases in tax revenues will not be used to reduce deficits, given the contemporary political climate, but only to increase spending. There seems to be some reason to think that that is true, or at least that it was true until very recently.

Econometric studies of budgeting regimes

Hoover and Sheffrin (1992) carefully investigated the joint causality of taxing and spending, and they argued that a fundamental shift took place in the late 1960s or early 1970s. They found that in the earlier period, taxes and spending were causally linked, with "some mild evidence in favor of taxes causing spending." In the later

20. See White and Wildavsky (1989).

period, however, taxes and spending became "causally independent" (1992, p. 245). The Budget and Impoundment Control Act of
1974 and the GRH law were unsuccessful efforts to counteract the
absence of causal interdependence between taxing and spending in
the more recent period.

The implications are relevant to partisan differences concerning
the relative reliance on taxes and spending cuts to achieve deficit
reduction. Republicans have argued that increased taxes would not
reduce the deficit so much as they would simply facilitate a larger
public sector. Accordingly, they oppose tax increases, in part, as a
strategy to keep public spending from rising. Democrats are left in
the uncomfortable position of advocating tax increases to help
pay for existing programs. Hoover and Sheffrin undermined the
Republican argument that new taxes would simply cause new
spending, though they suggested implicitly that such might have
been the case before the change in spending regimes that they identified.

The research of Hoover and Sheffrin does suggest that behavioral patterns can shift without institutional change and that institutional change may not be enough to overcome an autonomous
change in behavioral patterns. We still do not know what broke the
causal linkage between spending and taxes that existed before the
late 1960s, but the acceptance of the Keynesian rationale for intentional deficits is a likely candidate.

ACCOUNTABILITY, RULES, DISCRETION, AND
THE POLITICAL PROCESS

We have identified numerous situations in which, intentionally or
otherwise, decisions have had consequences that have outlasted
the office tenure of those who created them, such as indebtedness
and the creation of a pay-as-you-go Social Security system. Under
such circumstances, elections do not provide a very effective
means of holding public officials accountable. Even when the dimensions of the consequences of decisions are visible, as in the
savings and loan crisis, the separation of powers precludes any
clear process for holding incumbents accountable, unless it is to
throw all of the rascals out. But when much of the responsibility

lies with former presidents and members of Congress who have been out of office for years, wholesale punishment of those currently in office makes less sense.

Efforts to change the rules and procedures of the political process usually are efforts to change outcomes. Charles Stewart has shown that efforts to centralize control of the spending process, such as the Budget and Accounting Act of 1921, may have been victories for the effort to limit expenditures. A coalition that succeeds in doing that not only can enjoy its victory at the time the change is passed but also can enjoy an extension of that victory, for the rules it creates will constrain and guide future majorities that may have different preferences. However, rules can merely guide the aggregation of preferences; they may not prevail over new majorities that are determined to go in a different direction, such as to spend more generously. This is apparent in the failure of the 1974 Budget and Impoundment Control Act to eliminate the deficits.

Recalling Plott's fundamental equation of social choice, we see that the institutions process preferences into outcomes:

$$\text{preferences} \times \text{institutions} \rightarrow \text{outcomes}$$

Advocates of procedural change hope that a new procedure will process the preferences into outcomes that they prefer. However, certain preferences may not be translatable into certain outcomes by any procedure, and so long as we consider the preferences as fixed and given (i.e., exogenous), there may be little that can be done to improve outcomes. Preferences for keeping entitlements up and taxes down cannot be translated though any existing institution into balanced budgets when automatic policy keeps expenditures rising and taxes constant.

Yet, as I have argued in Chapter 6, voter preferences are not always fixed, and voters may adapt their preferences to what they think is possible, or even to what they think is inevitable. Indeed, most people have a variety of opinions, some of which may be incompatible with one another, and this is not necessarily evidence of irrationality. A good example concerns preferences for spending, wherein individuals want, simultaneously, low taxes, high expenditures, and balanced budgets – incompatible combinations. As David Stockman has shown with the "budget quiz" he gave to

Ronald Reagan, even presidents are not immune to such inconsistency (1986, pp. 356–7). It may be useful to consider individuals as
composed of multiple "selves" with multiple, and not necessarily
compatible, desires.

Efforts to impose rules for outcomes, such as the GRH law, are
efforts to elevate one "self" and one set of preferences above
others. This effort seems to have failed on the federal level, but
this kind of provision seems to have worked on the state level. As
Poterba (in press) has shown, there is a great variety of provisions
for budgetary restraint among the states, and many of them seem
to work. One difference between the state and federal experiences
is that most state rules have been in place throughout the contemporary era and thus have been operating to avoid massive buildup
of debt. It is not clear that they would have worked as well as they
have if they had been imposed *after* the creation of large debts.[21]
In any case, the states and their experience can provide a valuable
laboratory for investigating what kinds of fiscal rules may be more
effective than those that have been tried on the federal level.

The political process in a democracy aggregates fluid preferences
into collective decisions through institutional processes that are
themselves subject to change and manipulation. The outcomes that
result are functions of the collective decisions interacting with the
constraints of a world that is imperfectly understood. There is in
all this interaction no Archimedean point, no firm bedrock for
analysis and evaluation. The process legitimizes the outcomes, and
when the outcomes are viewed as unsatisfactory, the process may
be changed, or the preferences may be changed.

We are able to learn about democratic processes by creating
models in which certain features, such as preferences, are artificially held as fixed. In the real world, some things are more change-
able than others, but little is truly fixed. Democratic processes
provide for continuous feedback from outcomes to preferences and
procedures. We have seen ways in which this feedback process
can produce pathological outcomes, as with electoral cycles or
with budget deficits. The shift to pathological outcomes is not
inevitable, and broader experience shows that it is not irreversible.

Still, it appears that the formal institutions and the informal

21. Actually, Brown (1990) suggested that the rules were created in the 1830s after
massive deficits had been built up in the states.

norms of fiscal policy have not provided adequate restraints against the temptation to let expenditures outpace revenues, or against the unprecedented peacetime expansion of debt as a fraction of GNP. The institutions of electoral accountability, which are fundamentally the institutions of restraint against governmental arbitrariness or tyranny, have not been notably effective in curbing the temptations to permit expenditures to outpace revenues and to allow short-term perspectives to override the long view. In the next chapter we raise the same questions regarding monetary policy.

8 Discretion and accountability in the monetary policy process

Monetary policy is the alternative to fiscal policy for stabilization purposes. By default, it is currently the main instrument of American economic stabilization policy, because the flexibility of fiscal policy is severely limited by large deficits. The possible actions available to monetary authorities have to do with the levels of interest rates and the rate of growth of the money supply, which in turn may affect the level of economic activity and rates of inflation.

Good and successful monetary policy can bring an appropriate balance between economic growth and stable prices, but of course the meaning of "appropriate" is contestable. Poor or unsuccessful monetary policy runs two main risks. If the money supply grows much faster than real economic activity, the result will be inflation or even hyperinflation. The opposite risk is that there will not be enough financial liquidity to support the real economic activity that would take place if credit were more readily available. The United States has never experienced hyperinflation, but monetary policy has been at least partly responsible for the sustained increases in price levels since World War II.[1] The second risk was experienced in the banking panics and recessions of the nineteenth and early

---

1. With 1967 = 100, the price index varied between 30 and 60 for the 80 years between 1860 and 1940, but it has risen to about 300 since 1940. Broz (1993) described the experience of the "Continental" paper currency of the revolutionary war as hyperinflation. See also Sachs and Larrain (1993, p. 728).

184

twentieth centuries, and the Great Depression itself has been attributed to poor monetary policy.[2]

Just as there are two main risks inherent in poor monetary policy, there are two basic alternative strategies for good policy. One of these is to make monetary policy automatic, in the same sense that entitlements and tax rates are automatic fiscal policy. The other is for policymakers to use their discretion in manipulating the instruments available to them. The strategy of making monetary policy automatic has never really been tried. One version is a mythical reconstruction of the gold standard that has little basis in historical reality. Another is an untested proposal for a fixed rate of money growth that has no track record in experience. Either way, this strategy reflects a belief that some kind of automatic pilot would be better than human judgment and discretion.

The strategy of discretion, of course, involves no single set of procedures, but rather an enormously mixed bag that incorporates virtually all of American monetary history, including the successes and the failures. Some of the reasons for such an eclectic mixture are that policymakers' understanding of the alternative instruments available for discretionary choice has changed over time, their conceptions of the possibilities for active discretionary stabilization and control have varied with macroeconomic theory and over time, and the institutions through which discretionary choices are made have also changed.

Several of these observations will be documented and elaborated in this chapter, with examples from the entire span of American history. Most of the chapter will focus on the Federal Reserve System, the current institution for monetary policymaking, which was established in 1913.

INSTITUTIONS AND ISSUES IN MONETARY POLICY

Article I of the Constitution gives Congress the power to "coin money and to regulate the value thereof," but goes no further in specifying how such actions should be carried out. There are many

2. See Friedman and Schwartz (1963).

institutional alternatives for handling monetary policy. Some of the most fundamental considerations concern the backing of the currency, the existence of central banks, and the independence of central banks.

The backing of the currency

For much of American history, the money supply was backed by precious metals, usually gold.[3] The money supply was decoupled from gold in two major steps, one domestic and the other international. Before 1933, the "gold clause" in many business contracts provided that payment should be made in gold or in currency backed by a designated quantity of gold. In that year, Congress abrogated the gold clause in public and private contracts.[4] Subsequently, under the postwar Bretton Woods agreement on a system of international monetary relations, the American dollar was the standard against which exchange rates were set, and the United States was committed to exchanging gold for foreign holdings of dollars at the rate of $35 per ounce. In 1971, President Nixon suspended that policy.

That first decision broke a restraint against a potentially inflationary expansion of the money supply. The second stemmed an outflow of gold that had resulted from such expansion. The result is a complete uncoupling of the money supply from any commodity standard. The American currency is now "fiat money," legal tender that is produced and authorized by the government, wherein the government's capacity to print increasing quantities of money is not restrained by any commitment to convert money into any commodity in limited supply, such as gold or silver.

The elimination of commodity standards was no doubt related to the sustained increases in price levels since World War II, which were unprecedented in American history. That fact occasionally inspires arguments in favor of a return to the gold standard as a way to restore an automatic discipline over monetary policy and to avoid the inflationary bias of fiat money. This book will not consider such proposals in depth, but two points should be made.

3. A bimetallic gold and silver standard was used during some periods in the nineteenth century.
4. Friedman and Schwartz (1963, pp. 468–9).

First, a commodity standard did not prevent public officials from creating discretionary fluctuations in the money supply. Second, several prominent economic historians blame the rigidity of the gold standard for many of the mistakes in public policy during the Great Depression of the 1930s.[5]

The existence of central banks

The other main institutional issue for monetary policy is the existence of central banks. There had been two instances of a "Bank of the United States" before the establishment of the Federal Reserve in 1913. The first bank, which was chartered in 1791 and lasted until 1811,

was not intended to be a central bank; it was not to control the quantity of money. Nor was it to act as a centralized depository, an office of discount for commercial banks, or a lender of last resort. (Timberlake, 1993, p. 4)

The same was true of the second Bank of the United States, which was chartered in 1816. However, under the leadership of Nicholas Biddle, the second bank took on some countercyclical activities (largely in response to foreign exchange disturbances) that went beyond the powers delegated to it. Timberlake pronounced Biddle's manipulations of the money stock as "mostly good," even though they went beyond the delegated authority (1993, ch. 3, esp. p. 33). The second bank's charter expired in 1836, when President Andrew Jackson vetoed its renewal. The experience with the second bank made it clear that even under rudimentary institutional arrangements, some discretionary control of the money supply was possible. That experience occurred in an era that predated by perhaps a full century any widespread awareness of the possibility of systematic monetary policy.

The United States had no formally constituted central bank from 1836 until 1913, when the Federal Reserve System, the current central bank, was established. The experience in the three-quarters of a century without a formal central bank is relevant for evaluating the arguments of two kinds of critics of the Federal Reserve: those who criticize discretionary monetary policy under a relatively independent central bank, and those who advocate a return to the gold

5. See Eichengreen (1992a) and Temin (1989).

standard as a rule-based way of imposing automatic discipline on monetary policy.

During the 1836–1913 hiatus, several regimes were operative. The currency was backed by a bimetallic (gold and silver) standard until 1862, when the convertibility of paper money into specie (coin) was suspended by the U.S. (Union) government, which financed the Civil War in part by printing money. Accordingly, the period between 1862 and 1879, when specie payment was resumed, is called the greenback era. Not surprisingly, that period saw substantial inflation. Because specie payment was resumed at the prewar standard, the resumption involved substantial deflation.

The "golden age" of the gold standard as an international monetary system was between 1879 and 1914, when it collapsed with the outbreak of World War I. Kenneth Dam (1982) characterized as a "myth" the view that the gold standard was a rule-based, self-adjusting system that worked automatically to restore equilibrium after a disturbance. The system operated under discretionary changes in the "bank rate" or discount rate, which made the gold standard "far from automatic and self-adjusting" (p. 17).

A further discretionary aspect of the pre-1914 gold standard had to do with what in the 1920s came to be known as the "rules of the game." . . . But these *rules* of the gold standard game were strictly *discretionary,* and . . . central banks not only did not always abide by them but sometimes acted perversely. . . . (Dam, 1982, p. 18; emphasis added)

Dam acknowledged that the gold standard worked well for a number of decades, but he argued that it was a short-lived "incident in the history of international monetary organization" and that the common view of it confuses the gold standard as an international monetary system and as a domestic monetary regime (1982, p. 19). As a domestic monetary regime, the gold standard in the United States was complex and varied substantially in the period between 1879 and 1914 (Dam, 1982, pp. 28–9).[6]

If it had not been apparent earlier, the innovative policies of Leslie Shaw, secretary of the Treasury from 1902 to 1907, showed that a central bank, as such, was not necessary for the government to be able to carry out discretionary monetary policy, nor did the presence of the gold standard preclude such policy. In Shaw's words,

6. See also Eichengreen (1985).

if the Secretary of the Treasury were given $100 million to be deposited with the banks or withdrawn as he might deem expedient, and if in addition he were clothed with authority over the reserves of the several banks, with power to contract the national-bank circulation at pleasure, in my judgment no panic as distinguished from industrial stagnation could threaten either the United States or Europe that he could not avert. (Friedman and Schwartz, 1963, pp. 149–50)

The Treasury's powers of debt management were comparable to the open market operations that have become the most important of the Federal Reserve's monetary policy instruments.[7]

The banking panic that occurred in 1907 and the subsequent recession also illustrated that not everything was ideal in the golden age of the gold standard. Indeed, it was that experience that crystallized a broad recognition of a need for monetary reform. The emergence of the United States as a major world economic power had forced a recognition in the internationally oriented sector of the economy that changes were needed in America's monetary institutions. The panic of 1907 prompted many others to agree on the need for change.[8] In 1908, Congress provided for the creation of the National Monetary Commission, a bipartisan body "to inquire into and report to Congress . . . what changes are necessary or desirable in the monetary system . . . or in the laws relating to banking and currency."[9] Although the immediate recommendations of the commission were rejected by Congress, the plan that was accepted in 1913 bore considerable resemblance to the proposals of the commission.

The independence and decision procedures of central banks

In comparative studies, the Federal Reserve is consistently counted among the world's most independent central banks. Independence is seen as a device to insulate monetary policy from inflationary pressures for expansionary activity, and several studies have found an association between independence and low inflation.[10] It is therefore not surprising that the Federal Reserve is

7. See Friedman and Schwartz (1963, pp. 149–52, esp. note 24) and Timberlake (1993, pp. 186–95).
8. See Broz (1993) for a thorough and insightful treatment of the founding of the Federal Reserve that emphasizes the role of internationally oriented groups.
9. Quoted by Broz (1993, p. 353).
10. See Alesina and Summers (1993), Cukierman (1992, chs. 18–23), and Grilli et al. (1991).

criticized for being insufficiently expansionary, and for obstructing economic growth.[11] These criticisms are sometimes associated with demands that the Federal Reserve be more accountable, implying a continuum between independence and accountability.

The Federal Reserve is also criticized for the opposite failing of being too responsive to inflationary pressures.[12] For critics who take this view, the existing degree of independence is not enough. For many of them, a major institutional alternative would be "rules" for monetary policy, as opposed to the discretionary choices that characterize contemporary decisions. The most commonly proposed rule is that the money supply should grow at a known, fixed rate, regardless of economic conditions. This proposal is a monetary counterpart to the balanced budget "rule" for fiscal policy discussed in Chapter 7.

From some perspective or another, the Federal Reserve is regularly the subject of proposals for institutional reform.[13] The proposals that receive the most contemporary attention involve independence (vs. accountability) or rules (vs. discretion). Reform ideas regarding independence and accountability are common in both public and scholarly discourse. Reform ideas regarding rules and discretion are more subtle and are far more common in the academic literature than in the public forum.

The status of the Federal Reserve as one of the world's most independent central banks is measured largely by formal legislated features that were defined in 1913 and 1935. However, the Federal Reserve did not become as independent as it now is until an informal agreement was reached in 1951, known as the "accord." This fact suggests that its independence may be as much a matter of norms, or informal patterns of behavior, as of intentional changes in formal institutions. Changes in formal institutional arrangements may not have the consequences desired by their supporters unless they are accompanied by behavior patterns that cannot be created by legislative fiat.

Just as it may be difficult to legislate effective independence, it might be even more difficult to legislate adherence to rules for monetary policymaking, such as a rule for a fixed rate of money

11. See Greider (1987) for a prominent example.
12. For example, see Havrilesky (1993).
13. See Havrilesky (1993) for a recent sampling. See also Woolley (1984, ch. 7).

growth. Consider that independence involves insulation from accountability to elected officials, with a presumption that monetary authorities are more concerned about minimizing inflation than are elected officials. Such rules would be designed to limit the discretion of monetary authorities, and to make them even less responsive to the presumably inflationary pressures of the electoral process than they currently are under conditions of relative independence.

Originally, the case for rules ignored the problems of enforceability, because it was presumed that the rationale was so strong that the rules would be self-enforcing. However, more contemporary arguments recognize that enforceability is a serious problem. To whom would monetary authorities be accountable if they were to fail to follow a legislated rule? Elected officials and the public are unlikely sources of enforcement, because the incentives of the electoral process usually are considered *sources* of inflationary pressures. If that is the case, the practical argument for rules becomes tenuous, even though it has generated some very interesting scholarship.

Consideration of the enforceability of rules returns us to issues of accountability that are central to the democratic process, issues with which this book began. Accountability has at least two important meanings in political life. The most common is that one is subject to removal from office because of inadequate performance. As we saw in Chapter 3, institutions designed to ensure this kind of accountability may have their own problems. An alternative meaning is that officials must explain, report, and justify. I shall argue that at the same time that independence makes the Federal Reserve less accountable in the removability sense, independence can be associated with meaningful accountability in the explanation sense.

The motivations of monetary authorities

Although we can recognize that there is no reason to assume that the motivations of all monetary authorities need be the same, it will be useful to identify some of the leading possibilities and their implications. The most careful effort to elaborate monetary policy goals in a general theoretical way is seen in the work of Alex

Cukierman (1992), who identifies an employment motive and a revenue motive.[14] Although he gives it less explicit attention, Cukierman obviously considers inflation a comparably important motive. The goal of minimizing inflation is included in all of his objective functions, but the theme of his analysis is that the inclusion of other goals entails higher inflation.

The argument regarding the employment motive is the time-consistency argument first presented in Chapter 2. Recall that the key mechanism is that the monetary authorities have a target rate for unemployment that is below the natural rate, because of distortions in labor markets. (Equivalent arguments are easily made for growth targets above the natural rate.) Once labor contracts are signed, with a given level of expected inflation, the government has an incentive to create an inflationary surprise that will reduce unemployment or increase output. But according to this argument, labor contracts are signed with knowledge of the government's incentives. They anticipate the inflation, which is not a surprise. The result is no improvement regarding unemployment or output growth, and a positive rate of inflation.

The argument regarding the revenue motive is also a time-consistency argument, but it has different features. Government can gain purchasing power from the public by printing money. The amount of revenue it gains in this way will depend on the amount of cash the public chooses to hold. This amount is inversely related to the rate of inflation the public expects. The time-consistency problem takes the form that once the public has chosen the amount of money it will hold, the government can raise its revenues by printing more money and creating more inflation than was expected.

Cukierman's analysis of the motivations of monetary authorities is decidedly modern and reflects contemporary economic theory. For example, the time-consistency problem was not prominent in the economic literature before 1977, and we may wonder how motivations that were not recognized by economists may have affected the behavior of public officials.[15] This book itself is based on the presumption that politicians can have motivations other than

14. Cukierman also explains a balance of payments motive and a financial stability motive. Neither will be pursued in this book.
15. It is, of course, possible that public officials can be motivated by goals that are not recognized by economists.

maximizing the public interest, and as such it reflects a viewpoint and a systematic literature that scarcely existed in economics or political science 20 years ago. (Although I shall not explore it here, there is also a possibility that the motivations of public officials could be affected by what political economists write and think.)

Cukierman's analysis of motivations, as reported here, treats the government as if it were a single entity, though of course he acknowledges that "there may be differences of emphasis on alternative policy objectives between central banks and political authorities," and that "the actual course of policy usually represents a compromise between alternative views" (1992, p. 16). Normally we expect central bankers to be more inflation-averse than elected officials. This is often true because of the values that are associated "by coincidence" with the professional background of monetary authorities.[16] But there are reasons to make this a matter of choice as well. Kenneth Rogoff (1985) explains how it may make sense for political authorities to appoint a central banker whose inflation aversion is greater than their own or that of the public.

Neither the elected officials nor the central bankers themselves need be homogeneous. Just as in our discussion of political parties we recognized that not all politicians are alike, not all monetary authorities are alike. Chappell, Havrilesky, and MacGregor (1993) have documented differences among central bankers according to their professional backgrounds and partisan affiliations. Given these facts, we should recognize that the observed patterns of behavior might have been different if different people had been chosen.

The targets of monetary policy

The money supply and interest rates are inversely related in the short run, in that the interest rate is the price of borrowing money. The greater the supply, the lower the price. The monetary authority can try to control the money supply, or it can try to control interest rates, but it cannot do both at the same time. If it controls the money supply, interest rates will fluctuate with changes in the public's demand for money. If it controls interest rates, the money

16. See Woolley (1984, ch. 4).

supply will accommodate changes in money demand. Whichever target the monetary authority chooses, the other will fluctuate as an *epiphenomenon,* a secondary phenomenon that results from and accompanies another. In general, targeting the money supply is a more effective anti-inflationary strategy than targeting interests rates, because sustained increases in the money supply might be necessary to keep rates low. On the other hand, targeting the money supply may lead to interest rate fluctuations that create contractions in real economic activity.

Usually, it is not at all easy to see what a monetary authority is doing, that is, which aggregate it is targeting, if any. One reason for this is that monetary policy is inherently technical and difficult to understand. However, monetary authorities can make use of this complexity for a variety of purposes, some of which may be more defensible than others. One possibility is that ambiguous monetary policy can mask the adverse consequences of fiscal redistribution (Havrilesky, 1987). Another is that it can provide cover for elected politicians who do not wish to take the political heat for unpopular (but perhaps desirable) policies (Kane, 1990).

Alex Cukierman has shown that given the asymmetric information between the central bank and the public, that ambiguity may actually help it to achieve public purposes. However, "the politically optimal level of ambiguity" is conditional on the degree to which the bank's objectives are common knowledge (1992, p. 219). Cukierman also shows that a central bank may achieve its purposes more effectively using its discretion, rather than using a rule for a fixed rate of money growth. The intuition is that in spite of an acknowledged inflationary bias of discretionary policy, the employment and revenue goals might be better achieved when asymmetric information gives the bank a capacity to create monetary surprises (1992, pp. 219–21).

THE FEDERAL RESERVE SYSTEM

The basic formal institution of contemporary American monetary policy is the Federal Reserve System ("the Fed"), established in 1913 specifically to deal with monetary issues. That specificity of institutional purpose distinguishes monetary policy from fiscal policy, whose formal institutions (Congress and the presidency) are among the most basic and general features of American government. Monetary institutions are therefore much more subject to reforms that are targeted to macroeconomic issues and not complicated by their consequences for other issues.

The founding of the Fed

At its founding, the Fed bore some resemblance to the recommendations of the National Monetary Commission, which had been established in 1908 in the wake of the previous year's panic, under the leadership of Republican Senator Nelson Aldrich. Although the banking panic was a precipitating event, it had been apparent for some time that American monetary institutions were not well suited to handle the nation's increasingly prominent position in the world economy. The internationally oriented sector of the economy led a campaign to build support for the creation of a central bank. However, the commission's proposals were blocked in the Democratic Congress elected in 1910, and it was left to the Wilson administration, with unified Democratic control, to create the new institution.

Congress's intentions in 1913 for the new central bank are not totally clear, and on many issues it is likely that there was no clear intent.[17] Congress represented Republicans and Democrats, nationalists and internationalists, creditors and debtors, and therefore many different interests in monetary policy. There does seem to have been a consensus that some reform was needed, but there was considerable disagreement about the roles to be played by government, by the New York financial center, and by the rest of the banking industry. The result was a compromise that provided limited influence for each of those elements. Broz has characterized previous American monetary history as a series of swings between easy money regimes and stable currency institutions (1993, pp. 219, 422–3). The newly established Fed had such diverse features that it was not easily characterized as a victory for any side.

The structure of the Fed reflected a compromise between those

17. See Shepsle (1992).

who feared the private power of Wall Street and those who feared the public power of Washington. A seven-member Federal Reserve Board in Washington reflected the desire for public control. Twelve privately controlled regional banks reflected the desire to limit political influence. The fact that the New York Fed was merely first among twelve equals reflected a desire to limit the power of Wall Street. Ten-year terms for the five congressionally appointed members of the Federal Reserve Board were meant to make them independent of elected officials. The secretary of the Treasury and the comptroller general were originally ex officio members.

That structure, with something for almost everyone, can be seen as an improved way of dealing with both international and domestic monetary problems without having to take a definitive stand or express a definitive intent on a variety of issues. As we saw in Chapter 5, the officially legislated goals of the Fed were vaguely defined: to "furnish an elastic currency." In the context of the early twentieth century, that meant that the Fed should be able to respond to the seasonal fluctuations in the demand for money. That capacity implied that Congress did intend to give monetary authorities some kind of discretion to respond to changing conditions.[18]

But that discretion was understood to be structured and restrained by the gold standard and the real bills doctrine. The gold standard meant that the supply of money was limited by the requirement that currency be redeemable in gold. The real bills doctrine provided the standard by which credit was to be extended: for projects that produced "real" commodities. No one would argue that Congress in 1913 *intended* to create an institution whose chairman would, at least occasionally, be seen as the second most influential person in the nation, after the president, nor an institution that would have the capacity to steer the economy.

The vagueness of the Fed's mandate and the decentralized character of its structure reflected the fact that the new reform institution was a response to a variety of needs, without a singular, easily definable purpose. Vagueness and decentralization were ways of resolving disagreement and avoiding conflict at the time of the legislation, but they would have consequences. The vagueness of

18. The United States had accumulated a massive gold stock in the preceding two decades, but under existing law that stock did not provide the flexibility that gold stocks did for European countries with central banks. See Broz (1993).

the goals has given Fed officials substantial autonomy and reduced their accountability, as compared with a situation in which the goals are clearly defined.[19] Vagueness also facilitates adaptation to changing circumstances, which can be a substantial advantage in the absence of a capacity to foresee how conditions, problems, and demands will change.

The development of institutions to control open market operations illustrates how the Fed and Congress adapted to newly discovered problems and possibilities. In particular, the decentralization that solved a political problem in 1913 was to have unanticipated consequences that would create a problem and lead to an adaptation.[20] The main instrument of monetary policy envisioned in the Federal Reserve Act was the "discount rate," the rate at which reserve banks would lend to member banks. Control of that rate was meant to provide the elasticity of the currency that would adjust to shifting credit demands. The act did not anticipate the importance of open market operations, the buying and selling of government securities, which have become the most important of the instruments of monetary policy.

Originally open market operations were designed mainly to give the reserve banks "a portfolio of earning assets out of which to pay their expenses" (Eichengreen, 1992b, p. 16). After it became apparent that such operations could have an effect on economic activity, it was recognized that there might be a need to coordinate the activities of the member banks. During the recession of 1920, member banks purchased large amounts of government securities to replenish their income. The Federal Reserve Board and the Treasury complained that the banks were bidding against each other and destabilizing the prices of government bonds. The result was the creation of an Open Market Investment Committee, later to be more broadly constituted as the Open Market Policy Conference (Eichengreen, 1992b, pp. 17–20). That experience involved some tests of strength between the board and the reserve banks, resolved largely in favor of the banks, which dominated the coordinating body until the banking acts of 1933 and 1935 reconstituted the institutions of open market operations. In those acts, Congress

19. See Kane (1990, p. 290).
20. This section draws on Eichengreen (1992b).

established a Federal Open Market Committee in which the reserve banks were clearly dominated by the government-appointed component, renamed the Board of Governors.

These developments illustrate some important points about monetary authority in the United States. Congress is the ultimate authority. However, it does not always specify exactly what it wants, surely in large part because it does not always know. Legislation creating monetary institutions is like an incomplete contract, allowing the Fed to adapt to changing conditions and unanticipated problems. The legislated institutions provide a structure in which tests of strength take place.

Even though the Fed was intentionally insulated from the influence of elected officials, it is still the agent of Congress, which is the principal in a principal-agent relationship.[21] Of course, as principal, Congress has the power to abolish the Fed or to make any other change in the structure within which its agent operates. Although abolition is a most unlikely possibility, its potential is a fundamental fact that underlies the relationship between Congress and the Fed.

Reforms of the 1930s

Congress passed significant amendments to the Federal Reserve Act in 1933 and 1935, after catastrophic economic performance. The Fed had failed to halt a banking panic that exceeded most previous panics in its severity, and that led to the Great Depression, the deepest in American history. Economic historians are still analyzing and debating the role of the Fed in the Crash and the Depression, but regardless of the analysis, the central bank was seen to be in need of significant reform after those events.

The changes of the 1930s shifted power from the regional banks to a reconstituted Board of Governors in Washington, and from private bankers to public officials. The Banking Act of 1935 extended the terms of the board members, now to be called "governors," to 14 years.[22] The act also removed the secretary of the Treasury and the comptroller of the currency from the board,

21. See Irwin Morris (1994) for a systematic treatment of the Fed as the agent of two principals, Congress and the president.
22. The Banking Act of 1933 had extended the original 10-year terms to 12 years.

making it more independent of the administration.[23] In addition to the power to set the discount rate, which had been granted in the 1913 act, the Banking Act of 1935 gave the Board of Governors the power to set reserve requirements, and it recognized the capacity to influence economic activity through open market operations, the buying and selling of government securities.

The new Federal Open Market Committee (FOMC) was created to carry out what has become the most important of the Fed's policymaking functions. The FOMC comprises all seven members of the Board of Governors and the twelve presidents of the regional banks, but only five bank presidents have voting powers at any time. Those changes made the Fed more "public" and better insulated it from the power of the private banks, but they also made it more independent of administration influence.

Reforms of the 1970s

Up until the late 1960s, the Fed defined the terms of its own accountability by what it chose to put in its annual reports. But in the turbulent economic times of the 1970s, Congress became restive and demanded more structured accountability. It incorporated its demands in House Concurrent Resolution 133, passed in 1975, in the Federal Reserve Reform Act of 1977, and in the Humphrey-Hawkins act of 1978.

The theme of those actions was to demand that the Fed become more systematically accountable to Congress on Congress's own terms. Members of Congress wanted the Fed to set specific targets for its actions. The proposals included targets for economic outcomes, such as unemployment rates, and intermediate targets, such as interest rates. The Fed, under the leadership of Chairman Arthur Burns, consistently resisted yielding to demands that it accept such targets, citing the need to retain flexibility and discretion to deal with changing conditions.

The compromise embodied in the three legislative acts mentioned earlier was that the Fed chairman would report to the House and Senate banking committees twice each year and that he would set targets for money growth. Burns succeeded in avoiding specific

23. See Kettl (1986) on how this was partly inadvertent.

targets. Instead, the Fed set target *ranges* for money growth, and it set such ranges for several different definitions of the money supply. In that way, there was latitude for the Fed to defend itself by shifting the emphasis in its reports to Congress.

Those changes of the 1970s did not significantly change the Fed's powers. The somewhat combative maneuvering between the banking committees and Chairman Burns obscured the fundamental fact that the Fed was a legislative creation of Congress and could be abolished or changed by Congress. However, in those interchanges, it was not clear that Congress had the upper hand, because the stature and reputation of the Fed restricted the realistic latitude that Congress had.[24]

In spite of Burns's protests, I would argue that the changes did not significantly weaken the Fed's independence. They may even have strengthened it by structuring its accountability. A powerful body created by Congress is vulnerable to major change if people become dissatisfied with its performance and there is no effective accountability. The Fed is not effectively accountable in the sense of being subject to sanction for poor performance, but since the reforms of the 1970s, it is more effectively accountable in the sense of having a regular forum in which it must report, explain, and justify its actions. The Fed did retain its independence by influencing the standards for the targets it was asked to defend.

INFORMAL INSTITUTIONS: PATTERNS OF DISCRETIONARY MONETARY POLICYMAKING

The actual patterns of monetary policymaking have varied over time, independently of formal legislative changes, just as in the case of fiscal policy. When there is a general change in the continuing government policy or strategy, we speak of a change in *regimes*.[25] The most clear-cut example of such a change in monetary policy was the accord of 1951 between the Treasury and the Fed.

During World War II, monetary policy was defined by the acquiescence of the Fed to the Treasury Department's goal of supporting the prices of government securities, and keeping interest rates low, the "peg," in order to accommodate the government's wartime

24. See Kettl (1986, ch. 6) for a thorough and insightful treatment of this episode.
25. See Sargent (1986, p. 41).

borrowing needs. In effect, monetary policy was set by the Trea-sury, and the Fed voluntarily cooperated. There was no question that the Fed had the legal authority to set monetary policy indepen-dently, regardless of Treasury preferences, but the central bank did not seek to move abruptly from its wartime position of voluntary subordination to independence. Instead, it made known its restive-ness incrementally in a series of moves culminating in the agreement designated the accord, in March of 1951.

The president and the Treasury Department resisted those moves, and the Fed acted with considerable caution. One reason for that was surely that its legal independence was based in legisla-tion and could be revoked at any time by new law. The position of Congress was in fact supportive of the Fed's efforts to free itself from its commitment to support the government bond market, as illustrated in hearings held by a subcommittee of the Joint Eco-nomic Committee. That group was chaired by Senator Paul Doug-las of Illinois, himself a distinguished economist. After a series of meetings and several misunderstandings, the following statement was issued:

The Treasury and the Federal Reserve System have reached full accord with respect to debt-management and monetary policies to be pursued in furthering their common purpose to assure the successful financing of the Government's requirements and, at the same time, to minimize monetization of the public debt.[26]

Although it was not immediately apparent, that agreement marked the beginning of the contemporary era of monetary policy. It is an era in which the Fed is consistently counted among the world's most independent central banks.[27]

The legal status of the Fed had not changed since 1935, but there is no doubt that the Fed did not exert its independence during the 10-year period between 1941, when the policy of supporting the government bond market was adopted, and 1951. Nor is there doubt that there was a significant change in the Fed's actual inde-pendence after the accord, even though some observers contend that the post-accord Fed is still significantly influenced by the executive branch and that its independence is limited.[28]

The general orientation of the Fed since 1951 has been to use

26. Quoted by Stein (1969, p. 277). This section draws heavily on Stein's analysis.
27. See Alesina and Summers (1993) and Cukierman (1992, chs. 19–24).
28. See, for example, Havrilesky (1993).

its discretion in stabilizing the economy. According to William McChesney Martin, appointed chairman of the Board of Governors soon after the accord, the task of the central bank is to "lean against the wind," and to follow a countercyclical monetary policy. However, it is often very difficult to infer just what the Fed is doing. Its policy is normally cloaked in considerable ambiguity. This ambiguity enhances the Fed's independence and allows it to limit its accountability in either of the two senses we have mentioned (to be subject to removal for inadequate performance, and to explain and justify). However, in the modern framework of time-consistency problems and asymmetric information, such ambiguity *can* enhance the possibility that the Fed can serve genuinely public purposes. As Cukierman suggests, there is a "politically optimal level of ambiguity" (1992, ch. 12).

The most clear-cut shift in Fed policy since 1951 occurred during Paul Volcker's chairmanship, beginning in October 1979 and ending in late 1982. Described as a new set of operating procedures, that shift involved more targeting of the money supply than had characteristically been the case. As assessed by Alt (1991, pp. 45–8), this period involved substantially less volatility in the money supply (M2) than at any time before or since, as well as considerable increases in interest rates. That policy is often credited with creating the recession of 1982 and the disinflation that accompanied it. It would be a mistake to consider it an experiment with a Friedman-type rule for a fixed rate of money growth, because no public commitment was made, and the possibility of discretionary change was preserved.

That episode is not universally admired. Some critics simply think of it as the deepest recession since the Great Depression. Others see it as a necessary step toward the desirable goal of reducing the inflation of the 1970s. The episode is a leading example of how independence and ambiguity can allow a monetary authority to bring about disinflation, which could be a difficult move for fiscal authorities. If a recession is necessary to reduce inflation, it will be difficult, if not impossible, for elected officials to take steps that will involve immediate pain in order to achieve a future goal. The insulation of an independent body can make such a step easier, and the ambiguity of monetary procedures can provide further cover.

These two examples of informal changes in American monetary policy regimes (1951 and 1979) are two of the most visible and clearly identifiable. There doubtless have been other, less dramatic shifts in operating procedures that have occurred much more often. My purpose is not to catalogue such shifts, but rather to establish two points. The first is that informal changes can be as important as formal, legal changes in monetary institutions. By legislated standards, the Fed was as independent before 1951 as after, but in reality its effective independence was not declared until that date. That experience should promote caution in efforts to measure independence by formal, legal criteria.

The second point is that within the context of the independence that has existed since 1951, there can be important and desirable shifts in policy that might not take place in the absence of a body that is insulated from electoral accountability. Fiscal and monetary authorities are not equally vulnerable to expansionary pressures. Fiscal authorities, who are accountable to electorates, find it easy to respond to demands for fiscal stimuli in the form of tax cuts or expenditure increases. They find it less easy to respond to a need for restraint or austerity, which may involve tax increases or expenditure cuts. Monetary authorities, who are insulated from electorates, are in a better position to respond to a need for restraint. To do so, they will not have to increase taxes or reduce expenditures, which might be an electoral liability. Their independence of the electoral process gives them more freedom to introduce austerity when needed than might be the case otherwise. (Of course this independence also gives them the same freedom when austerity is not needed. The identification of need is a matter of discretionary judgment.[29])

INDEPENDENCE AND ACCOUNTABILITY

As the preceding sections make clear, discretionary monetary policy has been available and has been used by public officials for well

---

29. According to the scapegoat hypothesis, an independent Fed helps elected officials to act responsibly with minimal political cost, by permitting them to blame the Fed for actions they may approve, but which it would be impolitic to defend. See Kane (1990).

over a century, with and without central banks. Yet there have always been concerns that such power over the management of money might not be used wisely, and some have argued that such discretion should be restrained, if not eliminated. The gold standard surely restrained the discretion of such officials to some degree when it was in effect, but it was not nearly so automatic as the entitlements and taxes discussed in Chapter 7. The gold standard has often been considered akin to a rule for monetary policy, but even if there had been a rigid and inflexible connection between the money supply and the stock of gold (and there was not), monetary policy could have fluctuated "automatically" (and arbitrarily) with the discovery of new sources of the precious metal, as in California, Alaska, and South Africa.

The main theoretical alternative to the use of discretion in monetary policy would be the use of rules that would specify in advance what public officials should do. Rules could be contingent or noncontingent. Contingent rules would specify what public officials should do in all situations that could be anticipated. Noncontingent rules would specify what should be done in all cases, regardless of conditions.

The leading example of a noncontingent rule for monetary policy is that there be a fixed rate for growth of the money stock. This is noncontingent in the sense that the rate is meant to be achieved regardless of fluctuations in economic conditions. An advantage of noncontingent rules for purposes of accountability is that the standards of performance are relatively unambiguous and clear – I say "relatively" because the money stock is measured in several different ways, and for a rule to be unambiguous, one specific measure and standard would have to be chosen.

The use of contingent rules is at least a theoretical possibility that could avoid the inflexibility associated with noncontingent rules. A contingent rule would try to anticipate all the important conditions on which given actions might depend and specify what should be done under these conditions. There are several problems with this. One is that it would be difficult to anticipate all the conditions on which an action might depend. Another is that the more elaborate the conditions become, the more likely it becomes that discretion will be necessary to determine whether or not a given contingency obtains. At the extreme, contingent rules and discretion merge and become almost indistinguishable. A third problem has to do with accountability. An advantage of fixed and noncontingent rules is that there is a clear basis of accountability. As contingent rules become more and more elaborate, it becomes increasingly difficult to determine whether or not they have been followed to a satisfactory degree. Here, too, the distinction between discretion and contingent rules becomes blurred.

Rationales for rules

No one has made a convincing case for contingent rules, but a noncontingent rule for a fixed rate of money growth is often proposed. There are several rationales for such a rule. The best-known proponent of this idea is Milton Friedman, who presented it in *A Program for Monetary Stability* (1960).[30] His rationale is that there are severe limitations to our knowledge about the causes of business fluctuations and the lags between policy action and economic response. Under such conditions, discretionary action is more likely to destabilize than to stabilize. A publicly known rule for a fixed rate of money growth would have avoided policy mistakes that Friedman documents, and would provide a clear-cut basis for accountability.

There are two other rationales for monetary rules. One is similar to the rationale for a balanced budget amendment, discussed in Chapter 7, which I shall designate the public choice rationale. The idea is that the central bank cannot be trusted to resist inappropriate pressures from elected officials. Thomas Havrilesky (1987, 1993) has the most elaborate theory for why such pressures are inappropriate. He argues that elected officials appeal for votes by enacting redistributive tax and transfer schemes that create costly inefficiencies in the economy. In order to disguise the slowdowns in growth and productivity caused by such programs, presidents (and, to a lesser extent, Congress) pressure the Fed to expand the money supply, with inflationary consequences.

The final rationale for rules is the time-consistency argument. In this argument, there are inefficiencies in the economy due to

---

30. That proposal differed from his first proposal, which was for an automatic dollar-for-dollar creation (retirement) of money to cover government deficits (surpluses) due to automatic stabilizers set in tax and transfer laws (Friedman, 1953a).

distortionary taxes, labor unions, or laws affecting the labor market (e.g., minimum wages and unemployment compensation). Such features are said to result in a rate of economic growth below the potential or "natural" rate, or unemployment rates above the "natural" rate. Monetary authorities operating in a rational expectations framework try to improve output to its natural rate, even though they know that they can do that only by surprising the public with an inflationary increase in the money supply. But the public knows that they will do that, and expects the increase. The result is that output does not increase, but inflation does. It is said that a rule for a fixed rate of money growth would help politicians resist the temptation to carry out such policy.[31]

The time-consistency rationale differs from Friedman's lack-of-knowledge rationale in that it is based on the strong presumption that both the public and the monetary authority understand how the economy works and understand each other's goals and strategies. The time-consistency rationale differs from the public choice rationale in that there is no misunderstanding or effort to mislead, though there is likely to be asymmetric information. (However, in some respects, the two arguments are similar, but use different language. The time-consistency argument is presented in the language of rational choice and enlightened self-interest, whereas the public choice argument uses language that emphasizes the venal or self-serving motivations of public officials and the failure of the public to understand the consequences of the policies it supports.)

Accountability

Friedman pointed out that a rule for a fixed rate of money growth would provide a clear-cut basis for accountability, which is a concept that is widely used as if it needed no definition, but in fact it is used in different ways. As we have seen, one meaning is that officials be subject to sanction for inadequate performance, such as by removal from office through defeat in election or through impeachment. The other is to be subject to the need to give account (i.e., to explain, report, or justify), such as through a state of the

---

31. See Kydland and Prescott (1977) for the seminal formulation. See also Barro and Gordon (1983). As several people have observed, a superior solution to this problem would be to eliminate the distortions.

union message or through a judicial opinion that embeds a court decision in the law. Like federal judges, central bankers have been intentionally shielded from the first kind of accountability by their long terms. (The current term for governors of the Fed is 14 years.) For much of this century, the Fed was in a position to use its own discretion to define its own standards for explaining, reporting, and justifying its actions in its annual reports.

In the absence of independent, authoritative standards for evaluating the performance of monetary authorities, that discretion to define the standards for its performance provided considerable latitude to Fed officials. For all three of the rationales for rules, a clearly defined standard is meant to provide a basis for knowing when the monetary authority has deviated from proper performance.

PART FIVE

Conclusion

9 The costs of democracy

This book has investigated macroeconomic policymaking in order to make inferences about the nature of democratic institutions, to get a grasp on problems that may be inherent in them, and to understand how alternative formulations of these institutions might affect performance. It has focused on recent experience in the United States. The concentration on macroeconomic issues has facilitated the evaluation of performance. The concentration on one nation has facilitated an understanding of the importance of process in democracy, and it has permitted an assessment of the consequences of institutional changes over time in that country.

However, economic performance is only one of the many values that may be facilitated or hindered by democratic institutions, and a focus on one country obscures an understanding of the ways in which alternative institutions that vary across countries can affect performance. In this final chapter, we shall consider some ways in which the single country focus may be complemented by further investigation, though without speculating beyond macroeconomic issues. But first a reflection on some of the implications of the methodological approach used in much of the analysis.

DEMOCRATIC POLITICS AND ECONOMIC METHOD

The book has used economic analysis in a sense that goes beyond the obvious character of the subject matter. A fundamental charac-

211

teristic of economics is the method of constrained optimization. Economics is about how to identify the choices that will maximize welfare functions or minimize loss functions, subject to the constraints of possibility. Much of the traditional economic approach to policy analysis is, in effect, about how to give advice to benevolent dictators, who are presumed to wish to optimize some publicly oriented objective function. Modern political economics has made great strides by recognizing that those who decide public policy may have other, private motivations, such as maximization of their prospects for reelection, of their incomes, or of some partial conception of what public policy ought to be. Models built on these features can predict the consequences of political motivations and compare them with what a benevolent dictator might do.

The optimizing methodology of economics has provided powerful leverage for understanding the nature of democratic politics. This book could not have been written without it. However, one central message of the book is that democracy cannot be adequately understood within the optimizing framework, which depends on externally defined goals for the objective functions. Chapter 5 argued that there is no authoritative or uncontestable welfare function that is not defined as part of a political process, and subject to revision in such a process. Optimizing analyses of democratic politics depend on arbitrarily defined objective functions that have no authority in the real world of democratic politics. Any theoretical comparison between the results of democratic processes and the choices of a benevolent dictator with respect to some welfare function presumes definitions of goals that in fact are defined only within the democratic political process.

Moreover, the diversity of views among leading macroeconomic theorists makes it clear that even if we wanted to delegate policy to a benevolent dictator, we might have to have a democratic election to decide whether she would be new Keynesian or new classical. If that election were not to be a once-and-for-all choice, we might evaluate the performances of the theories that guide these benevolent dictators with the models of electoral accountability and choice presented in Chapters 3 and 4. Thus, even the economic method of analysis of democracy is embedded in a kind of political choice, rather than being logically antecedent. Even the imaginary alternative of a benevolent dictatorship does not escape some of the problems that must be understood as issues of democracy.

Conceptions of the preferences of voters can be used to define objective functions that can be incorporated into models of the democratic political process. Such models may suggest the ironic possibility that democratic institutions distort these same preferences into inferior policy, as in the Nordhaus (1975) model of "the political business cycle." In fact, democratic politics incorporates the selection of broad goals, the implementation of specific policies, and the evaluation of government performance in a fluid and continuous process that can be decomposed only analytically. Fiscal policy and monetary policy processes can produce results that are disappointing or inferior to other possible outcomes. These processes can be revised by reforms of the relevant formal institutions, but these reforms are themselves likely to have unanticipated consequences and lead to demands for further revision.

The source of undesired results is likely to be found in norms and patterns of behavior (i.e., informal institutions). Reforms of formal institutions are likely to fail if they do not take into account the incentives involved in these norms and patterns of behavior. A balanced budget amendment to the Constitution would be unlikely to have much more effect than the Gramm-Rudman-Hollings law unless people realized the magnitude of the combination of tax increases and spending cuts that would be necessary to bring revenues and expenditures in line.

Democracy is inevitably about process. Democracy can be analyzed and better understood with economic models, but the economic models hinge on some set of preferences or some objective function defined outside of the economic framework. Thus, there is a circularity to the understanding of democracy that economic models can help to minimize, but from which they do not offer complete escape.

COSTS AND PATHOLOGIES

Still, our understanding of the costs and pathologies of democracy has depended very heavily on economic analysis. To repeat, costs are similar to prices and implicitly are to be compared to benefits.

They are to be minimized, but some costs are likely to be the price of anything valuable, and democracy is presumed to be valuable. Pathologies, on the other hand, are clearly undesirable and detrimental, associated with sickness or disease, and they need to be eliminated or cured if at all possible.

Costs

Some costs of democracy are inevitable parts of the principal-agent character of representative government and the asymmetries of information between the electorate as principals and public officials as agents. One form of cost has to do with the backward-looking accountability issue. Just as in any principal-agent framework, there will be ways in which the government agents will try to make their performance look misleadingly good at the time that contracts are renewed (i.e., at election time).

Another form of cost has to do with the forward-looking choice issue. Given the inevitable uncertainty about the consequences of choices that electorates make, there will always be ways in which the very possibility of choice carries with it costs that could be avoided only in some ideal world of perfect information. As William Bianco has observed, perfect control is impossible in all principal-agent situations in which there is asymmetric information. "The problem is not representative government; rather representative government is an example of a generic and intractable problem" (1994, p. 167).

There is another candidate for a cost of democracy that I have discounted, but should recognize as a possibility. This one involves the failure of the public to appreciate the consequences of the actions it supports. In this view, the public supports or demands activity that makes it worse off than it might otherwise be. An example of an argument for such a cost is provided by Hibbs, who asserts that the "true" costs of inflation are not in the inflation itself, but in the recessions that are induced to curb inflation. The public is inflation-averse in a way that cannot be explained by Hibbs's assessments of the objective and measurable costs: Voters punish the politicians who create inflation, and they reward the politicians who create disinflationary recessions, which have more readily measurable costs (1987, pp. 118, 178). I discount that view as one that depends heavily on Hibbs's own values, which are contestable in the framework laid out in Chapter 5. His argument does not give the public enough credit for seeing real costs in inflation, even if we do not fall back on the argument that the public is the authoritative resolver of disputes of fundamental values. However, I do not mean to rule out the possibility of reasonable arguments that the public does not know the consequences of its preferences. Furthermore, when we consider preferences as endogenous, we do not need to consider observed behavior as a complete description of possible behavior. Just as individuals may change their preferences (say for cigarettes) after learning the consequences of their preferences, so might the public change its preferences regarding something like inflation.

Pathology

Democracy has been associated with patterns that some people do not like, such as redistribution of income or wealth through tax and transfer programs, a large public sector, inflation, and deficits. Opponents of these patterns may think of them as pathological tendencies of democracy, but democracy is neither necessary nor sufficient for the occurrence of such phenomena. As a general rule, such assessments are too contingent on the tastes and preferences of the observer or analyst, as distinguished from those of the electorate. The nature and extent of tax and transfer programs and the size of the public sector are matters of preference and judgment that are to be decided in a political process. Also, within certain ranges, nonzero values of inflation and government deficits may be legitimate and defensible products of democratic politics.

However, inflation and public indebtedness can go beyond tolerable ranges, though the definition of a boundary between the tolerable and intolerable is itself a matter of political judgment. Hyperinflation and unsustainably rising debt/GNP ratios are conditions that I have judged to be pathological, and democratic experience includes instances of both these conditions. For example, in the twentieth century, democratic regimes in Germany, Israel, and several Latin American countries have experienced hyperinflations,[1] and Germany, Italy, Belgium, and Ireland have experienced rapidly rising debt/GNP ratios in peacetime.[2]

But there is no necessary connection between democracy and either hyperinflation or explosive public indebtedness. The greatest hyperinflations have occurred in countries devastated by wars (Cagan, 1987), whether the countries were democratic or not. The institutional variable that is necessary (but obviously not sufficient) for hyperinflation is paper money, that is, fiat currency unbacked by and unconvertible into a commodity, such as gold. Explosive growth of public debt is also associated with wars. In the twentieth century, large debts have been experienced in third-world nations that have only intermittently been democratic.[3] Most democratic experience in the United States and many other countries has not involved either hyperinflation or public debt crises. Clearly, there is little reason to believe that normal democratic processes have an inherent or systematic tendency to generate such pathological results.

However, among democratic institutions there is evidence of asymmetry between the creation and elimination of problems. That is, there is reason to believe that democratic processes can systematically obstruct the resolution of pathological situations such as hyperinflation or debt crises. This is because one of the main features of democracy is the capacity to protect one's self against the unwanted imposition of costs. Certain forms of democratic institutions do this more than others. Some democratic institutions facilitate majorities, whereas others enhance the prospects that minorities will be able to block change. There is reason to believe that the latter kind may better approximate popular preferences in general, while at the same time they may obstruct stabilization programs that would make everybody better off.

INSTITUTIONAL ALTERNATIVES

The form of democracy in the United States is one of many alternatives. A useful way of classifying the alternatives was provided by

1. See Sargent (1986) and Cagan (1987).
2. See Alesina (1988b) and Roubini and Sachs (1989a,b).
3. See Frieden (1991).

Arend Lijphart (1984), who identified two pure types: majoritarian and consensus democracy. Majoritarian democracy involves the concentration of executive power, cabinet dominance of a fused relationship between the cabinet and the legislature, a legislature dominated by the lower house, a two-party system organized along a single dimension, plurality elections, and centralized government. Great Britain is the classic case of this model, but Lijphart shows that New Zealand actually approximates it better. Whereas this "Westminster model" facilitates majority rule, consensus democracy restrains majorities in several ways.

Consensus democracy involves the sharing of power through grand coalitions, separation of executive and legislative powers, balanced power in bicameral legislatures, multiparty systems organized along multiple dimensions, proportional representation, and federalism. Switzerland and Belgium are leading examples of this model. Lijphart described and classified 22 democracies according to the characteristics of these models.

The United States is obviously a hybrid, having features that facilitate and features that hinder majorities. In terms of partisan competition over the issues of inflation and unemployment rates, the United States is effectively modeled as a two-party majoritarian system, because the main differences in outcomes hinge on control of the presidency. However, for the purpose of understanding fiscal policy, the United States is more like the consensus model, because legislative changes demand agreement among dispersed powers.

Several studies have suggested that there are relationships linking such characteristics of the alternative democratic systems to macroeconomic performance. Roubini and Sachs have investigated the relationship between political conditions and budget deficits in OECD economies. They suggest that

when power is dispersed, either across branches of the government (as in the U.S.), or across many political parties in a coalition government (as is typical in Italy), or across parties through the alternation of political control over time, the likelihood of intertemporally inefficient budget policy is heightened. (1989a, p. 905)

Their argument is based on the recent experience of budget deficits in the industrial democracies. They contend that these nations were hit in the early 1970s by an exogenous shock that involved a growth slowdown and rising unemployment and, in the late 1970s, rising interest rates. Their argument about political institutions is not that they caused the deficits that resulted from those shocks but that they affected the efforts to reverse the deficits. This asymmetry is explained by the difficulty that coalition governments have in securing the cooperation of the several parties whose agreement is necessary for choosing and implementing a budget reduction package.

Grilli et al. (1991) offer a related argument in which they find that governments with unsustainable debt growth tend to be countries with short-lived coalition governments. These authors distinguish possible sources of such patterns. One prediction is that public debts should be larger in unstable and polarized societies. This view is grounded in the theories of Alesina and Tabellini (1990) and Persson and Svensson (1989). The idea is that a government that expects to be replaced by a new government with very different preferences will actively use deficits to limit the choices of its successor in a conscious strategic move. A second prediction is more like the Roubini and Sachs view, in which unpopular but desirable policies can be blocked when the agreement of several decisionmakers is necessary in order to change policy. The first situation is characterized as instability, and the second as weakness.

The empirical analysis of Grilli and associates does not distinguish between the two views, but it does emphasize that government debts are highest in countries they characterize as "representational democracies," which are countries that are closer to the consensus democracy pole of Lijphart's analysis. They have a high degree of "proportionality" of representation, which is indicated by the number of parliamentary seats per district:

All the countries that seem to have an unsustainable debt, except Ireland and Portugal, are governed by representational systems. Conversely, all representational democracies except Denmark have unsustainable fiscal policies. (Grilli et al., 1991, p. 351)

In the studies by Roubini and Sachs and Grilli and associates there is a recognition of more than one source for the characteristics associated with undesirable debt policies. One source may be institutions that disperse power, as in the consensus model. Another may be the diversity or polarization of preferences within the system. There can be dispersed powers in a two-party system, as in the United States, but multiparty systems are likely to reflect a diversity and perhaps a polarization of preferences. Diversity of preferences and electoral systems that reflect rather than suppress diversity are unlikely to generate parties that win majorities on their own. Governments are likely to be either minority governments or coalitions of several parties.

George Tsebelis (forthcoming) has brought both these elements into a single framework with the concept of the veto player. He shows how either institutional actors (such as a president with a veto) or partisan actors (such as a party whose support is needed to create a parliamentary majority) can act as veto players and can have similar effects on the possibility that a political system will produce policy change. In a world in which unsustainable debts are imposed on governments by exogenous shocks, changes in policy are most likely to be obstructed in systems that enhance the power of the veto player, whether the source of veto power is institutional or partisan.[4]

Whereas Tsebelis's argument hinges on the likelihood of a policy change away from an undefined status quo, Huber and Powell (1992) identify a different set of possible consequences of institutional alternatives. They distinguish between two "visions" of democratic processes in terms of how they may create congruence between citizen preferences and public policies. The alternatives are the "majority control" and "proportionate influence" visions, and they parallel the differences between Lijphart's majoritarian and consensus models of democracy. However, Huber and Powell show how the political process in each might lead government policy to approximate popular preferences, after which they compare the cases empirically. From a test involving 38 governments in 12 nations, they conclude that the proportionate influence vision of democratic processes does a better job of assuring congruence of popular preferences and government policy.

The research reported in this section is provocative, though not conclusive. Even if we were to conclude that one set of institutional alternatives was inferior with respect to some indicator of macroeconomic performance, as two articles suggest, we would

4. Note echo of the McCubbins (1991) argument.

have to be prepared to consider that that set might have advantages with respect to other criteria of democratic values.[5]

REFLECTIONS

I have tried to minimize the degree to which my own values have influenced the message of this book, but there are limits to how successful such an effort can be. This book reflects a deep and fundamental faith in democratic institutions. It is an attempt to confront honestly the worst that can be said about democracy in the context of macroeconomic performance, and to recognize and acknowledge the costs and pathologies of democratic practice in the real world.

Democratic governments have produced plenty of policies and outcomes that I would not seek and do not approve of, but in many of those cases the people were getting what they wanted. That is what democratic government is about. Occasionally we find that people do not like the consequences of their choices, and the analyst trained in political economy may be able to suggest institutional changes that can improve the situation. But another message of this book is that institutional reforms often have unanticipated consequences, and that it is not easy to "fix" the undesired consequences of deeply held preferences with a new procedure or a new rule.

This book has emphasized the importance of informal institutions, or norms. The informal, unwritten norms regarding budget balance that prevailed before the 1960s were far more powerful in constraining deficits than were the written rules of the Gramm-Rudman-Hollings law, and I am convinced that they cannot be regenerated simply by putting a version of that deficit reduction rule into the Constitution. It would be best of all, perhaps, to re-create the old norms, but that task would be comparable to putting toothpaste back into a tube.

In many respects this is a conservative book. I believe that there is always a risk of expecting too much from democratic government. I have recognized the foresight of the Republicans of

5. See Shepsle (1988).

the 1930s who opposed Social Security by entitlement. I have defended the instincts, if not the stated arguments, of those who insisted on watering down the "full employment bill" into the Employment Act of 1946. In hindsight, I believe that undermining the norm of balanced budgets in the 1960s was regrettable (though I did not think so at the time), because the ensuing lack of fiscal discipline is not, in my view, worth the extra stimulus. And I have defended the independence of the Federal Reserve as a monetary counterweight to the popularly based biases that now exist in fiscal institutions.

But though it is a conservative book, this book is even more a defense of democratic institutions, in which an attempt has been made to step back from the preferences of observers and to recognize that many of the features of democratic politics involve people getting what they want. What they want is often different from what the observer or analyst wants, but in a framework of democratic values it must be respected. And what "the people" want is no easier to pin down than any other element of the fundamental equation relating preferences, institutions, and outcomes. People learn to want what they see they can get, but they can also change their minds if they see that they do not like what they wanted and got. In this way, changing patterns of preferences can lead to improvements or to deterioration in economic performance under democratic institutions.

There are no Archimedean points in democratic politics.[6] Even public preferences, which are fundamental, do not provide bedrock for analysis and evaluation. Rather, democratic politics is inherently about process. The process aggregates and filters preferences via institutions into outcomes, but the process also modifies the preferences in a public discourse.

In teaching the material in this book, I have occasionally found that I have either created or reinforced cynicism about democratic institutions. Although that has not been my intention, I can see how cynicism might emerge from a systematic review of the possibilities and consequences of selfishness and opportunism in democratic politics. A certain amount of cynicism is a healthy thing; it is surely better than naïveté. Yet I see in this material a far more

6. Grafstein said that "we have met the Archimedean point and it is us" (1990, p. 178).

222   *Conclusion*

positive and hopeful view of democratic institutions, even though opportunism does occur in democratic institutions, as it does in markets and bureaucracies.

Adam Smith pointed out, two centuries ago, that the market guides individual selfishness into social well-being, and modern microeconomic theory has developed Smith's insights into a coherent theory of competitive markets that is the crowning achievement of the social sciences.[7] There is no comparable theory that shows that competitive politics in a democracy has the same optimizing features as perfect markets under pure competition.[8] Indeed, Kenneth Arrow, one of the theorists who demonstrated the optimizing qualities of markets, demonstrated the "impossibility" of similarly perfect democratic institutions.[9] However, more than any other known institutional arrangement, democracy is a self-correcting feedback mechanism. If perfection is impossible, that fact suggests

7. See Arrow and Hahn (1971).
8. But see Wittman (1989).
9. Arrow (1963).

References

Alesina, Alberto. 1987. Macroeconomic Policy in a Two-Party System as a Repeated Game. *Quarterly Journal of Economics* 102:651–678.

Alesina, Alberto. 1988a. Credibility and Policy Convergence in a Two-Party System with Rational Voters. *American Economic Review* 78:796–805.

Alesina, Alberto. 1988b. The End of Large Public Debts. In Francesco Giavazzi and Luigi Spaventa (eds.), *High Public Debt: The Italian Experience,* pp. 34–89. Cambridge University Press.

Alesina, Alberto. In press. Elections, Party Structure and the Economy. In Jeff Banks and Eric Hanuschek (eds.), *Modern Political Economy: Old Topics, New Directions.* Cambridge University Press.

Alesina, Alberto, Gerald D. Cohen, and Nouriel Roubini. 1992a. Macroeconomic Policy and Elections in OECD Democracies. In Alex Cukierman, Zvi Hercowitz, and Leonardo Leiderman (eds.), *Political Economy, Growth, and Business Cycles,* pp. 227–262. Cambridge, MA: MIT Press.

Alesina, Alberto, Gerald D. Cohen, and Nouriel Roubini. 1992b. Macroeconomic Policy and Elections in OECD Democracies. *Economics and Politics* 4:1–30.

Alesina, Alberto, and Alex Cukierman. 1990. The Politics of Ambiguity. *Quarterly Journal of Economics* 105:829–850.

Alesina, Alberto, and Allen Drazen. 1991. Why Are Stabilizations Delayed? *American Economic Review* 81:1170–1188.

Alesina, Alberto, John Londregan, and Howard Rosenthal. 1993. A Model of the Political Economy of the United States. *American Political Science Review* 87:12–33.

Alesina, Alberto, and Howard Rosenthal. 1994. *Partisan Politics, Divided Government, and the Economy.* Cambridge University Press.

Alesina, Alberto, and Jeffrey Sachs. 1988. Political Parties and the Business Cycle in the United States, 1948–1984. *Journal of Money, Credit, and Banking* 20:63–82.

223

Alesina, Alberto, and Lawrence H. Summers. 1993. Central Bank Independence and Macroeconomic Performance. *Journal of Money, Credit, and Banking* 25:151–162.

Alesina, Alberto, and Guido Tabellini. 1990. A Positive Theory of Budget Deficits and Government Debt. *Review of Economic Studies* 57:403–414.

Alt, James E. 1979. *The Politics of Economic Decline: Economic Management and Political Behaviour in Britain since 1964.* Cambridge University Press.

Alt, James E. 1985. Political Parties, World Demand, and Unemployment: Domestic and International Sources of Economic Activity. *American Political Science Review* 79:1016–1040.

Alt, James E. 1991. Leaning into the Wind or Ducking out of the Storm: U.S. Monetary Policy in the 1980s. In Alberto Alesina and Geoffrey Carliner (eds.), *Politics and Economics in the Eighties,* pp. 41–82. University of Chicago Press.

Alt, James E., and K. Alex Chrystal. 1983. *Political Economics.* Berkeley: University of California Press.

Alt, James E., and Robert Lowry. In press. Divided Government and Budget Deficits: Evidence from the States. *American Political Science Review.*

Alt, James E., and Charles Stewart III. 1990. Parties and the Deficit: Some Historical Evidence. Unpublished manuscript, Department of Government, Harvard University.

Alt, James E., and John T. Woolley. 1982. Reaction Functions, Optimization, and Politics: Modelling the Political Economy of Macroeconomic Policy. *American Journal of Political Science* 26:709–740.

Aluise, Joseph. 1991. The Microeconomic Foundations of the Natural Rate of Unemployment and the Leverage of Political Parties. Unpublished manuscript, University of North Carolina at Chapel Hill.

Alvarez, R. Michael, Geoffrey Garrett, and Peter Lange. 1991. Government Partisanship, Labor Organization, and Macroeconomic Performance. *American Political Science Review* 85:539–556.

Andrabi, Tahir. 1993. Seignorage, Taxation, and Weak Government. Unpublished manuscript, Department of Economics, Pomona College.

Arndt, H. W. 1978. *The Rise and Fall of Economic Growth: A Study in Contemporary Thought.* University of Chicago Press.

Arrow, Kenneth J. 1963. *Social Choice and Individual Values,* 2nd ed. New York: Wiley.

Arrow, Kenneth J., and F. H. Hahn. 1971. *General Competitive Analysis.* San Francisco: Holden-Day.

Asher, Martin A., Robert H. DeFina, and Kishor Thanawala. 1993. The Misery Index: Only Part of the Story. *Challenge* 36(2):58–62.

Bailey, Stephen K. 1950. *Congress Makes a Law: The Story Behind the Employment Act of 1946.* New York: Columbia University Press.

Balke, Nathan S. 1991. Partisanship Theory, Macroeconomic Outcomes, and Endogenous Elections. *Southern Economic Journal* 57:920–934.

Baron, David P. 1991. Majoritarian Incentives, Pork Barrel Programs, and Procedural Control. *American Journal of Political Science* 35:57–90.

Barro, Robert J. 1973. The Control of Politicians: An Economic Model. *Public Choice* 14:19–42.

Barro, Robert J. 1979. On the Determination of the Public Debt. *Journal of Political Economy* 87:940–971.

Barro, Robert J. 1986. U.S. Deficits since World War I. *Scandinavian Journal of Economics* 88:195–222.

Barro, Robert J., and David Gordon. 1983. Rules, Discretion, and Reputation in a Model of Monetary Policy. *Journal of Monetary Economics* 12:101–122.

Beck, Nathaniel. 1982. Parties, Administrations, and American Macroeconomic Outcomes. *American Political Science Review* 76:83–93.

Bianco, William T. 1994. *A Proper Responsibility: Representatives, Constituents, and Decisions about Trust.* Ann Arbor: University of Michigan Press.

Blais, Andre, Donald Blake, and Stephane Dion. 1993. Do Parties Make a Difference? Parties and the Size of Government in Liberal Democracies. *American Journal of Political Science* 37:40–62.

Blanchard, Olivier, and Stanley Fischer. 1989. *Lectures on Macroeconomics.* Cambridge, MA: MIT Press.

Blinder, Alan S. 1987. *Hard Heads, Soft Hearts: Tough Minded Economics for a Just Society.* Reading, MA: Addison-Wesley.

Blinder, Alan S., and Douglas Holtz-Eakin. 1984. Public Opinion and the Balanced Budget. *American Economic Review, Papers and Proceedings* 74:144–149.

Blinder, Alan S., and Robert M. Solow. 1974. Analytical Foundations of Fiscal Policy. In Alan S. Blinder et al. (eds.), *The Economics of Public Finance,* pp. 3–115. Washington: Brookings Institution.

Bratton, Kathleen A. 1994. Retrospective Voting and Future Expectations: The Case of the Budget Deficit in the 1988 Election. *American Politics Quarterly* 22:277–296.

Brown, E. Cary. 1956. Fiscal Policy in the "Thirties": A Reappraisal. *American Economic Review* 46:857–879.

Brown, E. Cary. 1990. Episodes in the Public Debt History of the United States. In Rudiger Dornbusch and Mario Draghi (eds.), *Public Debt Management: Theory and History,* pp. 229–262. Cambridge University Press.

Broz, J. Lawrence. 1993. Wresting the Scepter from London: The International Political Economy of the Founding of the Federal Reserve. Doctoral dissertation, University of California at Los Angeles.

Bryant, Ralph C. 1980. *Money and Monetary Policy in Interdependent Nations.* Washington: Brookings Institution.

Buchanan, James M., Charles K. Rowley, and Robert D. Tollison (eds.). 1986. *Deficits.* Oxford: Basil Blackwell.

Buchanan, James M., and Richard E. Wagner. 1977. *Democracy in Deficit: The Political Legacy of Lord Keynes.* New York: Academic Press.

Budge, Ian, and Richard I. Hofferbert. 1990. Mandates and Policy Outputs:

U.S. Party Platforms and Federal Expenditures. *American Political Science Review* 84:111–132.

Cagan, Phillip. 1987. Hyperinflation. In John Eatwell, Murray Milgate, and Peter Newman (eds.), *The New Palgrave: A Dictionary of Economics*, vol. 2, pp. 704–706. London: Macmillan.

Chappell, Henry W., Jr., Thomas M. Havrilesky, and Rob Roy MacGregor. 1993. Partisan Monetary Policies: Presidential Influence through the Power of Appointment. *Quarterly Journal of Economics* 108:185–219.

Chappell, Henry W., Jr., and William R. Keech. 1985a. A New View of Accountability for Economic Performance. *American Political Science Review* 79:10–27.

Chappell, Henry W., Jr., and William R. Keech. 1985b. The Political Viability of Rule-based Monetary Policy. *Public Choice* 46:125–140.

Chappell, Henry W., Jr., and William R. Keech. 1986a. Party Differences in Macroeconomic Policies and Outcomes. *American Economic Review, Papers and Proceedings* 76:71–74.

Chappell, Henry W., Jr., and William R. Keech. 1986b. Policy Motivations and Party Differences in a Dynamic Spatial Model of Party Competition. *American Political Science Review* 80:881–899.

Chappell, Henry W., Jr., and William R. Keech. 1988a. The Unemployment Consequences of Partisan Monetary Policy. *Southern Economic Journal* 55:107–122.

Chappell, Henry W., Jr., and William R. Keech. 1988b. Choice and Circumstance: The Consequences of Partisan Macroeconomic Policies. Paper presented at the annual meeting of the American Political Science Association, Washington, DC.

Collender, Stanley E. 1992. *A Guide to the Federal Budget, Fiscal 1993*. Washington: Urban Institute Press.

Cukierman, Alex. 1992. *Central Bank Strategy, Credibility, and Independence*. Cambridge, MA: MIT Press.

Cukierman, Alex, and Allan Meltzer. 1986. A Positive Theory of Discretionary Policy, the Costs of Democratic Government, and the Benefits of a Constitution. *Economic Inquiry* 24:367–388.

Cukierman, Alex, and Allan Meltzer. 1989. A Political Theory of Government Debt and Deficits in a Neo-Ricardian Framework. *American Economic Review* 79:69–95.

Dahl, Robert A. 1989. *Democracy and Its Critics*. New Haven: Yale University Press.

Dam, Kenneth. 1982. *The Rules of the Game*. University of Chicago Press.

Downs, Anthony. 1957. *An Economic Theory of Democracy*. New York: Harper.

Dryzek, John S. 1990. *Discursive Democracy: Politics, Policy, and Political Science*. Cambridge University Press.

Edwards, George C., III. 1990. *Presidential Approval: A Sourcebook*. Baltimore: Johns Hopkins University Press.

Eichengreen, Barry (ed.). 1985. *The Gold Standard in Theory and History*. New York: Methuen.

Eichengreen, Barry. 1992a. *Golden Fetters: The Gold Standard and the Great Depression.* Oxford University Press.
Eichengreen, Barry. 1992b. Designing a Central Bank for Europe: A Cautionary Tale from the Early Years of the Federal Reserve System. In Matthew B. Canzoneri, Vittorio Grilli, and Paul R. Masson (eds.). *Establishing a Central Bank: Issues in Europe and Lessons from the U.S.*, pp. 13–48. Cambridge University Press.
Eisner, Robert. 1986. *How Real Is the Federal Deficit?* New York: Free Press.
Erikson, Robert S. 1989. Economic Conditions and the Presidential Vote. *American Political Science Review* 83:567–573.
Erikson, Robert S. 1990. Economic Conditions and the Congressional Vote: A Review of the Macrolevel Evidence. *American Journal of Political Science* 34:373–399.
Fair, Ray C. 1978. The Effect of Economic Events on Votes for President. *Review of Economics and Statistics* 60:159–173.
Fair, Ray C. 1984. *Specification, Estimation, and Analysis of Macroeconomic Models.* Cambridge, MA: Harvard University Press.
Fair, Ray C. 1988. The Effect of Economic Events on Votes for President: 1984 Update. *Political Behavior* 10:168–179.
Fair, Ray C. 1990. The Effect of Economic Events on Votes for President: 1988 Update. Unpublished manuscript, Department of Economics, Yale University.
Fenno, Richard F. 1966. *The Power of the Purse: Appropriations Politics in Congress.* Boston: Little, Brown.
Ferejohn, John. 1986. Incumbent Performance and Electoral Control. *Public Choice* 50:5–25.
Fiorina, Morris. 1981. *Retrospective Voting in American National Elections.* New Haven: Yale University Press.
Fiorina, Morris. 1992. *Divided Government.* New York: Macmillan.
Fischer, Stanley. 1986. *Indexing, Inflation, and Economic Policy.* Cambridge MA: MIT Press.
Fischer, Stanley, and John Huizinga. 1982. Inflation, Unemployment, and Public Opinion Polls. *Journal of Money, Credit, and Banking* 14:1–19.
Fisher, Louis. 1975. *Presidential Spending Power.* Princeton University Press. Fisher, Louis. 1985. Ten Years of the Budget Act: Still Searching for Controls. *Public Budgeting and Finance* 5:3–28.
Forgette, Richard. 1993. Budget Balance and Government Party Control: Does Divided Government Matter? Paper presented at the annual meeting of the American Political Science Association.
Frey, Bruno S. 1983. *Democratic Economic Policy: A Theoretical Introduction.* New York: St. Martin's Press.
Frey, Bruno S., and Friedrich Schneider. 1978. An Empirical Study of Politico-Economic Interaction in the U.S. *Review of Economics and Statistics* 60:174–183.
Frieden, Jeffry A. 1991. *Debt, Development and Democracy: Modern Political Economy and Latin America, 1965–1985.* Princeton University Press.
Friedman, Milton. 1953a. A Monetary and Fiscal Framework for Economic

Stability. In Milton Friedman (ed.), *Essays in Positive Economics*, pp. 133–156. University of Chicago Press. Reprinted from *American Economic Review* 38:245–264 (1948).

Friedman, Milton. 1953b. *Essays in Positive Economics*. University of Chicago Press.

Friedman, Milton. 1960. *A Program for Monetary Stability*. New York: Fordham University Press.

Friedman, Milton. 1962. Should There Be an Independent Monetary Authority? In Leland B. Yeager (ed.), *In Search of a Monetary Constitution*, pp. 219–243. Cambridge, MA: Harvard University Press.

Friedman, Milton. 1968. The Role of Monetary Policy. *American Economic Review* 58:1–17.

Friedman, Milton. 1977. Nobel Lecture: Inflation and Unemployment. *Journal of Political Economy* 85:451–472.

Friedman, Milton, and Anna Jacobson Schwartz. 1963. *A Monetary History of the United States, 1867–1960*. Princeton University Press.

Froyen, Richard T. 1993. *Macroeconomics: Theories and Policies*, 4th ed. New York: Macmillan.

Garrett, Geoffrey, and Peter Lange. 1991. Political Responses to Interdependence: What's "Left" for the Left? *International Organization* 45:539–564.

Gerber, Elizabeth, and Arthur Lupia. 1993. Does Competition Matter? Political Campaigns and the Responsiveness of Electoral Outcomes. Unpublished manuscript, California Institute of Technology.

Gilmour, John B. 1990. *Reconcilable Differences? Congress, the Budget Process and the Deficit*. Berkeley: University of California Press.

Golden, David G., and James M. Poterba. 1980. The Price of Popularity: The Political Business Cycle Reexamined. *American Journal of Political Science* 24:696–714.

Grafstein, Robert. 1990. Missing the Archimedean Point: Liberalism's Institutional Presuppositions. *American Political Science Review* 84:177–194.

Gramlich, Edward M. 1983. Models of Inflation Expectations Formation: A Comparison of Household and Economist Forecasts. *Journal of Money, Credit, and Banking* 15:155–173.

Gramlich, Edward M. 1991. U.S. Budget Deficits: Views, Burdens, and New Developments. In James M. Rock (ed.), *Debt and the Twin Deficits Debate*, pp. 173–187. Mountain View, CA: Mayfield Publishing.

Greene, Jay P. 1993. Forewarned Before Forecast: Presidential Election Forecasting Models and the 1992 Election. *PS: Political Science and Politics* 26:17–21.

Greider, William. 1987. *Secrets of the Temple: How the Federal Reserve Runs the Country*. New York: Simon & Schuster.

Grier, Kevin D. 1989. On the Existence of a Political Monetary Cycle. *American Journal of Political Science* 33:376–389.

Grier, Kevin. 1993. On the Existence and (Constrained) Optimality of the Political Business Cycle. Unpublished manuscript, Department of Economics, George Mason University.

Grilli, Vittorio, Donato Masciandaro, and Guido Tabellini. 1991. Institutions and Policies. *Economic Policy* 13:341–392.

Hahm, Sung Deuk, Mark S. Kamlet, and David C. Mowery. 1993. The Political Economy of Deficit Spending in Parliamentary Democracies: The Role of Fiscal Institutions. Paper presented at the annual meeting of the American Political Science Association.

Hargrove, Erwin C., and Samuel A. Morley (eds.). 1984. *The President and the Council of Economic Advisors.* Boulder, CO: Westview Press.

Harrington, Joseph E., Jr. 1993. Economic Policy, Economic Performance, and Elections. *American Economic Review* 83:27–43.

Havrilesky, Thomas. 1987. A Partisanship Theory of Fiscal and Monetary Policy. *Journal of Money, Credit, and Banking* 19:308–325.

Havrilesky, Thomas. 1993. *The Pressures on American Monetary Policy.* Boston: Kluwer.

Havrilesky, Thomas, Henry Chappell, John Gildea, and Rob McGregor. 1993. Congress Threatens the Fed. *Challenge* 36(2):50–57.

Haynes, Stephen E., and Joe A. Stone. 1989a. Political Models of the Business Cycle Should Be Revived. *Economic Inquiry* 28:442–465.

Haynes, Stephen E., and Joe A. Stone. 1989b. Political Parties and the Variable Duration of Business Cycles. *Southern Economic Journal* 60:869–885.

Heller, Walter. 1966. *New Dimensions of Political Economy.* Cambridge, MA: Harvard University Press.

Hibbs, Douglas A., Jr. 1977. Political Parties and Macroeconomic Policy. *American Political Science Review* 71:1467–1487.

Hibbs, Douglas A., Jr. 1982. President Reagan's Mandate from the 1980 Elections: A Shift to the Right? *American Politics Quarterly* 10:387–420.

Hibbs, Douglas A., Jr. 1987. *The American Political Economy.* Cambridge, MA: Harvard University Press.

Hibbs, Douglas A., Jr. 1992. Partisan Theory after Fifteen Years. *European Journal of Political Economy* 8:361–373.

Hibbs, Douglas A., Jr. 1994. The Partisan Model of Macroeconomic Cycles: More Theory and Evidence for the United States. *Economics and Politics* 6:1–24.

Hibbs, Douglas A., Jr., and Christopher Dennis. 1988. Income Distribution in the United States. *American Political Science Review* 87:467–490.

Hirschman, Albert O. 1991. *The Rhetoric of Reaction.* Cambridge, MA: Harvard University Press.

Hoover, Kevin D. 1988. *The New Classical Macroeconomics: A Skeptical Inquiry.* London: Basil Blackwell.

Hoover, Kevin D., and Steven M. Sheffrin. 1992. Causation, Spending, and Taxes: Sand in the Sandbox or Tax Collector for the Welfare State. *American Economic Review* 82:225–248.

Huber, John D., and G. Bingham Powell, Jr. 1992. Congruence between Citizens and Policymakers in Two Views of Liberal Democracy. Paper presented at the annual meeting of the Midwest Political Science Association.

Huntington, Samuel P. 1968. *Political Order in Changing Societies*. New Haven: Yale University Press.

Jacobson, Gary C. 1990. Does the Economy Matter in Midterm Elections? *American Journal of Political Science* 34:400–404.

Jamieson, Kathleen Hall. 1992. *Dirty Politics: Deception, Distraction, and Democracy*. Oxford University Press.

Johnson, James. 1993. Is Talk Really Cheap? Prompting Conversation between Critical Theory and Rational Choice. *American Political Science Review* 87:74–86.

Kamlet, Mark S., David C. Mowery, and Tsai-Tsu Su. 1988. Upsetting National Priorities: The Reagan Administration's Budgetary Strategy. *American Political Science Review* 82:1293–1308.

Kane, Edward J. 1990. Bureaucratic Self-interest as an Obstacle to Monetary Reform. In Thomas Mayer (ed.), *The Political Economy of American Monetary Policy*, pp. 283–298. Cambridge University Press.

Keech, William R. 1992. Rules, Discretion, and Accountability in Macroeconomic Policymaking. *Governance* 5:259–278.

Keech, William R., and G. Patrick Lynch. 1992. Business Cycles and Presidential Elections in the United States: Another Look at Key and Downs on Retrospective Voting. Paper presented at the annual meeting of the American Political Science Association.

Keech, William R., and Kyoungsan Pak. 1989. Electoral Cycles and Budgetary Growth in Veterans' Benefit Programs. *American Journal of Political Science* 33:901–911.

Keech, William R., and Carl P. Simon. 1985. Electoral and Welfare Consequences of Political Manipulation of the Economy. *Journal of Economic Behavior and Organization* 6:177–202.

Kelley, Stanley, Jr. 1983. *Interpreting Elections*. Princeton University Press.

Kettl, Donald F. 1986. *Leadership at the Fed*. New Haven: Yale University Press.

Key, V. O., Jr. 1966. *The Responsible Electorate: Rationality in Presidential Voting 1936–1960*. Cambridge, MA: Harvard University Press.

Keynes, John Maynard. 1936. *The General Theory of Employment, Interest, and Money*. London: Macmillan. Reissued in 1964 by Harcourt Brace Jovanovich.

Kiewiet, D. Roderick. 1981. Policy-oriented Voting in Response to Economic Issues. *American Political Science Review* 75:448–459.

Kiewiet, D. Roderick. 1983. *Macroeconomics and Micropolitics*. University of Chicago Press.

Kiewiet, D. Roderick, and Mathew D. McCubbins. 1991. *The Logic of Delegation: Congressional Parties and the Appropriations Process*. University of Chicago Press.

Kingdon, John W. 1984. *Agendas, Alternatives, and Public Policies*. Boston: Little, Brown.

Klamer, Arjo. 1984. *Conversations with Economists: New Classical Economists and Opponents Speak Out on the Current Controversy in Macroeconomics*. Totowa, NJ: Rowman & Allanheld.

Klein, Martin, and Manfred J. M. Neumann. 1990. Seignorage: What Is It and Who Gets It. *Weltwirtschaftliches Archiv* 126:205–221.

Kotlikoff, Laurence J. 1992. *Generational Accounting: Knowing Who Pays, and When, for What We Spend.* New York: Free Press.

Kramer, Gerald H. 1971. Short-Term Fluctuations in U.S. Voting Behavior, 1896–1964. *American Political Science Review* 65:131–143.

Kramer, Gerald H. 1983. The Ecological Fallacy Revisited: Aggregate- versus Individual-Level Findings on Economics and Elections and Sociotropic Voting. *American Political Science Review* 77:92–111.

Kreps, David M. 1990. *A Course in Microeconoic Theory.* Princeton University Press.

Krugman, Paul. 1992. *The Age of Diminished Expectations: U.S. Economic Policy in the 1990s.* Cambridge, MA: MIT Press.

Kuklinski, James H., and Darrell M. West. 1981. Economic Expectations and Voting Behavior in United States House and Senate Elections. *American Political Science Review* 75:436–447.

Kydland, Finn, and Edward C. Prescott. 1977. Rules Rather than Discretion: The Inconsistency of Optimal Plans. *Journal of Political Economy* 83:473–491.

Lewis-Beck, Michael S. 1988. *Economics and Elections: The Major Western Democracies.* Ann Arbor: University of Michigan Press.

Lijphart, Arend. 1984. *Democracies: Patterns of Majoritarian and Consensus Government in Twenty-One Countries.* New Haven: Yale University Press.

Lohmann, Susanne. 1992. Optimal Commitment in Monetary Policy: Credibility vs. Flexibility. *American Economic Review* 82:273–286.

Lowi, Theodore J. 1979. *The End of Liberalism: The Second Republic of the United States,* 2nd ed. New York: Norton.

Lucas, Robert E., Jr. 1981. *Studies in Business Cycle Theory.* Cambridge, MA: MIT Press.

McCallum, Bennett. 1978. The Political Business Cycle: An Empirical Test. *Southern Economic Journal* 45:504–515.

McCubbins, Mathew D. 1991. Party Governance and U.S. Budget Deficits: Divided Government and Fiscal Stalemate. In Alberto Alesina and Geoffrey Carliner (eds.), *Economics and Politics in the 1980s,* pp. 83–122. University of Chicago Press.

MacKuen, Michael B., Robert S. Erikson, and James A. Stimson. 1992. Peasants or Bankers: The American Electorate and the U.S. Economy. *American Political Science Review* 86:597–611.

Majone, Giandomenico. 1989. *Evidence, Argument, and Persuasion in the Policy Process.* New Haven: Yale University Press.

Mankiw, N. Gregory. 1990. A Quick Refresher Course in Macroeconomics. *Journal of Economic Literature* 28:1645–1660.

Mankiw, N. Gregory, and David Romer (eds.). 1991. *New Keynesian Economics,* 2 vols. Cambridge, MA: MIT Press.

Mashaw, Jerry L. 1989. The Economics of Politics and the Understanding of Public Law. *Chicago-Kent Law Review* 65:123–161.

May, Kenneth O. 1952. A Set of Independent, Necessary, and Sufficient Conditions for Simple Majority Decision. *Econometrica* 20:680–684.

Mayhew, David R. 1991. *Divided We Govern: Party Control, Lawmaking, and Investigations 1946–1990*. New Haven: Yale University Press.

Meltzer, Allan H. 1988. *Keynes's Monetary Theory: A Different Interpretation*. Cambridge University Press.

Miller, Arthur H., and Martin P. Wattenberg. 1985. Throwing the Rascals Out: Policy and Performance Evaluations of Presidential Candidates, 1952–1980. *American Political Science Review* 79:359–373.

Modigliani, Andre, and Franco Modigliani. 1987. The Growth of the Federal Deficit and the Role of Public Attitudes. *Public Opinion Quarterly* 51:459–480.

Morris, Irwin L. 1994. Congress, the President, and the Federal Reserve: The Politics of American Monetary Policy. Doctoral dissertation, University of North Carolina at Chapel Hill.

Mosely, Paul. 1984. *The Making of Economic Policy: Theory and Evidence from Britain and the United States since 1945*. New York: St. Martin's Press.

Mueller, Dennis. 1989. *Public Choice II*. Cambridge University Press.

Nordhaus, William. 1975. The Political Business Cycle. *Review of Economic Studies* 42:169–190.

Nordhaus, William. 1989. Alternative Approaches to the Political Business Cycle. *Brookings Papers on Economic Activity* 2:1–68.

Okun, Arthur. 1973. Comment on Stigler's Paper. *American Economic Review, Papers and Proceedings* 63:172–180.

Okun, Arthur. 1975. *Equality and Efficiency: The Big Tradeoff*. Washington: Brookings Institution.

Olson, Mancur, Jr. 1982. *The Rise and Decline of Nations*. New Haven: Yale University Press.

Olson, Mancur, Jr. 1984. Beyond Keynesianism and Monetarism. *Economic Inquiry* 22:297–322.

Olson, Mancur, Jr. 1993. Dictatorship, Democracy, and Development. *American Political Science Review* 87:567–576.

Paldam, Martin. 1991. How Robust Is the Vote Function: A Study of Seventeen Nations over Four Decades. In Helmut Norpoth, Michael S. Lewis-Beck, and Jean Dominique Lafay (eds.), *Economics and Politics: The Calculus of Support*, pp. 9–31. Ann Arbor: University of Michigan Press.

Peltzman, Sam. 1991. Voters as Fiscal Conservatives. *Quarterly Journal of Economics* 107:327–361.

Persson, Torsten, and Lars E. O. Svensson. 1989. Why a Stubborn Conservative Would Run a Deficit: Policy with Time-Inconsistent Preferences. *Quarterly Journal of Economics* 105:325–345.

Persson, Torsten, and Guido Tabellini. 1990. *Macroeconomic Policy, Credibility and Politics*. Chur, Switzerland, and New York: Harwood Academic Publishers.

Peterson, Paul. 1985. The New Politics of Deficits. In John Chubb and Paul

Peterson (eds.), *New Directions in American Politics*, pp. 365–397. Washington: Brookings Institution.

Peterson, Peter. 1993. *Facing Up: How to Rescue the Economy from Crushing Debt and Restore the American Dream.* New York: Simon & Schuster.

Phelps, Edmund S. 1990. *Seven Schools of Macroeconomic Thought.* Oxford: Clarendon Press.

Phillips, A. W. 1958. The Relation between Unemployment and the Rate of Change of Money Wage Rates in the United Kingdom, 1861–1957. *Economica* (NS) 25:283–299.

Plott, Charles R. 1991. Will Economics Become an Experimental Science? *Southern Economic Journal* 57:901–920.

Portney, Paul R. 1976. Congressional Delays in U.S. Fiscal Policymaking: Simulating the Effects. *Journal of Public Economics* 5:237–247.

Poterba, James M. In press. State Responses to Fiscal Crises: The Effects of Budgetary Institutions and Politics. *Journal of Political Economy.*

Quattrone, George, and Amos Tversky. 1988. Contrasting Rational and Psychological Analyses of Political Choice. *American Political Science Review* 82:719–736.

Quinn, Dennis P., and Robert Y. Shapiro. 1991. Economic Growth Strategies: The Effects of Ideological Partisanship on Interest Rates and Business Taxation. *American Journal of Political Science* 35:656–685.

Rawls, John. 1971. *A Theory of Justice.* Cambridge, MA: Harvard University Press.

Reischauer, Robert D. 1990. Taxes and Spending under Gramm-Rudman-Hollings. *National Tax Journal* 44:223–232.

Remmer, Karen E. 1993. The Political Economy of Elections in Latin America, 1980–1991. *American Political Science Review* 87:393–407.

Richards, Daniel J. 1986. Unanticipated Money and the Political Business Cycle. *Journal of Money, Credit, and Banking* 18:447–457.

Riker, William H. 1982. *Liberalism Against Populism: A Confrontation Between the Theory of Democracy and the Theory of Social Choice.* Prospect Heights, IL: Waveland Press.

Rivers, Douglas. 1988. Heterogeneity in Models of Electoral Choice. *American Journal of Political Science* 32:737–757.

Rock, James M. (ed.). 1991. *Debt and the Twin Deficits Debate.* Mountain View, CA: Mayfield Publishing Co.

Rogoff, Kenneth. 1985. The Optimal Degree of Commitment to an Intermediate Monetary Target. *Quarterly Journal of Economics* 100:1169–1190.

Rogoff, Kenneth. 1990. Equilibrium Political Budget Cycles. *American Economic Review* 80:21–36.

Rogoff, Kenneth, and Anne Sibert. 1988. Elections and Macroeconomic Policy Cycles. *Review of Economic Studies* 55:1–16.

Roubini, Nouriel, and Jeffrey D. Sachs. 1989a. Political and Economic Determinants of Budget Deficits in the Industrial Democracies. *European Economic Review* 33:903–938.

Roubini, Nouriel, and Jeffrey D. Sachs. 1989b. Government Spending and Budget Deficits in the Industrialized Countries. *Economic Policy* 4:100–132.

Sachs, Jeffrey D., and Felipe Larrain B. 1993. *Macroeconomics in the Global Economy*. Englewood Cliffs, NJ: Prentice-Hall.

Samuelson, Paul A., and Robert M. Solow. 1960. Analytical Aspects of Anti-Inflation Policy. *American Economic Review, Papers and Proceedings* 50:177–194.

Sargent, Thomas. 1986. *Rational Expectations and Inflation*. New York: Harper & Row.

Sargent, Thomas, and Neil Wallace. 1976. Rational Expectations and the Theory of Economic Policy. *Journal of Monetary Economics* 2:169–183.

Savage, James D. 1988. *Balanced Budgets and American Politics*. Ithaca: Cornell University Press.

Schick, Allen. 1993. Governments versus Budget Deficits. In R. Kent Weaver and Bert A. Rockman (eds.), *Do Institutions Matter? Government Capabilities in the United States and Abroad*, pp. 187–236. Washington: Brookings Institution.

Schlozman, Kay L., and Sidney Verba. 1979. *Injury to Insult: Unemployment, Class, and Political Response*. Cambridge MA: Harvard University Press.

Schneider, Friedrich, and Bruno S. Frey. 1988. Politico-Economic Models of Macroeconomic Policy: A Review of the Empirical Evidence. In Thomas D. Willett, (ed.) *Political Business Cycles: The Political Economy of Money, Inflation, and Unemployment*, pp. 239–275. Durham: Duke University Press.

Scitovsky, Tibor. 1992. *The Joyless Economy*, rev. ed. Oxford University Press.

Sen, Amartya K. 1993. The Economics of Life and Death. *Scientific American* 268: 40–47.

Shepsle, Kenneth A. 1988. Representation and Governance: The Great Legislative Trade-off. *Political Science Quarterly* 103:461–484.

Shepsle, Kenneth A. 1991. Discretion, Institutions, and the Problem of Government Commitment. In Pierre Bourdieu and James S. Coleman (eds.), *Social Theory for a Changing Society*, pp. 245–265. Boulder, CO: Westview Press.

Shepsle, Kenneth A. 1992. Congress Is a "They," not an "It": Legislative Intent as Oxymoron. *International Review of Law and Economics* 12:239–256.

Shepsle, Kenneth A., and Barry R. Weingast. 1981. Political Preferences for the Pork Barrel: A Generalization. *American Journal of Political Science* 25:96–112.

Shepsle, Kenneth A., and Barry R. Weingast. 1984. Political Solutions to Market Problems. *American Political Science Review* 78:417–434.

Simon, Herbert. 1978. Rationality as Process and as Product of Thought. *American Economic Review, Papers and Proceedings* 68:1–16.

Simon, Herbert. 1983. *Reason in Human Affairs*. Stanford University Press.

Sniderman, Paul M., Richard A. Brody, and Philip E. Tetlock. 1991. *Reasoning and Choice: Explorations in Political Psychology.* Cambridge University Press.

Stein, Herbert. 1969. *The Fiscal Revolution in America.* University of Chicago Press.

Stein, Herbert. 1978. The Decline of the Budget-Balancing Doctrine or How the Good Guys Finally Lost. In James M. Buchanan and Richard E. Wagner (eds.), *Fiscal Responsibility in Constitutional Democracy,* pp. 35–58. Boston: Martinus Nijhoff.

Stein, Herbert. 1989. *Governing the $5 Trillion Economy.* Oxford University Press.

Stein, Herbert. 1994. *Presidential Economics: The Making of Economic Policy from Roosevelt to Clinton.* Washington: American Enterprise Institute.

Stewart, Charles. 1989. *Budget Reform Politics: The Design of the Appropriations Process in the House of Representatives 1865–1921.* Cambridge University Press.

Stigler, George J. 1973. General Economic Conditions and National Elections. *American Economic Review, Papers and Proceedings* 63:160–167.

Stockman, David. 1986. *The Triumph of Politics: Why the Reagan Revolution Failed.* New York: Harper & Row.

Su, Tsai-Tsu, Mark S. Kamlet, and David C. Mowery. 1993. Modelling U.S. Budgetary and Fiscal Outcomes: A Disaggregated, Systemwide Perspective. *American Journal of Political Science* 37:213–245.

Summers, Lawrence H. 1990. *Understanding Unemployment.* Cambridge, MA: MIT Press.

Sundquist, James L. 1983. *Dynamics of the Party System,* rev. ed. Washington: Brookings Institution.

Sundquist, James L. 1992. *Constitutional Reform and Effective Government,* rev. ed. Washington: Brookings Institution.

Suzuki, Motoshi. 1991. The Rationality of Economic Voting and the Macroeconomic Regime. *American Journal of Political Science* 35:624–642.

Suzuki, Motoshi. In press. Evolutionary Voter Sophistication and Political Business Cycles. *Public Choice.*

Tabellini, Guido, and Alberto Alesina. 1990. Voting on the Budget Deficit. *American Economic Review* 80:37–49.

Temin, Peter. 1989. *Lessons from the Great Depression.* Cambridge, MA: MIT Press.

Timberlake, Richard H. 1993. *Monetary Policy in the United States: An Intellectual and Institutional History.* University of Chicago Press.

Tinbergen, Jan. 1952. *On the Theory of Economic Policy.* Amsterdam: North Holland.

Tobin, James, and Murray Weidenbaum (eds.). 1988. *Two Revolutions in Economic Policy.* Cambridge, MA: MIT Press.

Tsebelis, George. 1990. *Nested Games: Rational Choice in Comparative Politics.* Berkeley: University of California Press.

Tsebelis, George. In press. Decision Making in Political Systems: Veto Players in Presidentialism, Parliamentarism, Multicameralism, and Multipartism. *British Journal of Political Science.*

Tufte, Edward R. 1978. *Political Control of the Economy.* Princeton University Press.

Weatherford, M. Stephen. 1983. Economic Voting and the "Symbolic Politics" Argument: A Reinterpretation and a Synthesis. *American Political Science Review* 77:92–111.

Weatherford, M. Stephen. 1987. The Interplay of Ideology and Advice in Economic Policy-Making: The Case of Political Business Cycles. *Journal of Politics* 49:925–952.

Weatherford, M. Stephen. 1988. An Agenda Paper: Political Business Cycles and the Process of Economic Policymaking. *American Politics Quarterly* 16:99–136.

Weaver, R. Kent. 1988. *Automatic Government: The Politics of Indexation.* Washington: Brookings Institution.

Weaver, R. Kent, and Bert A. Rockman (eds.). 1993. *Do Institutions Matter? Government Capabilities in the United States and Abroad.* Washington: Brookings Institution.

Weingast, Barry R., and William J. Marshall. 1988. The Industrial Organization of Congress; or, Why Legislatures, Like Firms, Are Not Organized as Markets. *Journal of Political Economy* 96:132–163.

White, Joseph, and Aaron Wildavsky. 1989. *The Deficit and the Public Interest.* Berkeley: University of California Press.

Whitely, Paul. 1986. *Political Control of the Macroeconomy: The Political Economy of Public Policy Making.* Beverly Hills, CA: Sage.

Wildavsky, Aaron. 1964. *The Politics of the Budgetary Process.* Boston: Little, Brown.

Williams, John T. 1990. The Political Manipulation of Macroeconomic Policy. *American Political Science Review* 84:767–796.

Wintrobe, Ronald. 1990. The Tinpot and the Totalitarian: An Economic Theory of Dictatorship. *American Political Science Review* 84:849–872.

Wittman, Donald. 1983. Candidate Motivation: A Synthesis of Alternative Theories. *American Political Science Review* 77:142–157.

Wittman, Donald. 1989. Why Democracies Produce Efficient Results. *Journal of Political Economy* 97:1395–1424.

Woolley, John T. 1984. *Monetary Politics: The Federal Reserve and the Politics of Monetary Policy.* Cambridge University Press.

Index

accord between Federal Reserve and Treasury Department, 8, 190, 200–2
Adams, Henry C., 177
adaptive expectations, 57, 83, 87, 88
agency, agent, 7, 8, 51, 67, 149, 156, 166, 198, 214. *See also* principal-agent
Alesina, Alberto, 32, 63, 66, 77–9, 87, 88, 91, 93, 96, 98, 117, 169, 189, 201, 216, 218
Alt, James, 61, 72, 91, 149, 164, 202
Aluise, Joseph, 82
Alvarez, Michael, 98
ambiguity, 78, 127, 129, 194, 202
anarchy, 4–6
Andrabi, Tahir, 175
appropriation, 170, 171
Archimedean points, 17, 159, 182, 221
Argentina, 114
Arndt, H. W., 110, 111
Arrow, Kenneth, 15, 103, 222
Asher, Martin, 103
asymmetric information, 59, 96, 194, 202, 206, 214
asymmetric-information, 60
asymmetry, 59, 216, 218
authorization, 130, 170, 171
automatic policy, 154, 155, 181
automatic stabilizers, 122, 124, 154, 170, 173, 178, 205
autonomy, 197

Bailey, Stephen K., 28, 105
balanced budget, 8, 11, 31, 107, 118–25, 144, 155, 156, 165, 168, 172, 176, 178, 190, 205, 213
Balanced Budget and Emergency Deficit Control Acts of 1985 and 1987. *See* Gramm-Rudman-Hollings Acts

Banking Acts of 1933 and 1935, 197, 198, 199
Bank of the United States, 187
Baron, David, 169
Barro, Robert, 36, 39–41, 51, 117, 122, 123, 153, 155, 160, 164, 175, 176, 206
Bartlett, Bruce, 160, 161
Beck, Nathaniel, 73, 78, 141
Belgium, 5, 216, 217
benign, 3, 4, 29
Bianco, William, 8, 214
Blanchard, Olivier, 24
Blinder, Alan, 24, 30, 119, 162
Bratton, Kathleen, 30, 119, 164
Bretton Woods, 186
Britain, 28, 135, 141, 217
Brody, Richard, 129
Brown, Cary, 28, 177, 178, 182
Broz, Lawrence, 184, 189, 195, 196
Bryan, William Jennings, 143
Buchanan, James, 23, 28–30, 35, 155, 178, 179
Budge, Ian, 146
Budget and Accounting Act of 1921, 166, 167, 181
Budget and Impoundment Control Act of 1974, 20, 157, 167, 168, 180, 181
Budget Enforcement Act of 1990, 108, 172, 173
Burns, Arthur, 199, 200
Bush, George, 51, 61, 108, 124, 135, 146, 161, 173, 174, 179

Cagan, Phillip, 117, 216
Campaign Finance Reform Act of 1974, 167
Carter, Jimmy, 49, 78, 80, 86, 144, 146, 174
central bank, 96, 175, 176, 187, 188, 194, 195, 198, 201, 202, 205